W9-AWW-672

THE GREEK AND ROMAN MYTHS

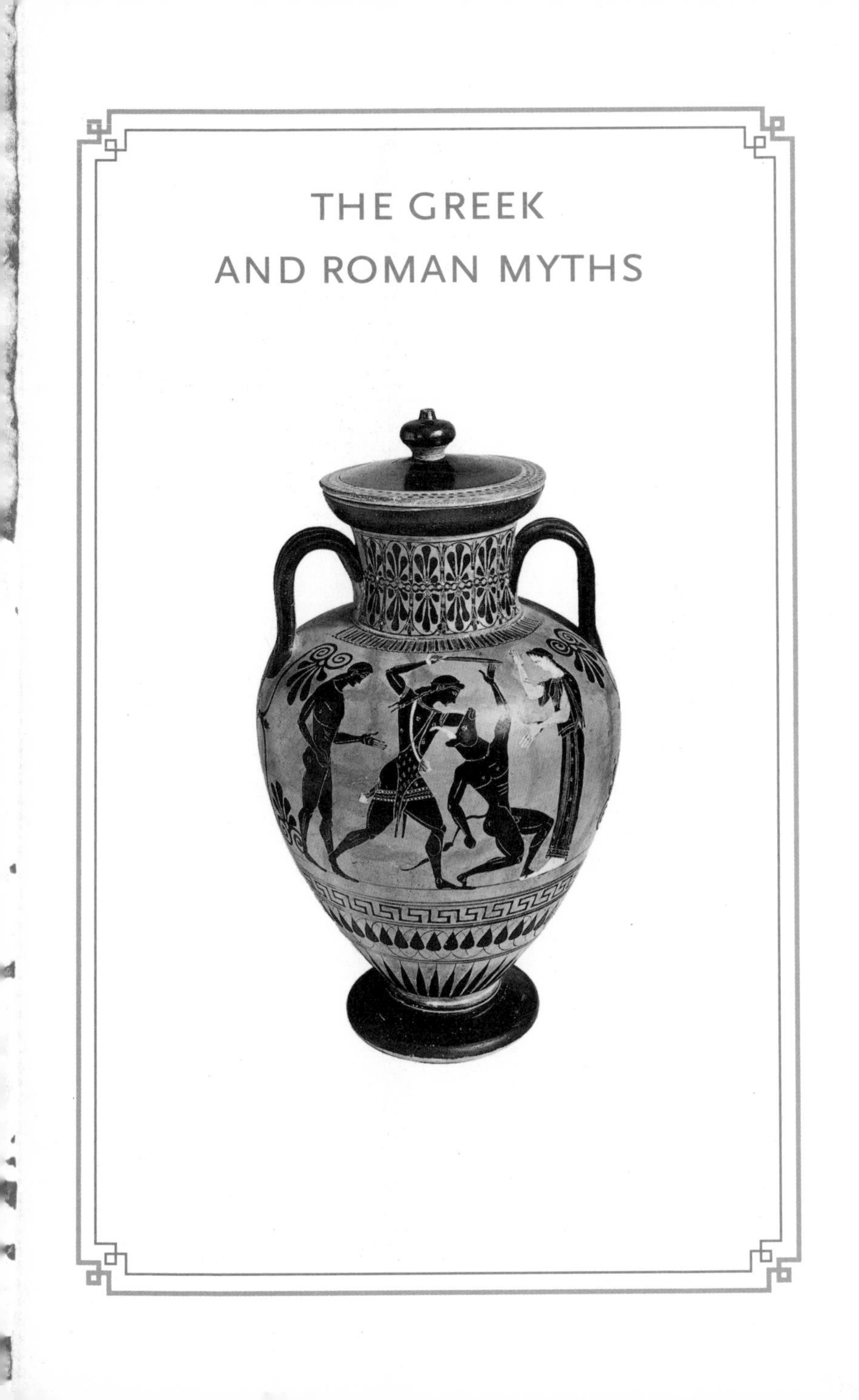

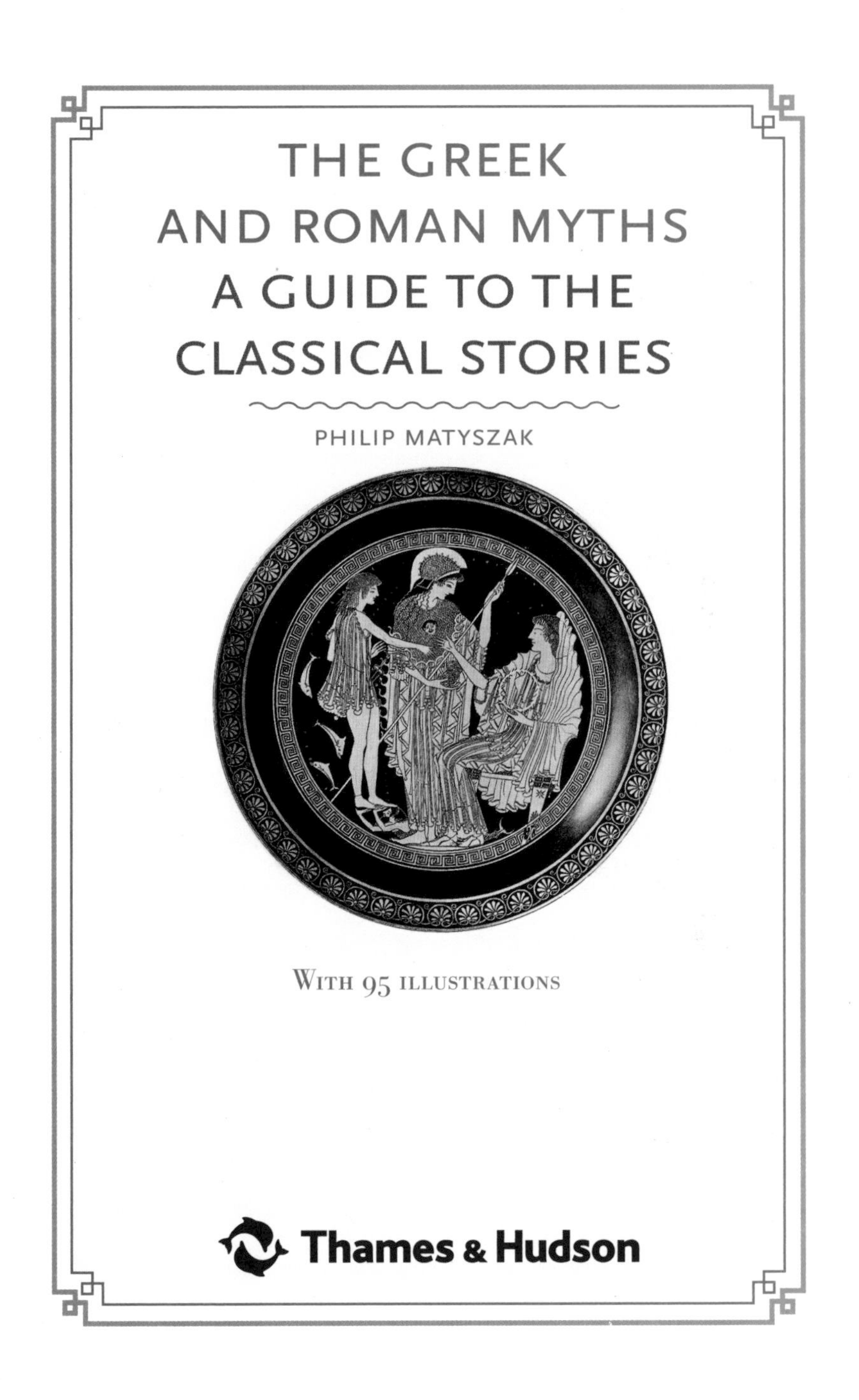

THE GREEK AND ROMAN MYTHS
A GUIDE TO THE CLASSICAL STORIES

PHILIP MATYSZAK

WITH 95 ILLUSTRATIONS

Thames & Hudson

This book is respectfully dedicated to Zeus, the Cloud-gatherer, Lord of Olympus, God of Storms. (Just in case.)

Acknowledgments

As ever this book was written with the help of friends and colleagues who made numerous helpful suggestions and comments. These include the awesomely knowledgable Robin Osborne and Rachel Peel, who both read the text from end to end and gently attempted to correct my ignorance. Where they have failed, the fault is mine.

Half-title: Theseus slays the Minotaur.
Frontispiece: Statue of Athena, a Roman copy of a Greek original.
Title-page: Theseus under the sea, receiving a wreath from Amphitrite.

First published in the United Kingdom in 2010 by
Thames & Hudson Ltd, 181A High Holborn, London WC1V 7QX

British Library Cataloguing-in-Publication Data
A catalogue record for this book is available from the British Library

ISBN 978-0-500-25173-7

Printed and bound in China by Toppan Leefung

Contents

Introduction

What are Greek and Roman myths? And Why is it Worth Studying them?

If the Greek and Roman myths were no more than a set of stories about magical transformations and squabbling gods there would be little point in reading about them. For a start, there are a huge number of such myths, all packed with bewildering names and genealogies. Why do we need to know these and why should we care?

We should care because the myths describe the ancients' view of the world, and the archetypes of heroes, wronged women and powerful yet frighteningly arbitrary gods shaped how the Greeks and the Romans saw themselves and their relationship with the universe. Indeed so powerful are many of these archetypes that they are still used today. When psychologists (who share their name with Psyche, a mythological princess) refer to an Oedipus complex or a narcissist they are using these archetypes, for the myths which feature Oedipus and Narcissus describe certain aspects of the human condition so powerfully that they have never been bettered.

And this brings us to a further reason for reading the myths: these stories have survived almost three thousand years not because they are cultural paradigms, thematic sequences of motifemes (or whatever buzzwords academics now favour), but because in the end they are powerful and hugely enjoyable narratives.

Nor is the world of mythology as chaotic as it seems at first glance. Many of the stories have a common theme. Heroes are afflicted, but receive compensatory gifts and powers, maidens suffer from love but are ultimately rewarded. The grimmer tales tell us that the inexorable threads woven, measured and cut by the Fates determine one's destiny, and the whole point of the exercise is to meet that destiny with fortitude and nobility.

There is also an overarching theme to the myths, one which tells us that, for all their conflicts, disagreements and misunderstandings, gods, demigods and humans stand together against the monsters and giants which represent the forces of disorder and wanton destruction. While modern tales are often about the triumph of good over evil, the ancient struggle was that of civilization and rationality contending with barbarism and chaos. Ultimately, the myths are about bringing human values to an arbitrary and unfriendly universe. And this is why, while blind hate, random destruction and irrationality may sometimes seem to be getting the upper hand in the world of today, the ancient myths have lost none of their power.

This is a companion or guide to understanding the common heritage of stories and belief which united the Greek and Roman worlds. It has three ultimate purposes:

Appreciating the Big Picture

In many ways, there is only one classical myth in its broadest sense. This is a story built over the course of a millennium or more, beginning before 800 BC with folk memories and tales from Greece and rounded off finally by Roman writers in the second century AD. It is the greatest collaborative tale ever told, and all the more awe-inspiring for being the collective effort of two different cultures. The result is a huge and rambling story with numerous sub-plots and thousands of characters, yet with a basic narrative, clear protagonists and a beginning, middle and end.

One purpose of this book is therefore to allow the reader to see the picture of myth as a whole, as a story that was familiar to every Greek and Roman child.

Understanding the Context

Yet this book has a further purpose, for in order to be a true guide it must explain not just the stories, but also how the people of antiquity understood them. We need to get inside the minds of the Greeks and Romans and to see their world and their gods as they saw them. We need to imagine the viewpoint of a Greek or Roman who is about to hear a particular myth for the first time. Here you will discover the background, most of the protagonists and their characters, where a particular tale fits into the overall story and how to understand the motivation of those involved. Because these myths are the foundation of the great tragedies of Euripides, Sophocles and others, to understand myth is to appreciate all the more deeply the monumental works of western culture such playwrights produced.

Modern Resonances

Finally, these myths are so powerful and so deeply embedded in western consciousness that they have never gone away. They have inspired countless painters, sculptors, composers and writers from the Renaissance onwards, and so separate box features highlight the post-classical afterlife of each myth. Moreover in our own time we use language and handle objects associated with the ancient gods, frequently while being totally unaware of the fact. This book brings out many of the allusions to myth that crop up in modern life – often in completely unexpected contexts – and in so doing will, it is hoped, add to the reader's understanding not just of the classical world, but of the modern world as well.

The source material from which this guide has been compiled ranges from the works of Homer and Virgil to the less well-known Hesiod and Ovid by way of lyric poets such as Bacchylides and Pindar, as well as the Orphic hymns. Where there has been some disagreement in the source material (especially on the topic of who begat whom) the tendency has been to go with those that allow the construction of a seamless narrative, though some of the more jarring dissonances are noted for those readers who want to take things further. All translations are by the author unless otherwise stated.

1

In the Beginning: From Chaos to Cosmos in Four Steps

To the Greeks and Romans, the world started bright, fresh and new. As with many young things, there was a large degree of disorder, but also immense vitality and energy. Those living later in the classical era considered that the golden age was done and their universe was relatively orderly only because it lacked the wild exuberance of youth.

The birth of myth

Just as the Romans believed newborn baby bears were without form until licked into shape by their mothers, it took the great storytellers of antiquity, from Homer to Virgil, to mould the inchoate stories of Greek and Roman myth into what became their standard forms. The pages which follow tell of the Creation much as it was given shape by Hesiod in about 720 BC. His version, called the *Theogony*, became for the Greeks and Romans the most widely accepted (but not the only) story of the creation of the universe.

Step 1
Chaos Theory

Before there was earth or sea or the sky that covers everything, all nature was the same the wide world across. [It was] that which we call chaos;

a raw confused mass, nothing but inert matter,
badly combined discordant atoms of things,
all mixed up in the same place.
OVID *METAMORPHOSES* 1.10ff

At first all was Chaos. Time, heaven, earth, the skies and the waters were all co-mingled and there was neither reason nor order in the mingling. Chaos was infinite and dark, a yawning chasm through which the jumbled elements that would later make up the world were forever falling. Chaos contained all things that ever were to be, though none yet existed in organized form. It was, as the followers of Orpheus later described it, 'the egg of the world'. It was here, in the uncountable space before time existed, that certain forces began to take shape which became the first organized entities in the universe. These were the big four: Eros, Gaia, Tartarus and Nyx/Erebus. Every divine entity among the thousands and thousands in the ages to come would be descended from these.

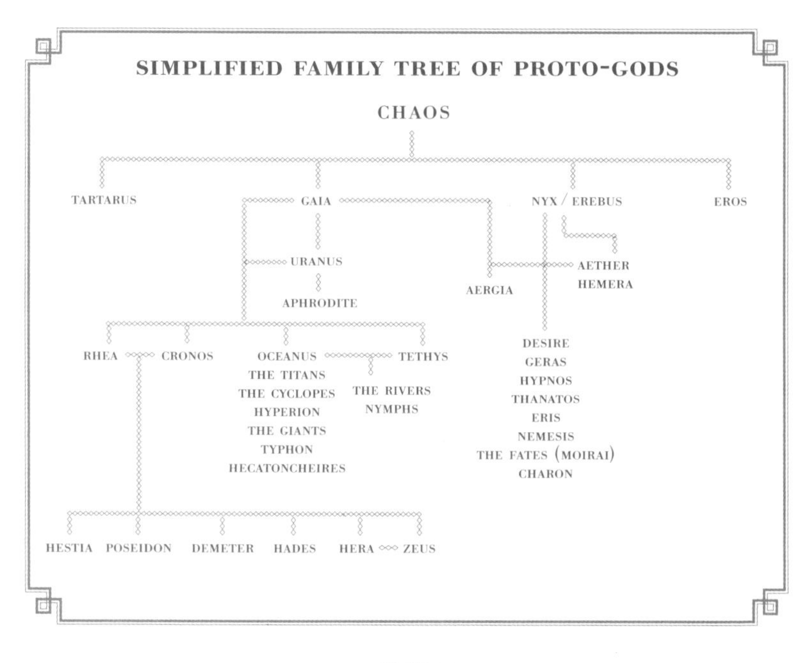

Eros

The first to emerge from Chaos was the proto-god Eros (Love). The primeval Eros was a mighty force, arguably the greatest of all, for without Eros the other beings who sprang from Chaos would have remained static and unchanging, eternal yet sterile. For Eros embodied not only love but also the entire reproductive principle. In later eras he would offload many of his duties to other deities and become the cuddly Cupid of Roman times. But we would do well to remember, through the occasionally gruesome tales that follow, that the universe of myth was created through Love.

Eros and his potent bow.

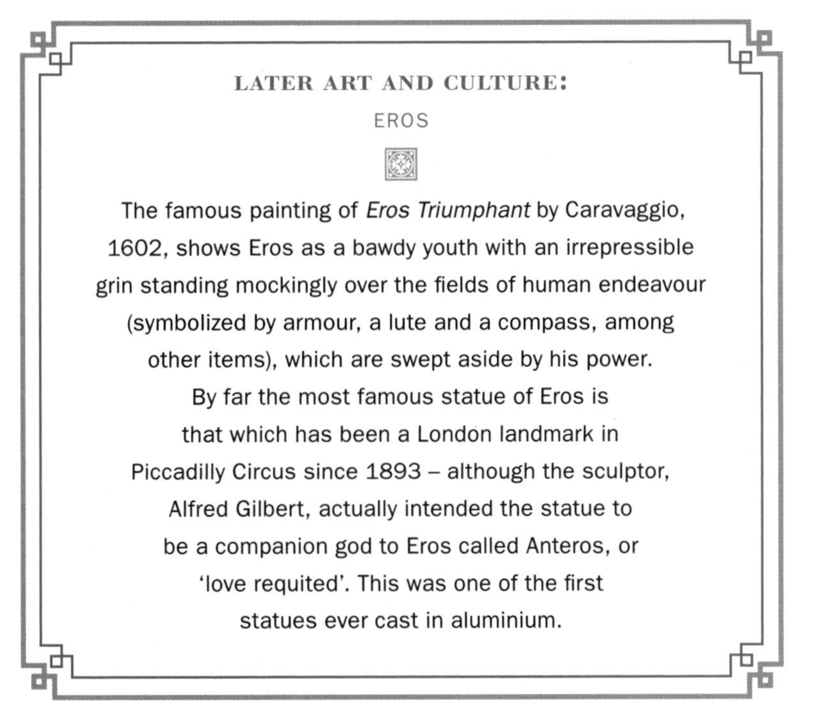

LATER ART AND CULTURE: EROS

The famous painting of *Eros Triumphant* by Caravaggio, 1602, shows Eros as a bawdy youth with an irrepressible grin standing mockingly over the fields of human endeavour (symbolized by armour, a lute and a compass, among other items), which are swept aside by his power.

By far the most famous statue of Eros is that which has been a London landmark in Piccadilly Circus since 1893 – although the sculptor, Alfred Gilbert, actually intended the statue to be a companion god to Eros called Anteros, or 'love requited'. This was one of the first statues ever cast in aluminium.

Gaia

The first upon whom Eros worked his magic was Gaia, the Earth, for only the Earth is able to bring things from itself by itself – a principle known to ancient Greeks and modern man alike as parthenogenesis, or 'maiden birth'. And so, says Hesiod, 'without the sweet union of love' Gaia brought forth from herself Uranus, who was the sky (Caelus to the Romans), and Pontus, the waters.

Tartarus

This was the dark opposite of Gaia. Where Gaia was fertile, and alive, Tartarus was sterile and dead. In later ages Tartarus would be the prison for giants and monsters (human or otherwise) too powerful or dangerous to walk the earth. Even Eros could do nothing with Tartarus, who produced no offspring.

Nyx

Eros had an easier time with Nyx, 'the black-winged night', which had already a certain duality, being also Erebus, the night of Tartarus. And, through Eros, Nyx and Erebus came together to produce Hemera, which became the Day, and Aether, which became the heavens, the upper air, the breath of the gods and the border between Tartarus and Gaia. (Aether was one of the primordial forces of the universe, but not a particularly creative one, so it is no surprise that when he did later come together with Gaia their offspring was Aergia, the goddess of Laziness.). With the birth of these entities, the basic foundations of the universe were complete.

Step 2
The Big Bang: The Line of Gaia and Uranus

Of Gaia I shall sing, mother of everything,
deep-rooted and eldest, who nourishes all.

HOMERIC HYMN 30

The dynamic duo of the early universe were Gaia and her 'son' Uranus; the earth and the sky. Like her fellow proto-gods, Gaia was not human in thought or nature, and each force acted upon the other with no regard for such human concepts as mother–son relations or incest. It was enough that Gaia was the female element and Uranus the male, who every night covered the earth in his starry splendour. Of course, there was no measuring the time in which this happened, for time was yet to be born, and Chaos, from which the four first forces had sprung, still lay between the earth and the heavens. And as we well know, chaos has never completely gone away.

Gaia today – literally everywhere

Gaia is best known today in the Gaia hypothesis, which postulates that the earth is in fact a single living organism. As a result, the Gaia name is now used in everything from government programmes to vegetarian sausages.

However, our dictionaries know Gaia best in her aspect of Ge (see p. 22 for aspects), the Earth. A picture (*graphe*) of Ge gives us geography, and we also have geostatic satellites and geophysical studies. The study of Gaia's bones gives us geology, and the measurement of the earth gives us geometry. Those farmers who work the earth – *ge-eurgos* – have given us the name of George, and the two states of Georgia.

Uranus today

Uranus is best known today as the seventh planet of the solar system. In fact, the planet was unknown to the ancients, being discovered only in 1781, and coincidentally was originally named after King George, who, as we have seen, had Gaia, Uranus' consort, as his namesake.

The metallic element uranium was discovered soon afterwards, and received its name as a tribute to the discovery of the planet. Just as Uranus was believed to be the last of the planets, uranium was once believed to be the last of the elements.

The Titans

The union of Gaia and Uranus was fruitful, and produced a horde of creatures who are collectively known as the Titans. These assumed different forms. Many were monstrous, and, being immortal, survived to trouble humanity in later ages. Others were integrated into the pattern of the universe as it continued to take shape, and became indispensable to its proper functioning. Among the latter were Oceanus, who embodied the world-river that flowed around all of Ge, or rather around the Eurasian landmass and north Africa, which is all the ancients knew of the earth. There was also Mnemosyne, mother of the Muses, and Hyperion, from whom in turn were born Helios (the sun), Selene (the moon) and Eos ('the rosy-fingered dawn').

Titans today

Titan is a large moon of Saturn, and a noun (titan) or adjective (titanic) meaning 'almost superhuman'. The strength of the Titans gave its name to the very strong metal titanium, and to the *Titanic* – a ship somewhat less strong than believed. The name was also used for a long-serving series of space rockets.

Monstrous offspring

Other children of Gaia and Uranus included the one-eyed race of Cyclopes, and the gigantic and terrible Hecatoncheires, each of which had fifty heads and one hundred arms and hands (Hecatoncheires means 'hundred-handers'). These latter creatures had considerable potential for trouble, and in some versions of the tale Uranus had them cast into Tartarus. Others claim that Uranus refused to let the monsters be born at all, keeping them confined in the womb of Gaia beneath the earth, never to directly trouble the world of men.

Gaia took a dim view of Uranus' treatment of their children, and decided it was time to do something about it. The Time in question was her youngest son Cronos, with whose birth chronology as we know it came into the universe. And just as time has a way of passing unnoticed for those having fun, so too did Cronos take Uranus unawares while he lay with Gaia and castrated him with a deft stroke of an adamantine sickle thoughtfully provided by his mother.

The discarded genitals fell into the waters and there seeded the birth of Aphrodite, the oldest of the deities who were to become the 'Olympians' (p. 54). 'She is called Aphrodite as she was born in foam [*Aphros*] … and Eros attended her birth along with sweet Desire, and they took her to the family of the gods, and to her allotted place in the whisperings of girls, the smiles, deceptions and the delectable tenderness of intimacy among humans and among the immortal gods' – so Hesiod tells us.

LATER ART AND CULTURE:
THE BIRTH OF APHRODITE

The legend of the birth of Aphrodite (known to the Romans as Venus) inspired in the 1480s one of the best-known works of Renaissance art – Sandro Botticelli's *Birth of Venus,* showing the goddess as she emerges from the waters. 'Venus' may be modelled on the beautiful courtesan Simonetta – especially as the seashell in Renaissance Italy was a metaphor for that part of the body that Venus conceals in the painting.

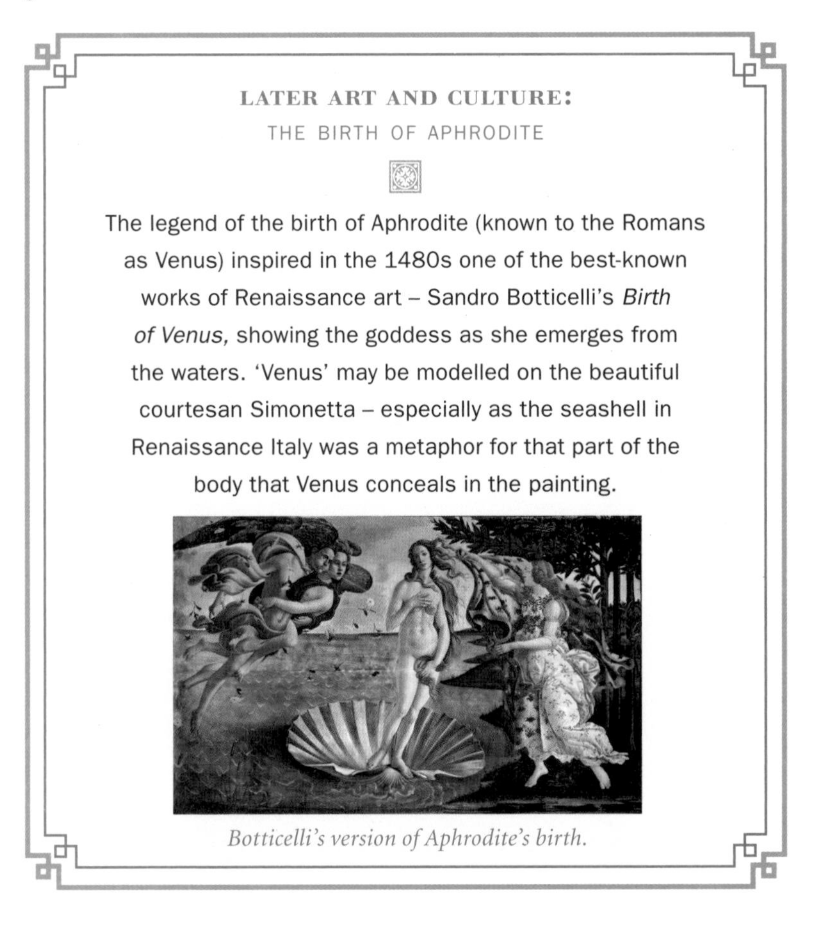

Botticelli's version of Aphrodite's birth.

Winged sleep and death carry off a mortally wounded hero (Attic vase c. 510 BC).

The Children of the Night

For those who wonder where 'sweet Desire' had come from to assist at the birth of Aphrodite, the answer is that Nyx had been busy as well. Desire was one of the more pleasant of a decidedly mixed bag of Nyx's children, which included Geras (Old Age), Hypnos (Sleep), Thanatos (Death), Eris (Discord) and Nemesis (Retribution), as well as the dread Moirai, or Fates, who wove the destiny of men and gods alike.

Step 3
The Neoptolemus Principle and the Birth of Zeus

The Neoptolemus Principle dictates that the harm a man has done will in turn be done to him. The Greeks took this almost as a law of nature and named it after a son of Achilles (p. 196) who was killed as brutally as he had slain many others. Although Neoptolemus himself lived much later, the principle at work can be seen even at this early stage in the attack on Uranus. Gaia and Uranus continued to consort, but the castrated Uranus ceased to interact meaningfully with the universe, and soon dropped from the record. Gaia too stepped into the background. In fact, she *became* and remains the background itself.

Cronos and Rhea

Cronos led a new generation of gods, taking as his consort his sister Rhea. Rhea is a minor character in Greek myth, but came back strongly in Roman religion as the Magna Mater, the Great Mother, being as she was the mother or grandmother of the Olympian gods. In the modern world Rhea is the largest of the moons of Saturn. This is appropriate, since for the Romans Cronos (with a touch of Hades) became Saturn, an agricultural god who is today worshipped as Saturday (Saturn's day).

Several significant women in early Roman myth were called Rhea. Rhea Silva was the mother of Romulus and Remus, and another Rhea was the mother of Aventius (with Heracles), after whom the Aventine Hill of Rome is named.

Sadly for Gaia, Cronos decided that, upon mature reflection, it might be better if her monstrous offspring stayed imprisoned in Tartarus. Having started along illiberal lines, Cronos remained consistent. He knew full well that Nemesis was already on his case after the castration of his father, and that the Neoptolemus Principle meant that he, in his turn, was likely to suffer at the hands of one of his children.

The (un)birth of the Olympians

Cronos attempted to avert retribution by his children for the attack on his own father, but since gods are immortal, killing his offspring was not an option. Uranus' experience suggested that stuffing them back into their mother did not work, so Cronos took matters into his own hands – indeed into his own stomach – by swallowing his children as they were born; a metaphysical reflection of the fact that in the long run, Time does indeed swallow up all his children.

Cronos receives a stone, instead of Zeus.

However, in attempting to avoid his father's example, Cronos still committed the identical error of not considering the maternal instincts of his wife. Like Gaia, Rhea was angered by the fate of her children, and like Gaia, she was prepared to do something about it.

Baby Zeus suckled by Amalthea, from the bas-relief of an ancient altar.

The birth of Zeus

Like any good Greek girl in all the ages to come, Rhea turned to her mother for advice. Gaia advised her daughter to come home. And so, when Rhea's pregnancy with her youngest came to term, she returned to the earth. And here Zeus was born, possibly at Lyktos, or maybe Mt Ida, or maybe Mt Dikte, but certainly in Crete. When Cronos duly turned up to swallow the newborn, he was given instead a large lump of Cretan stone wrapped in swaddling clothes. And so Cronos went away believing that he had consumed the latest of his children, while Gaia carried off Zeus, her grandchild, to be raised in secrecy, fed by the honey of the wild bees and nourished by the milk of Amalthea, one of the first goats ever to be.

LATER ART AND CULTURE:

THE BIRTH OF ZEUS

The great Flemish artist Rubens based many paintings on mythological themes. In Roman mythology it was Saturn who fathered Zeus (Jupiter) and consumed his other children, and Rubens' *Saturn*, 1636, is a horrifying picture of a man tearing a living child with his teeth. This theme developed into one of black insanity in the early 1820s with Goya's painting *Saturn Devouring One of his Sons*. By contrast, the escape of Zeus was charmingly depicted in 1615 by the Baroque master Gian Lorenzo Bernini in a small marble sculpture called *The Goat Amalthea with the Infant Jupiter and a Faun.*

Goya's nightmarish vision of Cronos.

Heavenly wars: the Titanic struggle

Though Zeus was quietly growing into his power away from his father's watchful gaze, Cronos was both powerful and crafty: if he were to be overthrown, Zeus would need allies. And so Gaia inveigled Cronos into regurgitating Zeus' brothers and sisters, from last to first – and as soon as Cronos vomited the stone he had believed to be Zeus, the game was up. Zeus freed the imprisoned sons of Gaia from Tartarus and Cronos called upon his brothers and sisters, the Titans, to defend his reign. War commenced in heaven and mighty was the struggle, which, according to Hesiod, for ten years 'made the vault of heaven shake and groan and the earth and boundless seas threw back the echoing roar; high Olympus was shaken to its base and the earthquakes came in endless succession'. But eventually Cronos was defeated, and the Titans who had fought with him were imprisoned in Tartarus.

War with the Giants

But before Zeus could be secure as master of the universe, he still faced great challenges, the first of which consisted of the Giants, who had sprung from the earth from the blood of Uranus, just as Aphrodite had risen from the sea. Led by Atlas, the Giants piled the mountains atop one another in an ultimately unsuccessful attempt to reach and storm Olympus, the mighty mountain in northern Greece which Zeus and his siblings had made their home and citadel.

Gods going to battle with Giants, from a Greek vase by Nikosthenes.

LATER ART AND CULTURE:

WAR WITH THE TITANS AND GIANTS

The wars of the gods against the Titans and Giants formed a theme in the Renaissance and later Enlightenment, with artists using the allegory of enlightened values set against ignorant barbarism for the propaganda purposes of their sponsors. Examples include Giulio Romano's *The Fall of the Gigants from Mount Olympus,* 1530–32, Joachim Wtewael's *The Battle Between the Gods and the Titans,* 1600, and Francisco Bayeu y Subías's *Olympus: The Fall of the Giants,* 1764.

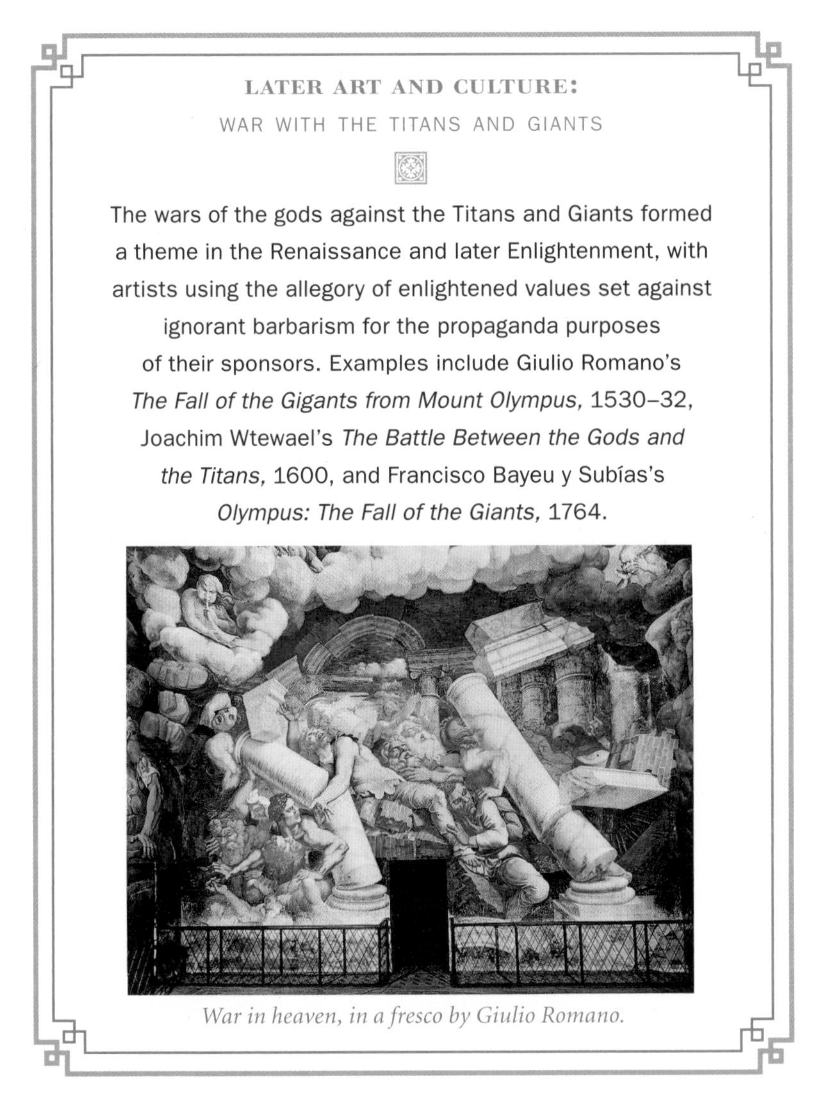

War in heaven, in a fresco by Giulio Romano.

Terrifying Typhon

The final and most awful challenger to the authority of Zeus was Typhon, the hundred-headed, the hurricane, the breather of fire. He was the youngest son of Gaia, and came closest of all to bringing the forces of disorder and darkness to victory on earth. But Zeus

Typhon smitten by Zeus' thunderbolt (detail).

discovered his skill with the thunderbolts the Cyclopes had made for him and with these he smote Typhon and cast him into the earth beneath Mt Etna in Sicily, from whence Typhon still periodically belches fire in his futile rage.

Step 4
The Cascade Effect

With Zeus, the embodiment of order, now securely on his throne on Mt Olympus, the world began to take its final shape. It was a numinous world, a world of great gods and lesser gods, and to each fell the responsibility of filling all that remained of creation.

Aspects of the gods

A divine being could fulfil the various roles ascribed to him or her in two ways. The first was by aspects – different facets of the god, each reflecting a different role that the god had assumed. Thus Zeus was the king of the gods, but he was also the bearer of thunderbolts and the gatherer of the clouds, the god of storms, and in other aspects a god of prophecy and healing and a protector of strangers. A mortal seeking divine favour would address himself to that aspect of the god he required, and indeed, if his prayers were comprehensively answered, he might even build a temple to that aspect of the god.

Children of gods

Gods could also hand on some of their responsibilities to their offspring. Thus one can imagine the world of myth as a cascade of gods flowing into every part of the world, each god creating and occupying a niche, and giving birth to children who filled the sub-niche under that. For example, Tethys, daughter of Gaia, became the consort of Oceanus, and from their union came the great rivers of Ge, and from them came thousands of nymphs, each to haunt her own grotto or pool.

Pontus, the waters, produced Nereus, the 'Old Man of the Sea' (who is also known as Proteus, whose ability to adapt himself to any task – or shape – has given us the adjective 'protean'). Pontus populated every bay and cove with his descendants, the Nereids, who live also in the deep water and sport with the dolphins. And as the great gods of the waters produced minor gods, who produced yet more, ever more localized and specialized deities, so too did the other gods bear offspring in their hundreds, until there was not a force in the universe, from the winds to the seasons, which had not its own god or goddess. Each abstract idea had – was – a deity, and every grotto had a nymph, and every grove a dryad.

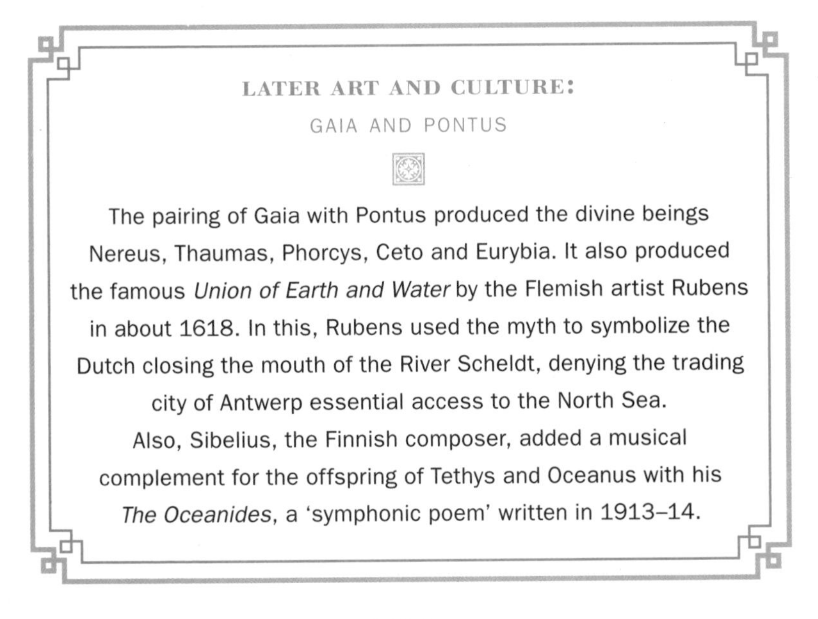

LATER ART AND CULTURE:

GAIA AND PONTUS

The pairing of Gaia with Pontus produced the divine beings Nereus, Thaumas, Phorcys, Ceto and Eurybia. It also produced the famous *Union of Earth and Water* by the Flemish artist Rubens in about 1618. In this, Rubens used the myth to symbolize the Dutch closing the mouth of the River Scheldt, denying the trading city of Antwerp essential access to the North Sea.

Also, Sibelius, the Finnish composer, added a musical complement for the offspring of Tethys and Oceanus with his *The Oceanides*, a 'symphonic poem' written in 1913–14.

A world of gods, a world of men

The world now created was both humanistic and numinous. Humanistic because the new gods were a part of the natural world: they were divine, but not omnipotent, and certainly not always wise. They shared the same values, aspirations and failings as humans. Although their food was ambrosia and their blood ichor, the gods ate, felt pain, jealousy and anger, and bled when injured. Yet unlike humans, the great gods were among the powers that the Greeks called daemons – normally invisible, yet omnipresent or able to travel great distances in no time at all. However, the motives behind their activities are humanly comprehensible and often far from laudable.

And as the gods were a part of the natural world, they were therefore on the same continuum that linked man with the beasts, so the division between human and divine was not clear-cut, as it is today.

Between gods and humans (the how and why of the creation of humanity is a topic for the next chapter) stood a host of beings, some of which, such as the satyrs, possessed elements of the divine while being less than human. Not only lesser divinities but even the great gods and goddesses were capable of interbreeding with humans, and did so with considerable enthusiasm.

The ancients were part of a world saturated with divine beings, and in which new divinities – even great gods such as Dionysus (see p. 103) – were constantly appearing. Fauns and satyrs frolicked in the forest glens, and dreadful creatures such as the vampire-like stryx haunted the night. Even apparent humans might be gods travelling incognito, or demigods, or the children of gods, for humans and their gods could interact at every level and in every way that it was possible for humans to interact between themselves. There was no division between natural and supernatural – the supernatural *was* natural. The world of myth was still taking shape, and as will be seen, humans were fully involved in that shaping. But the order of the universe was complete – it had become a single, organized whole – or, as the Greeks would say, a 'cosmos'.

2

Pandora's Children: The Human Story

Because the world of myth is holistic, with everything a part of everything else, there is no simple narrative that can explain developments as they unfolded. Humans appear early in the creation of the cosmos, and their story is interwoven with that of the gods to form a complex tapestry. Disentangling the threads of this tapestry is difficult but essential if we are to understand the interaction of humans and the divine. Humanity was older than some of the gods, and therefore it is right that their place in the cosmos should be explained here before we go on to look at particular gods and their individual stories – not least because humans are an important element in most of these stories.

Part 1
The Ages of (Wo)Man

Two stones big enough to fill a cart lie at the ravine's edge.
These stones are clay-coloured – not the colour of earth-like
clay, but like that found in a ravine or a sandy stream;
and the stones smell very much like human flesh.
The locals say that these stones are remnants
of the clay from which humankind was
shaped by Prometheus.

PAUSANIAS *GUIDE TO GREECE* 4.1

Not all the Titans fought against Zeus. One who was his ally was Prometheus, who bears a name linked to the concepts of 'forethought' and 'planning ahead'. In the days when Cronos still ruled the heavens, Prometheus had fashioned a creature called man to walk the earth. As Ovid explains in his *Metamorphoses*: 'He took the rainwater, which has still something of the heavens, and mixed this with the earth into a creature never seen before. For, while other animals look to the ground, this creature could turn its face to the stars, and see there his likeness in the gods who are masters of all.' Nor was this merely a physical likeness, as will be seen below.

The Age of Gold

Let this age of iron cease, and a
[new] Golden Age arise.
VIRGIL *ECLOGUES* 4.9ff

Early humans were exclusively male. And in the 'Age of Gold' described by Hesiod, theirs was a bachelor existence. 'They lived without care or trouble ... their banquets were free from evil ... and all good things belonged to them.' What happened to end this idyll is confused, and the many different tellings of the tale can never fully be reconciled. But it would appear that a clash of divine wills brought about both the end of the Golden Age and, not coincidentally, the creation of woman.

Tricking Zeus

Prometheus wanted the best for his creation, yet he accepted that men must sacrifice to the gods. So he prepared an ox for the dinner of Zeus, arranging the bones in one portion artfully beneath a layer of fat, while the other portion had meat and nourishing innards all carelessly thrown down and covered by the ox's paunch. 'Take your pick of these portions, great Zeus,' said the cunning Titan, 'and after the sacrifice the other portion shall go to humans.' Zeus easily saw through the trick, and was angered by the attempt. Nevertheless he took the fat and the bones, and the gods ever after had to be content with these when an animal was sacrificed. But there was a price to be paid for offering the gods the lesser share, and for the presumption of Prometheus. Zeus decided that this punishment would be harm to mankind, the Titan's beloved creation.

Prometheus steals fire

Zeus decreed that humans were to be denied the secret of fire, a lack that would keep them in primitive savagery and barely one step ahead of the animals. But stubborn Prometheus sneaked fire to his protégés, by hiding it in a hollow reed. And when Zeus later looked out over the earth and saw the stars in the heavens mirrored by fires in human settlements on the ground, he knew that Prometheus had defied him.

His wrath was terrible. He ordered the gentle Titan to be chained to a rock in the distant Caucasus mountains and then sent there an eagle to eat the prisoner's liver. The immortal Prometheus could not die, and overnight his liver grew back, to be agonizingly eaten again the next day.

The wrath of Zeus – the excruciating punishments of Atlas and Prometheus.

LATER ART AND CULTURE:

PROMETHEUS

The legend of Prometheus has powerful themes of self-sacrifice, altruism, suffering and redemption, which, unsurprisingly, have evoked responses in all the arts. In drama and verse Percy Bysshe Shelley produced his dramatic reworking of the ancient Greek playwright Aeschylus' *Prometheus Unbound.* In the twentieth century *Prometheus* was an opera by the German composer Rudolf Wagner-Régeny. In painting there have been many interpretations of the myth, from Piero di Cosimo's *Myth of Prometheus*, 1515, to Dirck van Baburen's *Prometheus Being Chained by Vulcan,* 1623. Gustave Moreau gave an expressionist twist to the theme in the nineteenth century, a time when the partition of Poland also evoked *The Polish Prometheus* (1831), in which the artist Horace Vernet depicted Poland as a recumbent soldier on whom the Russian eagle is feeding. The theme is best depicted in marble by the 1762 statuette by Nicolas-Sębastien Adam, which is now in the Louvre.

Prométhée Enchaîné, *which took the sculptor Adam twenty-seven years to produce.*

Pandora

Hephaestus, at Zeus' command, made a woman's body from clay. Athena gave it life, and the rest of the gods each gave some other gift. Because of these gifts they named her Pandora ['All-giving']. ... Pyrrha was her daughter.

HYGINUS *FABULAE* 142

Still furious, Zeus now turned his attention to mankind itself. In order to harm them, Zeus prepared 'a beautiful evil to balance the blessing of fire', namely Pandora. Zeus' fellow gods – some of whom were, after all, female – gave to the creation of Hephaestus a dowry of many gifts for mankind so as to soften the blow. But the gifts Pandora received needed to be trained to serve humanity, and until then were kept in a huge urn – which later ages have refigured as 'Pandora's box'.

Zeus, however, gave to Pandora a 'gift' that would undo the work of his fellow gods: an unshakeable curiosity. Hardly had Pandora arrived on the earth when she opened the lid to see what the urn contained. Immediately the creatures in the container flew out, and being as yet untrained to serve humanity they became instead despair, jealousy and rage and the myriad diseases and infirmities that afflict humanity. All that remained was hope, which became trapped under the unbreakable rim of the urn, and which mankind was able to train and make a friend, as the other 'gifts' in the urn had been intended to be, though in ways which we cannot now imagine.

Pandora emerges from the ground.

'So,' says Hesiod, at his crabby, inexcusably misogynistic best, 'from Pandora came the ruinous breed of women, an affliction to live with men … and take the fruits of his toil into her own belly.' And subtle and cunning indeed was Zeus, for 'whoever flees marriage comes yet to a pitiful end, alone and destitute of family'.

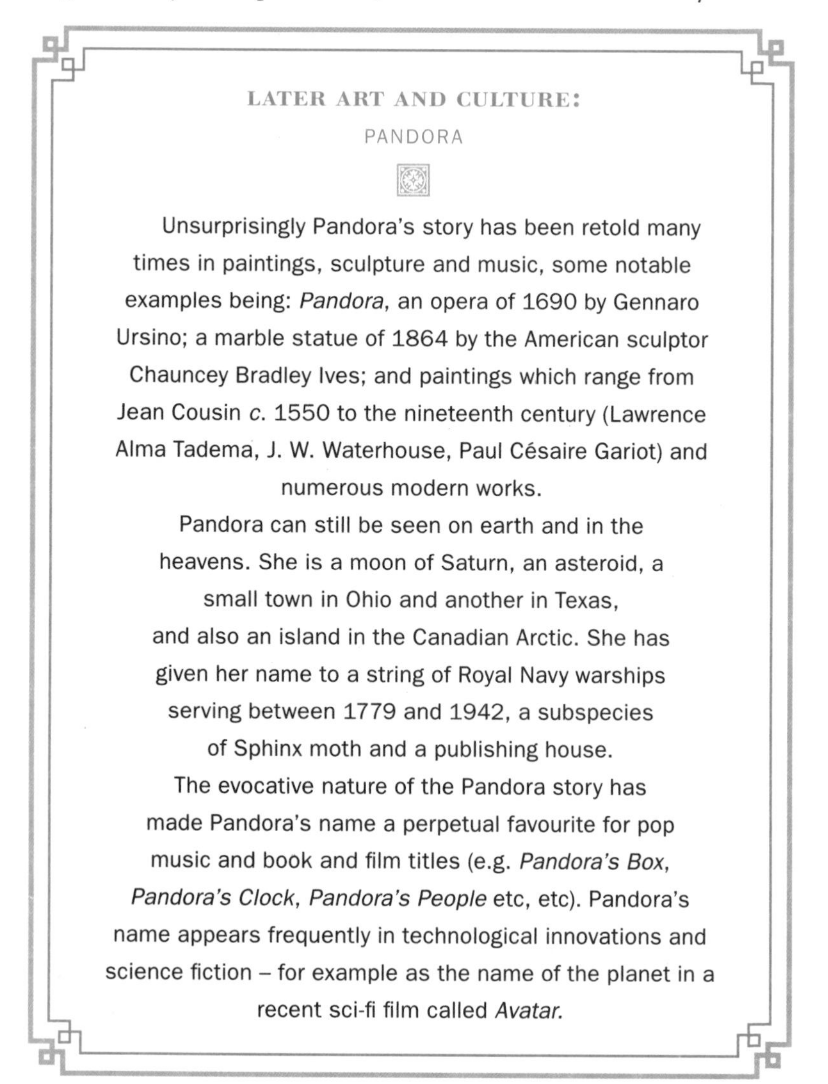

LATER ART AND CULTURE:
PANDORA

Unsurprisingly Pandora's story has been retold many times in paintings, sculpture and music, some notable examples being: *Pandora*, an opera of 1690 by Gennaro Ursino; a marble statue of 1864 by the American sculptor Chauncey Bradley Ives; and paintings which range from Jean Cousin *c.* 1550 to the nineteenth century (Lawrence Alma Tadema, J. W. Waterhouse, Paul Césaire Gariot) and numerous modern works.

Pandora can still be seen on earth and in the heavens. She is a moon of Saturn, an asteroid, a small town in Ohio and another in Texas, and also an island in the Canadian Arctic. She has given her name to a string of Royal Navy warships serving between 1779 and 1942, a subspecies of Sphinx moth and a publishing house.

The evocative nature of the Pandora story has made Pandora's name a perpetual favourite for pop music and book and film titles (e.g. *Pandora's Box*, *Pandora's Clock*, *Pandora's People* etc, etc). Pandora's name appears frequently in technological innovations and science fiction – for example as the name of the planet in a recent sci-fi film called *Avatar*.

The Age of Silver

The torrent of evils that Pandora had unwittingly unleashed into the world ushered in the Age of Silver – which, as might be imagined, was less than satisfactory in comparison with the Age of Gold. Children were brought up by their mothers, and kept firmly secured to the maternal apron strings until they went out into the world as fully fledged adults, unable (due to the excessive feminine influences of their upbringing) to keep faith with each other or with the gods. Violence, wanton treachery and sacrilege followed, and those fully grown babies did not live long after leaving the sanctuary of their maternal home. Eventually Zeus ruled the breed a failure, and removed the peoples of the Age of Silver from the earth.

The Age of Bronze

The Age of Silver was followed by the Age of Bronze, an age of war. So seldom did the warriors of this era remove their brazen armour that some later poets described them as being literally made of bronze. War and battles raged in endless succession, and while Ares, the god of war (p. 92), was in his element, even he had to accept that one could have too much of a good thing. The other gods, particularly mighty Zeus, soon wearied of the Age of Bronze, and it became a question of whether this race of indefatigable warriors would wipe themselves out before Zeus did it for them.

It was a close thing. According to Hesiod, the peoples of the Age of Bronze succeeded in their drive for self-obliteration, but this raises the question of why Zeus went ahead with his plans anyway – for all the tellers of myth are agreed that the King of the Gods raised a mighty flood and the waters swept over the earth and wiped mankind from its face. According to some versions of the tale, the last straw came when a king sacrificed his own son in the perverse belief that this would please Zeus rather than appal him.

Deucalion's Ark

Prometheus, still in pain-wracked captivity, nevertheless kept abreast of events and watched over his creations – in particular over a child of his own called Deucalion, who had married flame-coloured Pyrrha, the daughter of Pandora. The children of gods are long-lived, and evidently this couple had survived the vicious Age of Silver and the violent Age of Bronze. Prometheus was determined that they would also survive the flood. So Deucalion was ordered to construct an ark for himself and his wife, and in this they rode out the great inundation. Eventually, as the waters receded, Deucalion and Pyrrha found their ark had come to rest on a mountain. Precisely which mountain was much disputed in later ages, with Sicilians, Chalcidians and Thessalians each proposing outstanding bits of their landscape for the honour. However, popular opinion settled, as perhaps the ark of Deucalion did itself settle, upon Mt Parnassus near Delphi, summer home of Apollo and later the home of his oracle.

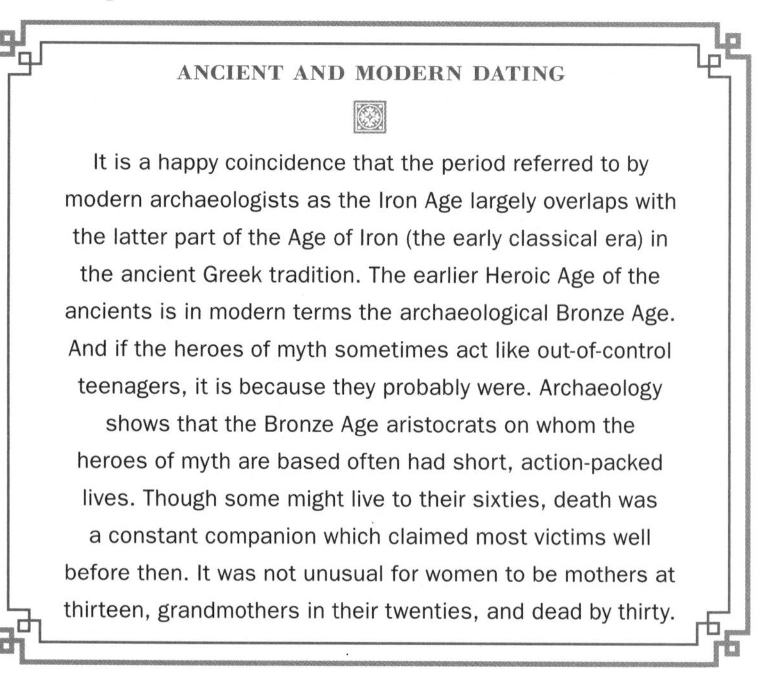

ANCIENT AND MODERN DATING

It is a happy coincidence that the period referred to by modern archaeologists as the Iron Age largely overlaps with the latter part of the Age of Iron (the early classical era) in the ancient Greek tradition. The earlier Heroic Age of the ancients is in modern terms the archaeological Bronze Age. And if the heroes of myth sometimes act like out-of-control teenagers, it is because they probably were. Archaeology shows that the Bronze Age aristocrats on whom the heroes of myth are based often had short, action-packed lives. Though some might live to their sixties, death was a constant companion which claimed most victims well before then. It was not unusual for women to be mothers at thirteen, grandmothers in their twenties, and dead by thirty.

The Age of Iron: Humankind Reborn

Zeus had been calmed somewhat after seeing the dramatic effects of his actions, and sent a message to the castaway pair, Deucalion and Pyrrha, through an oracle: 'Cover your heads and throw the bones of your mother over your shoulder'. After initial puzzlement – for no one knows what had become of Pandora – the pair realized that the mother in question was Gaia, the mother of all – and her bones were the stones that lay plentifully about. Deucalion and his wife did as instructed, and as the stones hit the ground they softened and changed shape. Those thrown by Deucalion became man, and those stones thrown by Pyrrha became woman. Thus were born the first generations of the Age of Iron, the men and women of the Heroic Age whose lives and deeds became the main substance of the mythological corpus.

The Heroic Age was followed by the time in which the tellers of the myths first wove their tales – the age of Homer and of Hesiod. The 'iron' of the age referred less to the development of iron tools, for even in Homer's day bronze was still commonly used, and more to the fact that iron was mundane in comparison to gold, silver or bronze.

Those living centuries afterwards in the later Age of Iron – or as one ancient historian poignantly put it, in the 'Age of Rust' – regarded their universe as complete and orderly. The last monsters were gone, slain by the last heroes, and while the gods and other supernatural entities still had a deep interest in and influence on human affairs, they now worked through human or natural agents rather than by hands-on personal intervention.

For those living after 600 BC the world was mature, indeed even elderly. There was no speculation about what age would follow the Age of Iron, because insofar as they thought about it at all, those living in that era believed that it would be followed by the world generally falling into ruin and the end of all things.

Part 2
The Landscape of Myth

The effect of mythology on the Hellenistic world can easily be confirmed by a glance at an atlas. In fact, both 'Hellenistic' and 'atlas' derive their names from two characters in Greek mythology, Hellen and Atlas.

The Hellenes

We have already seen how Deucalion, the first man, survived the flood and repopulated the world. His son was called Hellen. The children of Hellen settled in Thessaly, and later spread out across the land that became known to the Greeks by the name they still call it today – Hellas.

Other regions of the Greek world were partly named from where the grandchildren and descendants of Deucalion settled:

Dorus moved south and from his name come the Dorian people, who were later to include the Spartans. (The Dorians also give their name to a distinctive type of architecture, 'Doric', of which the most striking example is the Parthenon in Athens.)

Xuthus fathered Ion (though others say that he adopted him, and Ion's true father was Apollo, who seduced Creusa, Xuthus' wife). Ion became the war leader of the Athenians, who thereafter called themselves Ionians. So too did those people of the islands of the Aegean Sea and the Greeks of Asia Minor, who collectively called their lands Ionia.

Yet in Delos do you most delight your heart, Phoebus [Apollo];
for there the Ionians in their long robes gather with their shy
wives and children to do you honour.

HOMERIC HYMN TO APOLLO 2.145ff

Like Doric, Ionic is a style of architecture which has survived the ages – as can be confirmed by a glance at the Ionic columns of many grand buildings, including the British Museum in London and the US Treasury building in Washington.

Achaeus gave his name to the people of the lands west of Athens, notably of the area about Argos and Mycenae – which is why Homer describes those who fought the Trojans as Achaeans. In later years, those who claimed Achaean descent struggled bitterly with the Aetolians, who claimed to be the descendants of Aeolus, another child of Hellen, who settled the lands of southern Thessaly and the far east of Greece.

Hermes steals Io away on a sixth-century BC *Greek amphora.*

The children of Io

In time beyond memory, Greek culture had already spread over much of the eastern Mediterranean. While today we might put this down to trade routes and wars, the ancient Greeks credited these peregrinations to Io, a beautiful princess from Argos. According to mythology, her children helped shape not just Greece but also many other nearby countries. Her descendants form one of the over-arching family trees of mythology, intimately intertwined with the other two great family trees, which are those of Atlas and Hellen.

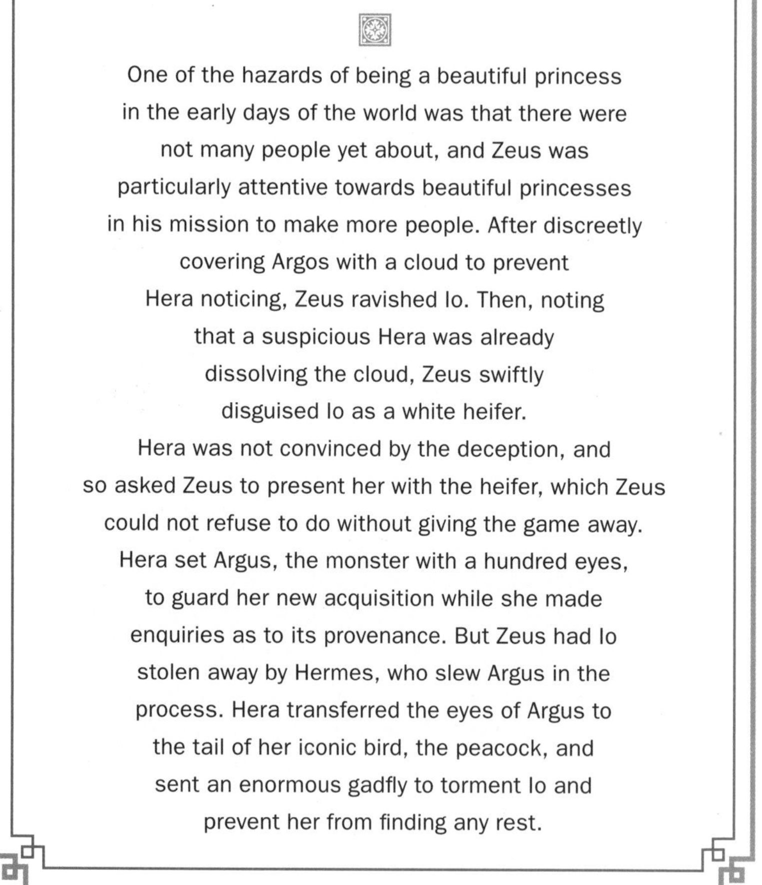

ZEUS AND IO

One of the hazards of being a beautiful princess in the early days of the world was that there were not many people yet about, and Zeus was particularly attentive towards beautiful princesses in his mission to make more people. After discreetly covering Argos with a cloud to prevent Hera noticing, Zeus ravished Io. Then, noting that a suspicious Hera was already dissolving the cloud, Zeus swiftly disguised Io as a white heifer.

Hera was not convinced by the deception, and so asked Zeus to present her with the heifer, which Zeus could not refuse to do without giving the game away. Hera set Argus, the monster with a hundred eyes, to guard her new acquisition while she made enquiries as to its provenance. But Zeus had Io stolen away by Hermes, who slew Argus in the process. Hera transferred the eyes of Argus to the tail of her iconic bird, the peacock, and sent an enormous gadfly to torment Io and prevent her from finding any rest.

After being transformed into a heifer (see box), Io crossed over to Asia Minor by swimming the strait named after that occasion: the 'cow-crossing' or Bosporus. Unable to settle in the east, she moved south, where she finally bore the child by Zeus that she had been carrying. Aegyptus, who gave his name to that country, was one of her descendants. (Another descendant of Io, to whom Zeus also took a fancy, was Europa, who gave her name to a continent.)

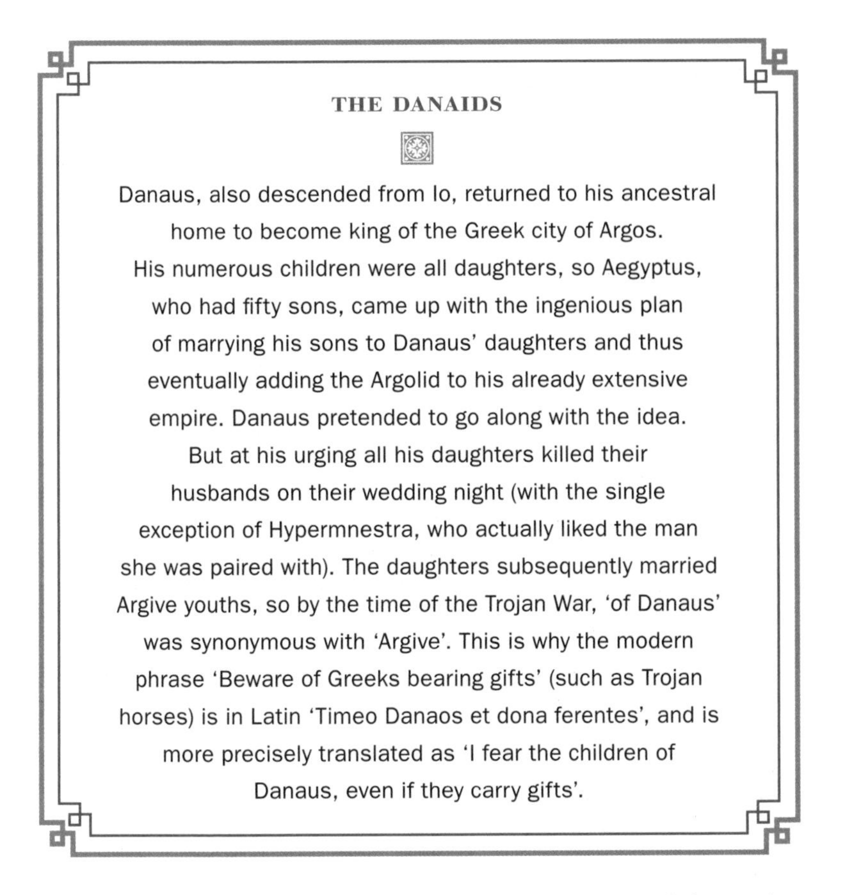

THE DANAIDS

Danaus, also descended from Io, returned to his ancestral home to become king of the Greek city of Argos. His numerous children were all daughters, so Aegyptus, who had fifty sons, came up with the ingenious plan of marrying his sons to Danaus' daughters and thus eventually adding the Argolid to his already extensive empire. Danaus pretended to go along with the idea. But at his urging all his daughters killed their husbands on their wedding night (with the single exception of Hypermnestra, who actually liked the man she was paired with). The daughters subsequently married Argive youths, so by the time of the Trojan War, 'of Danaus' was synonymous with 'Argive'. This is why the modern phrase 'Beware of Greeks bearing gifts' (such as Trojan horses) is in Latin 'Timeo Danaos et dona ferentes', and is more precisely translated as 'I fear the children of Danaus, even if they carry gifts'.

Agamemnon, the king of the Argolid at the time of the Trojan War (see p. 183) was another descendant of Io, but this time by way of Pelops (see p. 75), an immigrant from Lydia in Asia Minor who went on to give his name to the Peloponnese.

Io also numbered several heroic sons in her line, perhaps the most notable being Perseus and Heracles – the latter being significant in this geographical investigation because a number of towns called Heraclea sprang up in honour of the demigod's feats. One Roman version of such a town – Herculaneum – was preserved for posterity under a mudslide from Vesuvius at the same time as Pompeii was buried in ash.

Of Troy and Asia

The Titan Atlas, the brother of Prometheus, has given his name to a mountain range and a major mountain in North Africa. It was he who led the assault on Olympus in the battle between gods and Giants (p. 20). As punishment, Zeus gave him the task of carrying the sky on his shoulders.

Before he took up the heavens, Atlas found time to father several children, including the seven sisters known as the Pleiades (p. 90) and a daughter called Dione. The Pleiad Electra had a descendant called Dardanus, who gave his name to the Roman province of Dardania, and who was in turn the progenitor of Ilus, who founded the city of Ilium, known today as Troy. Some believe that Dardanus also gave his name to the nearby Dardanelles, scene of ferocious fighting during the First World War.

The Farnese Atlas, from Rome.

Since Pelops, ancestor of Agamemnon, was of the line of Dione, it can be seen that the Trojan War was something of a family affair (albeit very distant family). In later ages the Romans traced their ancestry back through Aeneas the Trojan to Dardanus, and ultimately to Atlas. The mother of Atlas was Clymene, or as some accounts have it, Asia, which to the Greeks meant a part of what is now Turkey, but in the modern vocabulary is now the most populous home of mankind.

Part 3
The Human Journey

For the Greeks and Romans, the human spirit, like that of the gods, was immortal and indestructible. The human body, on the other hand, was distressingly mortal. It was prone to decay and eventual death even if the gods did not decree an even more dramatic end. Yet to the ancients, death marked but another step in the development of the spirit. It is with such concepts that ancient myth merges with classical religion, and we realize that the theology of the ancient world embodied a clear and logical belief system as sophisticated as any that exists today. This is nowhere so evident as in the journey of every human from birth to death and far beyond.

Life on Earth

In classical mythology, all living things were at the moment of their creation filled with the spirit of the divine. Virgil, the Roman poet of the first century AD, puts this most clearly in his epic poem the *Aeneid*:

From the divine essence that moves the universe
all life arises, human beings, animals, birds
and even the monsters which move below the
marbled surface of the ocean deep.
The origins of each mind and spirit have
their beginnings and their power in
the fiery heavens.
AENEID 6.725ff

But though the spirit of man was of the heavens, the body was shaped by Prometheus from earthly clay. And though the body was necessary for a human to experience life on earth, the body also acted as 'a windowless prison' for the soul. Held within the body, the soul could only experience external reality through the crude filters of the flesh, and was subject to the rough passions and coarse desires of an earthly existence. As Plato famously put it, our perception of reality is as close to reality's true nature as the shadows that the outside world throws on to a cave wall. The spirit was tainted in the body, and then slowly purified in the underworld.

The underworld was not Hell, which is a place designed specifically for suffering and punishment. How a person lived life while on earth certainly had a bearing on what happened in the afterlife, but by and large the classical world was less judgmental than many other contemporary and later cultures. Partly this was because even as a human lay in the maternal womb, Clotho of the Moirai wove the threads of his or her life and Lachesis, the second of the Dread Sisters, measured its length. (The Moirai are those children of Nyx also called the 'Fates', but the actual Greek means something more like 'allotters'.) Thanks to the Moirai, what happened to a human during his mortal days was largely preordained – the important thing was instead how a person's immortal spirit coped with whatever destiny threw at it.

But in a further twist, one's character was considered as fixed from birth, which is how the Fates were able to factor a person's reactions into his predestined path through life. The best a human could do was to assume that he had an inherently noble nature, and to be true to that nature when his character was tested (and the nature of most heroes – especially in Greek tragedy – was tested in an intense crucible indeed). In short, you were measured not by what you made of your life, but by how well your character stood up to it. In this respect, the Greeks and Romans had a different concept of what it meant to be human. Success or failure was preordained, and indeed, what the fates had in store might be ascertained by diligent enquiry at an oracle. What mattered was how you coped with it.

To the ancients, the earthly sojourn was the equivalent of taking the soul for a vigorous workout in the gym. It was a brief period spent at an unsustainable intensity which left you either a better person or a total wreck. When your ordained time was up, you had to leave, and in classical myth time was called by the third of the Fates who cut the thread and brought a human's life to a close. This third fate was Atropos, whose name 'the inexorable' has been passed to atropine, the poison in deadly nightshade.

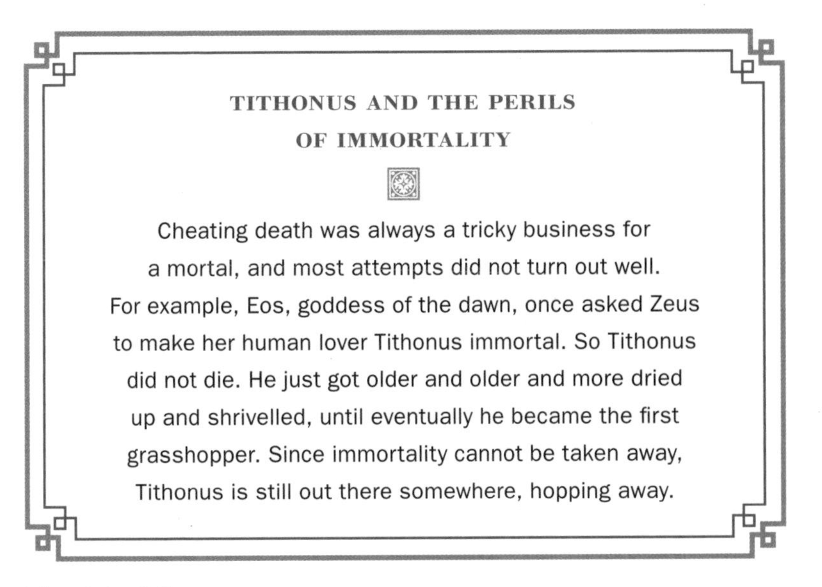

TITHONUS AND THE PERILS OF IMMORTALITY

Cheating death was always a tricky business for a mortal, and most attempts did not turn out well. For example, Eos, goddess of the dawn, once asked Zeus to make her human lover Tithonus immortal. So Tithonus did not die. He just got older and older and more dried up and shrivelled, until eventually he became the first grasshopper. Since immortality cannot be taken away, Tithonus is still out there somewhere, hopping away.

The Afterlife

Yours is the sleep eternal by which the soul
breaks the bonds of the body
Be it man, woman or child, none escapes
if you would gather them in
Youth finds no mercy, strength and
vigour eventually succumb
Here is found the end of nature's work,
in you who passes no judgment
Whom no prayers can weaken, whose
purpose no vows can turn aside.
ORPHIC HYMN TO DEATH 86

To the Greeks and Romans, death was a new beginning. If the relatives of the deceased had done their work and performed the proper rituals, the deceased would be met by Hermes, god of those who pass boundaries. Hermes guided the recently departed to the banks of a river at the border of the underworld which they had to cross.

A ferryman guards these waters. This is dreadful Charon, unkempt and filthy, his tangled white beard dangling from his chin and his ragged cloak loosely knotted about his shoulders. He is aged, but a god is still vigorous and green in age, and a steady flame burns in his glowing eyes. He poles his boat along and tends to the sail, and his battered craft takes each soul across.

VIRGIL *AENEID* 6.290ff

Charon, the ferryman, was the child of the two aspects of night, Nyx and Erebus (p. 12), and thus himself a god. He was a servant of Hades (the brother of Zeus), and once, when Heracles forced the boatman to ferry him across though yet alive, an outraged Hades had the boatman bound in chains for a year. Charon's services were not free, and the riverbank was packed with those who had suffered an irregular burial and therefore had not the coin to pay their fare. (For the Greeks this coin was an obol – a low denomination coin that was placed over the eyelids or in the mouth of the deceased.) What Charon did with the money is unknown – certainly boat maintenance and personal grooming were not over-represented in his budget.

Most believed the river bordering the underworld to be the Styx ('the hateful'), though another candidate was the River Acheron, in northwestern Greece. This was believed to flow from the earthly to infernal realms because, not far from its headwaters, the river plummets through a series of terrifying gorges. The ancients thought that some part of the torrent plunged straight into the underworld, while the remainder went on to wind its peaceful way to the sea.

It is hard for living souls to enter the underworld because the entry to it is guarded by the great three-headed watchdog Cerberus. If the living stumble across the portal he guards, Cerberus makes sure that the trespassers continue their journey as the recently and messily deceased.

LATER ART AND CULTURE:

CHARON

So powerful is the image of Charon that he appears in Michelangelo's otherwise Christian *Last Judgment* in the Sistine Chapel, 1537–41. There, Charon is depicted rather as he is in Dante's *Inferno*, which describes a trip to the Hades of antiquity as seen through a Christian perspective. Charon has been depicted in his own right in pictures such as *Charon Ferrying the Shades* by Pierre Subleyras in the 1730s, and the wonderful Joachim Patinir painting in the Prado Art Gallery in Madrid, 1515–24, but he is probably best known in modern times from the 1982 pop song by Chris de Burgh *Don't Pay the Ferryman*.

Charon, a sole mythological character in Michelangelo's Last Judgment.

The shades of the dead

King Minos (the son of Europa, p. 36) was famed as a law-giver in life and in the underworld he was the judge of the dead. Mostly he arbitrated disputes among the dead themselves, but some felt he also had a say in the rough triage that followed the arrival of a new soul. For not all entered the halls of Hades. Some passed on to the Isles of the Blessed, the Elysian Fields. This destination was reserved for those souls who had acquitted themselves with such distinction and nobility in life that they were removed altogether from the mortal plane. Short of being asked to join the company of the gods themselves, this was the best a mortal could hope for.

On the other hand, there were those who had shown themselves unfit to be a part of the human stock at all. The human spirit is as indestructible as that of any god, so destroying these reprobates was not an option. Instead, they were tossed into the cosmic dustbin of Tartarus. There they joined the imprisoned Giants, Titans and others deemed unfit ever again to set foot on mother Gaia.

The vast majority of humanity ended in the underworld, as shades. A shade was essentially the same person as the deceased, but in greatly attenuated form. It remembered, indeed yearned for, the intense sensations and passions of an earthly existence. With the right ritual a shade could be evoked from the infernal realms, and converse with the living. Thus Odysseus once sought counsel from the dead (p. 204), feeding them with blood from sacrificial victims, which he poured into a small pit dug in the earth.

I took the sheep and cut their throats over the pit,
and let the dark blood flow.
Then there gathered the spirits of the dead,
brides and unwed youths, old men worn
out by labour, and tender maidens with hearts
still new to sorrow.

HOMER *ODYSSEY* 11.20ff

The counsel of the dead might be of limited use, for the wits of the shades were as attenuated as the rest of them, but at least their memories were often clear. Those who had lived most intensely, such as Achilles, suffered most in the pale, tasteless world of Hades. 'I would rather be the slave of the poorest bonded servant on earth than king of the underworld', the hero famously lamented.

One's time in the underworld was variable – some philosophers considered a thousand years a reasonable period to cleanse the soul of the accretion of human passions and earthly cravings it had acquired while in the body. Much depended on the quality of the life the person had lived.

A depraved individual needed a very long time for the contaminants of life to leach from his soul, while an ascetic required only the spiritual equivalent of a quick wash and brush-up. But for all, the period spent in the underworld was far longer than the time spent in the flesh, so the kingdom of Hades, rather than the earth above should be considered as mankind's true home.

Orpheus in the underworld

The son of Calliope, the muse of epic poetry, Orpheus learned from Apollo (p. 82) and was said to play the lyre so divinely that even the rocks and trees would listen to him. He passionately loved his wife Eurydice, and was so devastated by her death that he eventually decided to go to the underworld and bring her back. By his music he charmed his way past Cerberus and Charon, and presented his petition in song to Hades and Persephone.

The dread rulers of the underworld agreed to let Eurydice follow Orpheus out of the underworld, but only if Orpheus did not look back, even for a moment. But when Orpheus was about to leave the underworld, it occurred to him that this might be a trick to make him leave quietly. So he glanced to see if his Eurydice was indeed following him. She was, but at that glance the deal was broken and jealous Hades snatched her back into his power. Orpheus never saw her again.

Orpheus charming the savage Cerberus.

Orpheus became the basis of the cult called Orphism in later centuries. The cult's followers have left a series of moving hymns dedicated to the gods:

Hear, O Goddess, the voice of your supplicant
who prays to you by night and day,
And in this hour, give to me peace and health,
well-omened times, and such wealth as I require,
But above all, be but here for your worshippers,
you guardian of the arts, the maiden with blue eyes.

ORPHIC HYMN 31 TO ATHENA

LATER ART AND CULTURE:

ORPHEUS

A drama involving a fellow musician – how could Offenbach resist? Produced in the 1850s, *Orpheus in the Underworld* is a light-hearted take on the story with a thoroughly Gallic slant that first acquainted Parisians with the high-kicking cancan. The 1607 opera, Monteverdi's *Legend of Orpheus*, is truer to the original tale both in narrative and spirit. In sculpture, Eurydice and Orpheus are remembered by, for example, Antonio Canova's work of 1775, and the Renaissance *Orpheus* by Baccio Bandinelli in Florence. In painting we find Nicolas Poussin's classic *Orpheus and Eurydice* (1650–53), while Albert Cuyp created a version of the popular theme of Orpheus charming the animals with his music, *c.* 1640.

Eurydice follows behind Orpheus in Poussin's masterpiece.

Going back

When you come to that spring to the left of the
house of Hades … you shall tell them,
'I am a child of earth and the starry heavens,
but my generation is of the sky. Quick,
let me drink of that cold-running water …'
INSCRIPTION FOUND IN A TOMB IN PETELIA, ITALY

Eventually, each shade found itself drawn towards the far side of the underworld, where the waters of the little River Lethe trickled over the stones, and where Nyx herself had her home.

Here, Plato envisaged a sort of staging area, presided over by a Sphinx, where the spirits received their future role in life. There was an element of chance in this, and the lottery element is why we refer to our 'lot' in life. Not all lots were suitable for all. Some undemanding roles were needed for souls which had recently ascended from the animals (we have all met at least one of these), while others, after trying human life, might be keen to settle for some bucolic down time – for example, as a cow grazing peacefully in a meadow.

Those new to the business fancied they might find joy as kings or tyrants, whilst others chose short lives, packed with joy and pain and spiritual fulfilment. Plato tells us that Odysseus, having had his fill of worldly endeavour, searched for a lot that gave him the uneventful life of an ordinary man.

All now drank from the stream of Lethe. They immediately lost their memory of their previous life. They were again pure spirit, with the passions and misdeeds of their former lives purged, with the past erased, but with characters developed by previous experience. The spirits now lay down to sleep. They would awaken in the infant bodies they had chosen, and the adventure would begin anew.

Some Greek cults taught that by avoiding Lethe and drinking from the nearby stream of Mnemosyne (memory), one could emerge from the underworld with the recollection of a previous life intact.

LETHE

Lethe was personified as a daughter of Eris (p. 119) and was the goddess of oblivion. The idea of forgetting it all has made Lethe a powerful image in many modern poems, and when the chemical compound ether was used as an anaesthetic, it was originally called 'Letheron'.

APPLICATION OF THE WATERS OF LETHE COCKTAIL

STEP 1

Take 2 oz (approx. 30 ml) gin
1 oz (approx. 30 ml) strawberry liqueur
½ oz (approx. 15 ml) orange juice
½ oz (approx. 15 ml) pineapple juice
1 tsp superfine sugar

STEP 2

Shake vigorously with ice, strain into a cocktail glass and drink.

STEP 3

Repeat until you either don't remember your name, or you have forgotten how to lift the glass. Note that excessive imbibers risk going on to taste the real thing.

3

The Great Gods: The First Generation

Before we approach the great gods of antiquity as individuals, it is necessary to discuss what these gods were, for we cannot understand the nature of myth if we think of the gods merely as spiteful super-beings with poor impulse control. For the gods should not be seen as humans with exceptional powers, but as forces of nature which the ancients believed had a human aspect. Each god controlled or embodied one or more of these forces and it is this concept which we need to examine in some detail before going on to meet the first generation of the Olympian gods.

On the nature of the gods

From the Greek and Roman point of view, refusing to believe in the gods was like not believing in gravity while falling from something high – an odd concept, and irrelevant to the central issue. The existence of the gods was independent of belief in them.

For example, everyone will accept that a fertile seed placed in warm moist earth will put out shoots, and, conditions being right, will become a new plant. Today we call this 'genetic programming'. The Greeks called it Demeter (who was Ceres to the Romans). Belief in either is not essential for the growth of the plant.

Similarly, the seasons of the year change in regular succession whether we believe in them or not. To the Greeks this was but one manifestation of Zeus, the organizing principle. When you tidy your room and arrange the vases and ornaments on the mantelpiece just so – equidistant and showing the same face to the room – that's also Zeus at work.

Someone waking from a nightmare will tell himself that what seemed so terrible just moments before either does not exist or else is not immediately threatening. Or as the Greeks would say, that person invokes Athena, goddess of rational thought. On the other hand, if someone has abandoned rational thought to fall madly in love, them the ancients would consider that person touched by Aphrodite.

In other words, the forces represented by the gods of Greece and Rome are real. The only question is whether they are self-aware, intelligent and interested in human affairs. (Ancient philosophers wondered about this too.) But before rejecting the idea out of hand, remember that all major religions consider their gods to be self-aware, intelligent and interested in human affairs, so the belief of classical religion is in no way exceptional.

Therefore, Greek and Roman myth must be seen not as a collection of superstitions and comic-book superheroes, but as a genuine belief system deserving the same respect as other human efforts to comprehend and engage with the divine. (We might note that some of the more colourful episodes of – for example – the Old Testament might also seem somewhat odd if considered out of context by a non-believer.)

The problem with myth

So how are we to understand the role in myth of the great gods of Olympus? In classical religion the gods embody the primal forces of the cosmos. It is through them that the sun rises, and the rivers flow. It is the gods who oversee justice and the rational working of all things. Yet, in classical myth the gods seem to be silly, squabbling creatures, fond of playing cruel tricks on each other and on humanity, and pursuing vindictive feuds.

ZEUS AND SEMELE

Semele was a priestess of Zeus and, as she was ravishingly beautiful, Zeus promptly set about the concomitant ravishing. Naturally, Zeus appeared to Semele in mortal form; and after she had become pregnant by her lover, Semele began belatedly to wonder if she had been taken in by a smooth-talking human with a great chat-up line. She demanded that Zeus show himself to her in his true form. As Zeus was bound by a promise to do as the lady demanded, he reluctantly complied. Exposed to the true radiant glory of the god, Semele was instantly toasted to a crisp.

Dionysus shares a wine goblet with his mother, Semele.

Resolving the conundrum

In this apparent inconsistency lies an attempt to answer the age-old question of why a just and loving god can allow bad things to happen to good people.

Of course, Greeks and Romans partly answered the question by deciding that their gods were not loving (except in the sense which

Zeus applied to his female companions). Furthermore, as we have seen in Chapter 2, they believed that much of what happened to a person was not in the hands of the gods, but tied to an immutable destiny mapped out by the Fates.

However, rather than accept that their lives were dictated by blind, immutable forces, most people in antiquity wanted – demanded – that their gods should every now and then bend the inexorable laws of nature to give some deserving mortal a break.

We have already seen that the gods had aspects, particular facets of their powers that could be viewed separately from the others. Therefore, to deal with humans, each god had a human aspect – and being human, this aspect had its unattractive side, though it was as far from representing the entire nature of a god as Zeus' human appearance to Semele represented his whole being. (In fact, as will be seen, Semele was anyway fated to perish on seeing the true nature of Zeus, for it was through her death that the thrice-born god Dionysus would come into the world, p. 103.)

There was much more to the ancient gods than their loves, their jealousies and their minor feuds and favourites. Yet it is these that engage our attention, for being human, we are interested in the human side of the gods – especially as it is on this human aspect that the ancients blamed much of the random nastiness that is a sad but integral part of life. Thus the great gods were very interesting characters. As we shall now see.

LATER ART AND CULTURE: ZEUS AND SEMELE

Gustave Moreau painted *Jupiter and Semele* in 1894–95, and Rubens depicted *The Death of Semele* in 1636. *Semele* also became an oratorio in three acts by Handel, first performed in London in 1744.

Aphrodite (Venus), the Irresistible

Parents: Uranus (father) and an adamantine sickle

Spouse: Hephaestus (Vulcan)

Significant lovers: Ares (Mars), Hermes (Mercury), Adonis, Anchises

Children: Aeneas, Harmonia, Deimos, Phobos, Hermaphroditus, Priapus, Beroe

Primary aspect: Goddess of love and sex

Minor aspect(s): Rescuer of sailors, guardian of plants, goddess of marriage and civic harmony, but also of prostitutes

Identified with: Myrtle, the swan, the dove

Temples, oracles and shrines: At Aphrodisias (the city of Aphrodite, in Asia Minor), on the Acropolis of Corinth, the temples in Rome of Venus Genetrix and of Venus and Roma

The power of Aphrodite is irresistible ...
She moves through the air, she dwells in the
sea-wave, she plants the seed and brings that
love from which all of us on this earth are born.
EURIPIDES *HIPPOLYTUS* 445ff

In one sense, Aphrodite is among the elder gods, for she is of the generation before Zeus. In addition, all the gods (with three exceptions, whom we shall come to later) were as subject to her influence as mortals. And, as many mismatched and star-crossed lovers will testify, Aphrodite is perfectly capable of using her powers mischievously, or even maliciously.

The girdle of Aphrodite made its wearers irresistible to whomever they wished to charm, and the hand-mirror of Aphrodite, with its small cross-grip on the bottom, remains even today the symbol for her gender. Her hand is almost omnipresent in the myths of Greece and Rome, and Zeus often attributed his philandering to Aphrodite's influence (though the Roman Jupiter was somewhat more circumspect in his conduct). By some distance the most famous depiction of Venus/Aphrodite is a damaged 2,000-year-old statue in the Louvre known as the Venus di Milo.

One never has to look far to find Aphrodite even today: for example, in the night sky, since Aphrodite is Venus, the evening star. As Venus – the name Aphrodite took from a minor Roman fertility goddess – the lady is not only a planet, but also a crop of nasty diseases spread by the act of love. As Porne, the incarnation of carnal love, her pictures (*porne graphe*) have attracted the excited attention of censors over the ages, while foods that are supposed to increase sexual desire (e.g. oysters) are aphrodisiacs. The lady pops up in unexpected places, such as in connection with the blood-red anemone that represents the mortal remains of her beloved, the beautiful boy Adonis who was killed while hunting. Beroe, the daughter of Adonis and Aphrodite, became Beryut – the city known today as Beirut.

Aphrodite had an illicit romance with Ares, the god of war (for love and war are often paired). Two of her children from that dalliance, Deimos and Phobos (Panic and Fear), still circle their heavenly father, whom the Romans called Mars. Phobos is still frequently found on earth in hundreds of aspects, from ablutophobia (the fear of washing or cleaning) to zoophobia (fear of animals).

The iconic Venus di Milo.

Aphrodite also had a child by Hermes (who was Mercury to the Romans), and this child took the conjoined names of his parents – Hermaphroditus (p. 101). Another child (parentage disputed) was the unfortunate Priapus (p. 101), whose inability to consummate his overwhelming lust left him massively over-endowed. (He so passionately pursued a nymph called Lotus that the gods made her into the flower of that name.)

The Trojan War came about at least in part because Aphrodite excited the love of Paris and Helen (p. 177). Aphrodite took an active interest in the conflict because her son by a mortal called Anchises was a Trojan warrior. This son, Aeneas, was later to flee burning Troy after the Greek victory. His descendants would found the city of Rome, and among the direct descendants of Anchises and Aphrodite were numbered the Caesars of Rome's famed Julian family.

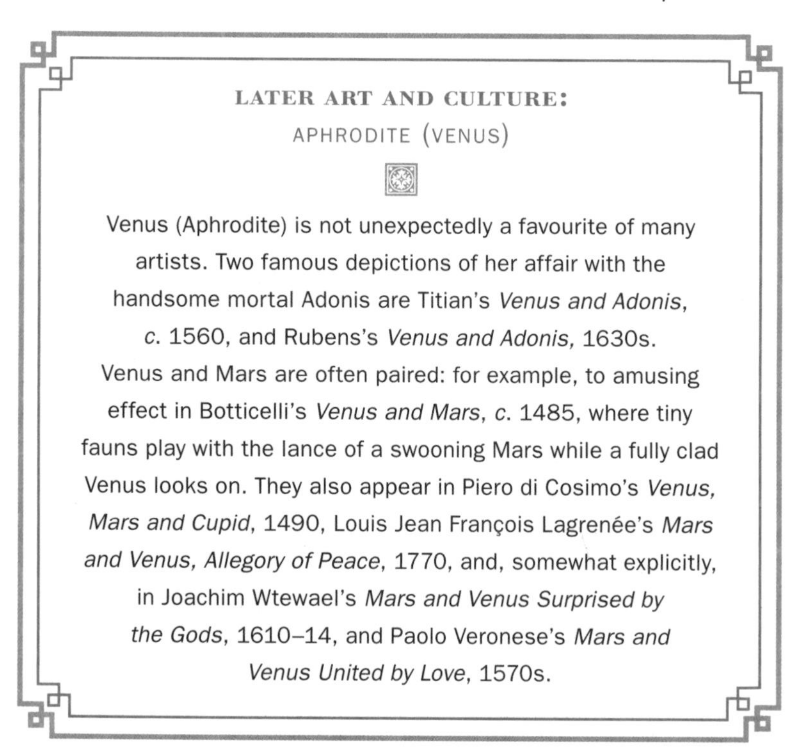

LATER ART AND CULTURE:
APHRODITE (VENUS)

Venus (Aphrodite) is not unexpectedly a favourite of many artists. Two famous depictions of her affair with the handsome mortal Adonis are Titian's *Venus and Adonis*, *c.* 1560, and Rubens's *Venus and Adonis*, 1630s. Venus and Mars are often paired: for example, to amusing effect in Botticelli's *Venus and Mars*, *c.* 1485, where tiny fauns play with the lance of a swooning Mars while a fully clad Venus looks on. They also appear in Piero di Cosimo's *Venus, Mars and Cupid*, 1490, Louis Jean François Lagrenée's *Mars and Venus, Allegory of Peace*, 1770, and, somewhat explicitly, in Joachim Wtewael's *Mars and Venus Surprised by the Gods*, 1610–14, and Paolo Veronese's *Mars and Venus United by Love*, 1570s.

Hestia (Vesta), Domestic Goddess

Parents: Cronos (father), Rhea (mother)

Spouse: None

Significant lovers: None

Children: None

Primary aspect: Goddess of the hearth

Minor aspect(s): Domestic happiness

Identified with: Fruit, oil, wine, cows of one year old

Temples, oracles and shrines: In the hearth of every home, in the civic centre of Greek cities, the shrine of Vesta in Rome

Hestia, in the high dwellings of all, both deathless gods and men who walk on earth, you have gained an everlasting abode and highest honour: glorious is your portion and your right. For without you mortals hold no banquet, where one does not duly pour sweet wine in offering to Hestia both first and last.

HOMERIC HYMN TO HESTIA 2.1-6
(TRANS. H. G. EVELYN-WHITE)

Hestia was the oldest child of Cronos (p. 17), and paradoxically also the youngest, as she was the last to be regurgitated. 'Hestia comes first' was the rule of the Greeks and Romans. It was in part because of her elder status that she preceded all other gods in ritual sacrifice, and also because Hestia represented the home and family.

Hestia, as the Roman Vespa.

As the representative of peace and conciliation, Hestia voluntarily yielded her place among the Olympian gods (generally to Dionysus, though not all Greco-Roman cultures had the same gods in their pantheon) to keep the sacred number of the Olympians at twelve. (Incidentally, the sacred number of twelve also explains the number of stars in the flag of the European Union.) Hestia has a stronger place in Greek and Roman religion than in mythology, since the goddess of the hearth seldom strayed far from home. Her fire did travel, however, as when every Greek city established a new colony, they took the sacred fire of Hestia with them to be nurtured in its new home.

As Vesta in Rome she kept the home fires of the nation burning, and it was deemed a massive misfortune to the state should her fire ever go out. Consequently a college of maidens called the Vestal Virgins were charged with preserving her cult and keeping the sacred fire alight in her shrine.

Unsurprisingly given her role as protector of a happy home, the hopeful founders of several American towns gave Vesta's name to their municipalities, and Vesta's association with fire remains today in a popular brand of matches.

Zeus (Jupiter), King of the Gods

Parents: Cronos (father), Rhea (mother)

Spouse: Hera

Significant lovers: Leto, Leda, Maia, Semele, Io, Europa, Demeter, Metis, Ganymede, Danae, Mnemosyne, Themis and Alcmene – among others

Children of particular note: Athena (Minerva), Persephone, Orion, the Muses, Ares (Mars), Apollo, Artemis (Diana), Heracles (Hercules), Dionysus (Bacchus), Hebe, goddess of youth, Perseus, the Dioscuri, Minos of Crete

Primary aspect: King of the gods

Minor aspect(s): Lord of storms, cloud-gatherer, protector of strangers, guarantor of oaths, smiter of liars, protector of Rome, sender of prodigies, stayer of armies

Identified with: The thunderbolt, the eagle, oak

Major temples, oracles and shrines: The temple of Capitoline Jupiter in Rome, the temple of Zeus at Olympia, the oracle of Zeus at Dodona

My child, deep-thundering Zeus holds the ends of
all in his hands, and disposes of everything by his will ...
we humans live from day to day and little know
what he holds in store.

SEMONIDES OF AMORGOS *LYRICS* 2.1

Mighty Zeus with thunderbolt and eagle, crowned by victory.

It is only partially true that Zeus was the father of the Olympian gods. Certainly he was 'father' in the sense of the *paterfamilias*, head of the household. But he was brother to other gods, including his wife Hera (Juno), Poseidon (Neptune) and Hades (Pluto). Neither Poseidon nor Hades deeply respected their younger brother, since, as Poseidon points out, each of the three gods became master of his realm by pure chance:

Zeus may be strong, but he is over-reaching himself if he threatens me with violence, as I am the same rank as he. We three brothers whom Rhea bore to Cronos – Zeus, myself and Hades who rules below – took each an equal share when heaven and earth were divided. We drew lots, and chance gave me my eternal dwelling in the sea, Hades the infernal realm, and Zeus the sky and the clouds. The earth and mighty Olympus are common to all, and Zeus cannot tell me where to go.... How dare he threaten me as if I were unimportant! If he wants to talk big, let him do so to his sons and daughters who must obey him.

HOMER *ILIAD* 15.191

God of the sky, Zeus was from earliest times a weather god, and his epithet 'gatherer of clouds' stayed with him well into the classical era. Yet as leader of the revolt against Cronos, Zeus was also accepted as king of the gods (albeit grudgingly by Hades and Poseidon), and thus was responsible for maintaining order on Olympus – and, by extension, throughout the cosmos.

Since ancient cities were subject to periodic bouts of disorder, the city authorities were fervent in their prayers to Zeus Poleius, the lord of cities. In everyday life, Zeus was the lord of hospitality, and travellers and strangers were made welcome in his name. And of course, none worshipped the king of the gods with more enthusiasm than those dedicated followers of discipline and order, the Romans. For them Zeus was Jupiter Optimus Maximus, Jupiter the Best and Greatest, who represented all that was right and worshipful in the cosmos. It was under the eagles of Jupiter that the legions spread the Roman version of civilization across the Mediterranean world and beyond. And it is fitting that today the largest of all the planets of the solar system is named after Jupiter, mightiest of all gods.

Zeus before Hera

Like the Greeks and Romans, the gods were not polygamous, and like the Greeks and Romans, the male gods firmly believed that marital fidelity applied to their wives rather than themselves. By the time he settled down with Hera, Zeus was already well into his 'father Zeus' role, with a prolific number of offspring. Despite his wife's best efforts, marriage hardly slowed his headlong promiscuity.

Courtship, Olympian style: Zeus and amoratrix.

THE IMMORTAL CHILDREN OF ZEUS (MOTHER'S NAME IN PARENTHESES)

- ATHENA (METIS)
- THE GRACES (EURYNOME)
- PERSEPHONE (DEMETER)
- THE MUSES (MNEMOSYNE)
- APOLLO, ARTEMIS (LETO)
- POLYDEUCES (LEDA)
- ARES, HEBE, ILEITHYIA (HERA)
- DIONYSUS (SEMELE)
- HERMES (MAIA)
- HERACLES (ALCMENE)

Zeus first consorted with **Metis**, the personification of thought, and needed some fast footwork to dodge the Neoptolemus Principle and avoid being overthrown by his child from that union (see p. 19 and p. 79). Next was **Themis,** the personification of tradition and good conduct. Among their daughters was Eirene (Peace). Then came **Eurynome**, the mother (some claim) of the three Charities or Graces (Brightness, Festivity and Cheerfulness).

The next consort was Zeus' sister, **Demeter**, from whom was born Persephone.

Then the Titan **Mnemosyne** (memory), from whom came the nine Muses. These Muses, including dance, theatre and poetry, have ever since been the source of human creativity and have seen their finest fruits preserved in temples dedicated to their inspiration: museums.

Hera was a serious love interest, if not already a wife, when Zeus began his dalliance with **Leto** (about whom we know appropriately little, since Leto means 'the hidden one'). When Leto became pregnant by Zeus, Hera prevented her from giving birth on either land or sea. However, a suitable spot was eventually found on sacred Delos in the Aegean, which being (allegedly) a floating island, was neither land nor sea. And here was born Olympian Apollo. Leto also bore Artemis (Diana), maiden goddess of the hunt, and this put Leto one up on Hera who only bore to Zeus one Olympian, the petulant and bloodthirsty Ares, god of war.

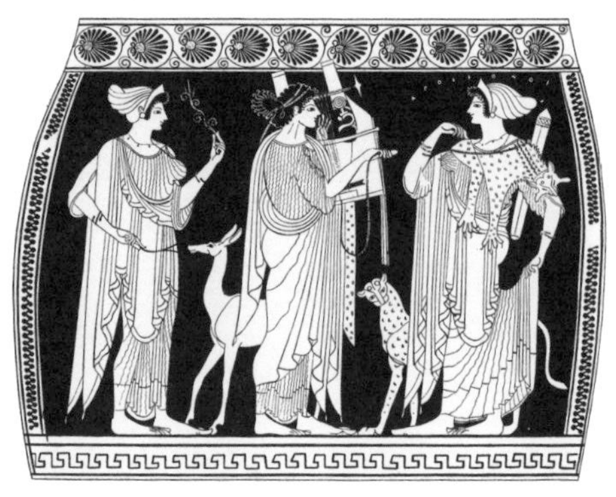

Apollo (with lyre), between his mother and Artemis (with leopard).

Zeus' philandering continued apace – indeed, the creation of womankind opened up for him a whole new world of marital misadventure. Much of what followed from Zeus' many seductions and Hera's vindictive reaction shaped the world of mythology and thus the modern world.

Hera (Juno), the Beautiful

Parents: Cronos (father), Rhea (mother)

Spouse: Zeus (Jupiter)

Significant lovers: None

Children: Ares (Mars), Hephaestus, Ileithyia, Hebe

Primary aspect: Consort of Zeus

Minor aspect(s): Protector of marriage, guardian of women, Juno who gives warning

Identified with: Peacocks, cuckoos, pomegranates

Temples, oracles and shrines: The temple of Hera near Argos, the temple of Hera at Agrigentum in Sicily, the temple of Juno Moneta in Rome

Hera, queen of heaven, daughter of mighty Cronos.

HOMER *ILIAD* BK 5

Hera, the long-suffering wife of Zeus, was unable to retaliate directly against her husband for his infidelities and so took it out on his unfortunate lovers, even though they were hardly in a position to refuse the King of the Gods. One might transpose Hera's character on to instances of the imbalance between the sexes in the real world, where, for example, masters might force themselves on slave girls in their household, and the girls might then be punished by the jealous wife for suffering something that both women were powerless to prevent.

A severe-looking Roman Hera.

Hera's name translates roughly as 'Lady', and probably comes from the same root as the masculine 'hero'. She is queen of the gods, and where Zeus is symbolized by the eagle, she is represented by the pride and ostentation of the peacock. Despite her royal status, Hera was very much subordinate to Zeus, and he once punished her by hanging her from the vault of heaven with anvils chained to her ankles for her vindictive persecution of his son Heracles.

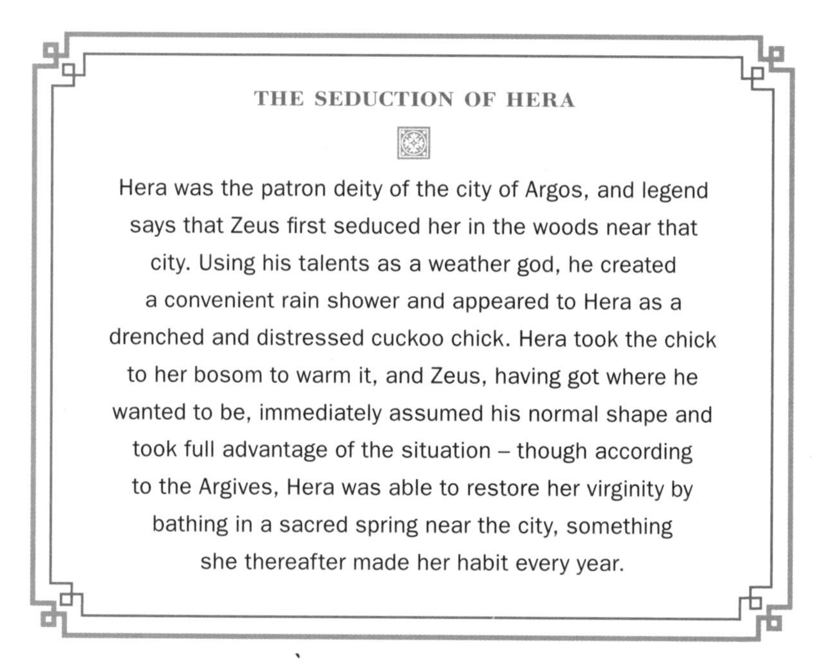

THE SEDUCTION OF HERA

Hera was the patron deity of the city of Argos, and legend says that Zeus first seduced her in the woods near that city. Using his talents as a weather god, he created a convenient rain shower and appeared to Hera as a drenched and distressed cuckoo chick. Hera took the chick to her bosom to warm it, and Zeus, having got where he wanted to be, immediately assumed his normal shape and took full advantage of the situation – though according to the Argives, Hera was able to restore her virginity by bathing in a sacred spring near the city, something she thereafter made her habit every year.

Gamelion, the month sacred to Zeus' queen, became a favourite for weddings in ancient Athens, and as Juno, the goddess has smiled on many a bride married in her month of June. Hera was a faithful wife to Zeus, and all who attempted to seduce her met a gory end. Her dedication to a dysfunctional marriage made her the protector of the entire institution, and Greek and Roman brides often received gifts of apples, in imitation of the golden apples given to Hera at her wedding by her grandmother Gaia, or pomegranates, a fruit also associated with the goddess. In her different aspects of virgin, wife and dowager, Hera covered the full gamut of what was expected of an ancient noblewoman, and was seen as the protector of her gender as a whole.

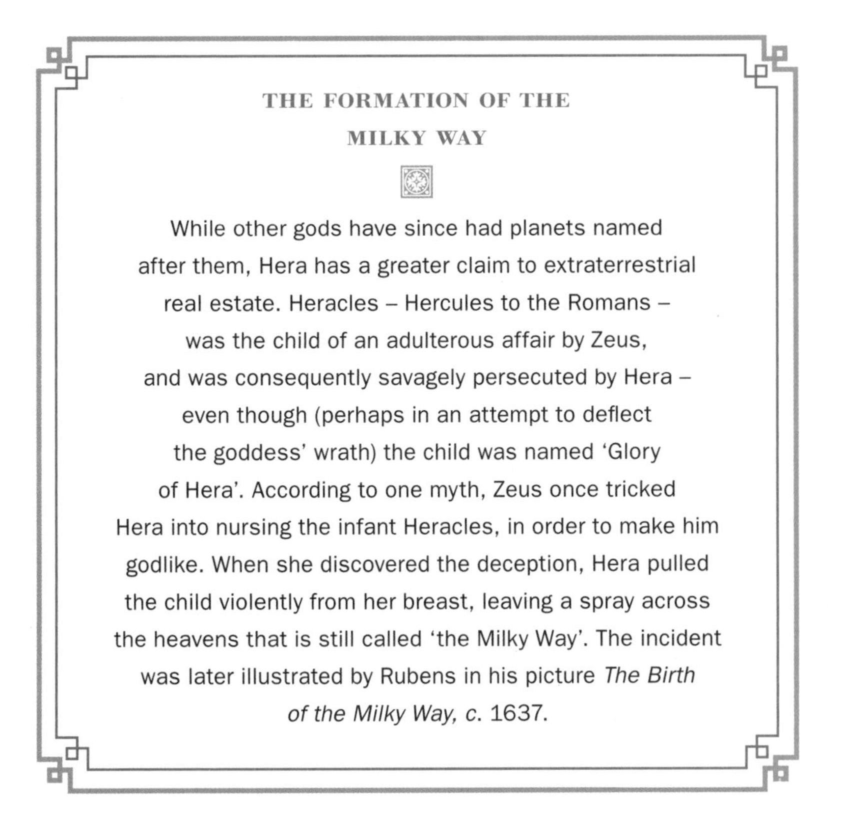

THE FORMATION OF THE MILKY WAY

While other gods have since had planets named after them, Hera has a greater claim to extraterrestrial real estate. Heracles – Hercules to the Romans – was the child of an adulterous affair by Zeus, and was consequently savagely persecuted by Hera – even though (perhaps in an attempt to deflect the goddess' wrath) the child was named 'Glory of Hera'. According to one myth, Zeus once tricked Hera into nursing the infant Heracles, in order to make him godlike. When she discovered the deception, Hera pulled the child violently from her breast, leaving a spray across the heavens that is still called 'the Milky Way'. The incident was later illustrated by Rubens in his picture *The Birth of the Milky Way, c.* 1637.

To one unfortunate nymph Zeus gave the job of diverting Hera's attention and so charming her with conversation that she would be unaware that her unfaithful husband had gone out womanizing. Hera discovered the ruse and cursed the nymph so that thereafter she was only able to repeat whatever was said to her. The nymph, Echo, has been doing this ever since.

As well as the Olympian Ares (Mars), Hera's other children with Zeus were Hebe, goddess of youth, and Ileithyia, the daughter who became the goddess of childbirth. There was a certain symmetry in this, as it was generally reckoned that a man going on campaign under the aegis of Ares endured pains and risks proportionate to those a pregnant woman suffered under Ileithyia. Hera also had a child on her own account without male intervention. This was Hephaestus (Vulcan) the smith, the god of craftsmen, who was ironically himself ill-made, ugly and lame, and therefore despised by his elegant and beautiful mother. Ultimately, however, through his cunning and strength of character, Hephaestus showed that he was quite capable of standing up for himself, at least in the metaphorical sense.

During the Trojan War, Hera was a steadfast supporter of the Greeks and even defied mighty Zeus for their cause. Later, she vindictively harassed Aeneas and the last survivors of the Trojan people. It was only after she was appeased that she allowed the refugees to settle in Italy and found the Roman race. As Juno, Hera took her position on the Capitoline hill as consort of Jupiter and the greatest goddess of Rome. The Roman mint in the temple of Juno Moneta on the capitol has given us the word 'money'.

Poseidon (Neptune), the Earth-shaker

Parents: Cronos (father), Rhea (mother)

Spouse: Amphitrite

Significant lovers: Caenis, Aethra, Demeter (Ceres), Alope, Theophane, Tyro, Medusa, Amymone

Children: Triton, Theseus, Pelias, Neleus, Nauplius, Arion, Polyphemus

Primary aspect: God of the sea

Minor aspect(s): Earth-shaker, lord of horses

Identified with: Horses

Temples, oracles and shrines: The temple of Poseidon at Sounion near Athens, the temple of Poseidon at Poseidonia (Paestum) in Italy, the altar to Neptune in the Circus Flaminius in Rome

Poseidon, the Great God, who moves the earth and
the barren sea ... two-fold the task gods have given you,
to be the tamer of horses and the saviour of ships.

HOMERIC HYMN 2.1ff

Poseidon contests with Athena for the patronage of Athens.

Like his brothers and sisters (though not including Zeus), Poseidon was probably swallowed by Cronos as soon as he was born. There is an element of doubt because there is a separate tradition that, like Zeus, Poseidon escaped swallowing and was raised in secrecy. According to this version of events, just as Zeus was replaced by a stone, Poseidon was replaced by a colt and grew up on the island of Rhodes, after which he joined his younger brother in the revolt against Cronos.

Poseidon approached his role as god of the sea with considerable enthusiasm, taking as consort a sea-goddess, Amphitrite, and building himself a palace of gold and gems on the seabed. He is associated with the three-pronged trident (literally 'the three-tooth'), a Cyclops-made fisherman's spear which he took as his symbol. Poseidon could be majestic and awe inspiring, or violent and capricious – attributes he shares with his watery domain. He jealously guarded his realm from interference by the other gods, and brooked no meddling, even from Zeus, whose authority elsewhere he only grudgingly acknowledged. He disliked the Trojans, but nevertheless once prevented Hera from usurping his privileges and sinking their ships.

THE CONTEST FOR ATHENS

Poseidon fell out with Athena when they disputed the patronage of Athens. Athena offered the citizens the olive tree and the arts of cultivation. Poseidon struck the rock with his trident and caused a spring to flow. However, as he was god of the sea, the spring water was salt and not terribly useful. The menfolk of Athens preferred Poseidon (suspecting that the sea god would make a bad loser), but the women opted overwhelmingly for Athena and their opinion carried the day. Rather as expected, when he heard the result of the poll Poseidon punished the Athenians with a vicious flood.

Poseidon became patron, not just of the city of Corinth but the entire Isthmus (bounded as it is between two seas), but he lost the patronage of Argos to Hera. As with the loss of the patronage of Athens (see box), Poseidon took this defeat very personally; all the more so since Argos had been founded by his son Nauplius, whom he fathered on the nymph Amymone. (Others among Poseidon's host of sons include Theseus, the slayer of the Minotaur, and Polyphemus, the one-eyed Cyclops blinded by Odysseus.)

Like most of the major male gods, Poseidon had an uninhibited libido and a complex love life. Medusa, once a beautiful girl, became a monster after an outraged Athena punished her for making love to Poseidon on the floor of her temple. Another lover, Theophane, was seduced by Poseidon in the form of a ram – and their offspring was also a ram, albeit one with a golden fleece (see p. 136). Reflecting the arbitrary and ungovernable nature of the sea, Poseidon was supremely unworried by taboos of either rape or incest. He once seduced his own granddaughter, and he raped a beautiful girl called Caenis (he afterwards granted her wish to become male so that she would never again suffer the experience). He broke both taboos simultaneously when he raped his sister Demeter (the Roman Ceres) in the guise of a stallion after she took refuge from him by hiding herself as a mare in a herd of horses.

Horses are a recurring theme with Poseidon, so much so that he is sometimes called 'Poseidon of the horses'. The sacrifice of a horse in the sea was regarded by Greeks and Romans as a sure way to win the favour of the god. Poseidon's favour was all the more important as he was not only lord of the sea, but he was also the shaker of the earth. Sometimes he combined his roles by shaking down cities with a violent earthquake and following this up with a devastating tsunami from the sea, literally mopping up any survivors.

To the Romans, Poseidon became Neptune through conflation with the Etruscan sea-god Nethuns. In the modern world he is the planet Neptune, and now that his brother Hades, as Pluto, has been demoted from full planet status, he is the outermost of the planets of the solar system. Triton, the fishtailed son of Neptune and Amphitrite (illustrated above), is now one of that planet's moons.

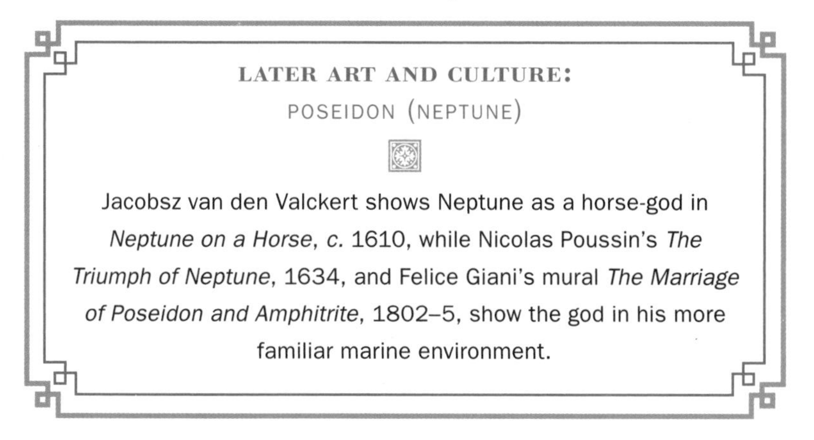

LATER ART AND CULTURE:

POSEIDON (NEPTUNE)

Jacobsz van den Valckert shows Neptune as a horse-god in *Neptune on a Horse*, c. 1610, while Nicolas Poussin's *The Triumph of Neptune*, 1634, and Felice Giani's mural *The Marriage of Poseidon and Amphitrite*, 1802–5, show the god in his more familiar marine environment.

Hades (Pluto), Lord of the Dead

Parents: Cronos (father), Rhea (mother)

Spouse: Persephone

Significant lovers: Minthe, Leuce

Children: The Furies

Primary aspect: God of the underworld

Minor aspect(s): The unseen, the rich one, receiver of all

Identified with: Black sheep, cypress, narcissus

Temples, oracles and shrines: The temple of Hades at Elis, the temple of Pluto in Dougga (modern Tunisia), the Necromanteion, 'the oracle of the dead' by the River Acheron in northwestern Greece

Hades, the lord of many, grim master of the underworld.

And the earth yawned open wide in the plain … and the Lord, the Host of Many, with his immortal horses sprang out … the Son of Cronos, he who has many names.

HOMERIC HYMN TO DEMETER 2.15ff

Hades is the god who rules the underworld, a kingdom with which his name has become synonymous. The name means 'the hidden one', for Hades possessed a helmet that made him invisible to all – even to his father Cronos, making the help of Hades crucial to Zeus' bid for power. Though he ruled the underworld, Hades was not Thanatos (Death), who was another of the children of Nyx (see p. 16).

There are few temples to Hades, and he never had many worshippers, for Hades was uninterested in the living. In any case, king or peasant, atheist or worshipper, Hades got them all in the end.

Hades was a chthonic (meaning 'of the earth') deity, for his kingdom, if not under the earth as such, was certainly approached from underground. Hades himself was coldly impartial, seldom unjust and certainly not evil. (In the same way, Greek daemons, though creatures with great powers, are not demons as understood today.) Just as it is not Hell, the kingdom of Hades is not exactly Tartarus either, that dark opposite of Gaia, but rather something that Hades created for himself – of which Tartarus is the deepest pit, reserved for the Titans and especially deserving cases among humans (see p. 12).

Proserpina (Persephone) abducted; relief from Villa Albani, Rome.

Given that it was particularly bad luck for humans to pronounce his name and thus cause Hades to take an interest in them, it is unremarkable that there are few tales in which the king of the dead is the protagonist.

Hades was a stern, dark-haired, elderly figure, in a chariot drawn by ink-dark horses. Thus he appeared in the most famous of his myths when he abducted Persephone, the daughter of Demeter, who ever since has spent part of every year in the underworld as his queen. During these months, Persephone's mother, the goddess of all that grows, goes on strike, and the fields lie fallow and the rain does not fall. So, rather like Saturn (a Roman god with whom Hades was often conflated), Hades had some influence on the weather and the crops. Furthermore, many of these crops are given additional flavour by Minthe, a nymph beloved of Hades whom a jealous Persephone changed into mint, a suitably spicy herb.

Hades was a grim figure whom few wanted to invoke (those who did, for whatever reason, did so by banging their palms on the ground). As so many souls ended up in his stewardship he was euphemistically called *plutos*, 'the rich', the name adopted by the ultra-superstitious Romans. In the modern world this version has mutated by way of the planet into an unexpected manifestation of the god as a ludicrous cartoon dog.

Hades is best known today from the metal that bears the Roman version of his name. The makers of plutonium chose to call it that because it is not only amongst the deadliest poisons known to man, but is also the substance most capable of turning Gaia into another Tartarus.

Demeter (Ceres), the Green Goddess

Parents: Cronos (father), Rhea (mother)

Spouse: None

Significant lovers: Poseidon, Zeus, Iasion

Children: Persephone, Arion, Plutus, Boötes (Philomelus)

Primary aspect: Goddess of plants and fruit

Minor aspect(s): Goddess of agriculture, fertility and newly married couples

Identified with: Corn, pigs, fruit, poppies

Temples, oracles and shrines: The site of the Mysteries at Eleusis, the temple of Ceres at Paestum, the temple of Demeter on Naxos

Demeter with her sceptre and garland of corn.

Rich-haired Demeter …
lady of the golden
sword and glorious fruits.
HOMERIC HYMN TO DEMETER 2.2ff

Demeter is a very old goddess, worshipped long before the twelve Olympians were canonized, and this is reflected in her name, an old form of the words 'earth-mother'. With Hestia, she was one of the two daughters of Cronos, and though she is one of the great goddesses of the ancient pantheon, she spent little time on Olympus, preferring to roam the earth. This was generally done in a variety of disguises, since her official regalia was somewhat conspicuous – she was a shining goddess in a chariot pulled by dragons.

One of Demeter's special responsibilities was to ensure that the corn grows from a seed to a full-grown crop, and indeed, Demeter has corn-blonde hair. Her only romance with a mortal occurred in a thrice-ploughed field, and one of the offspring of that union was elevated to the heavens as the constellation of Boötes, the ploughman.

The Eleusinian Mysteries of Demeter were celebrated near Athens. Initiates into the mysteries were forbidden ever to speak of what they had seen.

Both the Athenians and Sicilians claimed to have been the first to whom Demeter taught the art of cultivating grain, and as a bonus Demeter also gave the Athenians the fig tree; Athenian figs were generally considered superior to any others in the ancient world. The Romans knew Demeter as Ceres, and even today millions around the world commune with the goddess as they pour milk on their breakfast cereal.

In astronomy, like her son-in-law Pluto, Ceres is a dwarf planet, the largest in the asteroid belt. Appropriately, the symbol for Ceres is a sickle.

The most famous of the myths associated with Demeter is her search for her daughter Persephone (Proserpina to the Romans), who was abducted by Hades. Many tales are told of Demeter's wanderings during that search, including one in which she was raped by Poseidon in the guise of a horse (p. 69). The abduction also revealed Demeter's power, for if she permits nothing to grow on the earth (and during her wanderings she did not), then mankind will perish and the gods receive no sacrifices. It was this threat that forced Zeus to the negotiating table, and made Hades release his captive.

However, Hades was notoriously reluctant to give up any who entered his dark realm and this was all the more emphatically so in the case of his unwilling but beautiful wife. He therefore tricked Persephone into eating some pomegranate seeds, for all who eat in the house of Hades are doomed to stay in the underworld forever. Eventually a deal was worked out by which Persephone would stay with Hades for a part of the year, but at other times would rejoin her mother on the earth above.

THE ACCURSED FAMILY OF TANTALUS

The story of Tantalus and his descendants is a major sub-plot stretching across the entire Heroic Age of Greek myth in a gory and dramatic soap opera. Tantalus was king of Lydia on the western seaboard of what is now Turkey. While hosting a banquet for the Olympian gods, Tantalus committed an unforgivable offence. Serving one's son at table would have been considered odd by any Greek, divine or otherwise, but serving the son as the main course (due to a logistical oversight and the lack of any other meat dish) was in appallingly bad taste, even if the son apparently was not: Demeter, preoccupied by her missing daughter, absent-mindedly gnawed through an entire shoulder.

The boy, called Pelops, was restored to life, albeit with a prosthetic shoulder of ivory. For his revolting conduct, Tantalus was sentenced to an eternity of hunger and thirst in Tartarus, standing chest-deep in water that receded when he tried to drink it, and with grapes in front of his nose that lifted out of reach when he tried to eat them. (From which we get the word 'tantalize'.) Pelops inherited Lydia, but was driven from his kingdom, partly by King Ilus who had founded a nearby city called Ilium (Troy). Pelops fled to Greece, where he won the daughter of the king of Elis by beating the king in a chariot race – he sabotaged the king's chariot so effectively that the king died when it crashed. The charioteer, a son of Hermes, was a party to the plot. But as payment, Pelops killed him. Although he was purified by Hephaestus, and went on to conquer most of southern Greece (thus the Peloponnese), the enmity of Hermes was relentless and blighted the lives of Pelops' son Atreus (incest, fratricide and cannibalism), his grandsons – Agamemnon (murder, daughter-killing and adultery) and Menelaus (Helen and the Trojan War) – and his great-grandson Orestes (matricide).

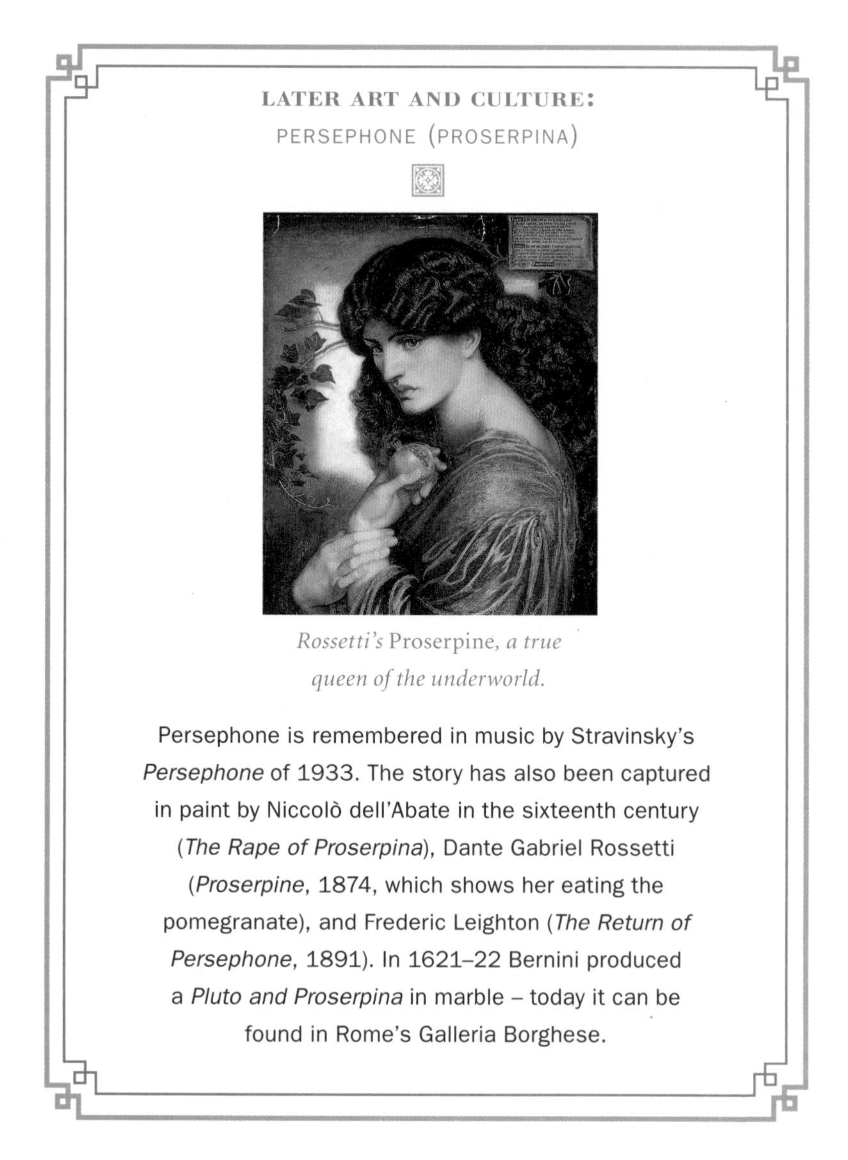

LATER ART AND CULTURE:
PERSEPHONE (PROSERPINA)

Rossetti's Proserpine, *a true queen of the underworld.*

Persephone is remembered in music by Stravinsky's *Persephone* of 1933. The story has also been captured in paint by Niccolò dell'Abate in the sixteenth century (*The Rape of Proserpina*), Dante Gabriel Rossetti (*Proserpine*, 1874, which shows her eating the pomegranate), and Frederic Leighton (*The Return of Persephone*, 1891). In 1621–22 Bernini produced a *Pluto and Proserpina* in marble – today it can be found in Rome's Galleria Borghese.

When her daughter Persephone is gone from her, Demeter shuts up shop, and the earth becomes dry and barren. But when Persephone returns, the rains bring riotous flowers and fertility, and the harvest takes root.

4

Olympus: The Next Generation

Certain gods arrived in the celestial big twelve of the Olympian pantheon by strange and varied routes. This is true both of the versions given by the ancient storytellers and of the sometimes barely more credible guesses of modern ethnographers and linguistic archaeologists. The background to the first generation of Olympian gods – Aphrodite, Zeus, Hera, Poseidon, Demeter and Hades – has been given in the previous chapter (though many Greeks and Romans felt more comfortable leaving Hades out of their versions of the pantheon). The remaining Olympians are children of this first generation, largely due to the indefatigable efforts of Zeus. Here we explore the lives and myths of this second generation.

Athena (Minerva), the Grey-eyed Goddess

Parents: Zeus (father), Metis (mother)

Spouse: None

Significant lovers: None

Children: None

Primary aspect: Goddess of reason

Minor aspect(s): Battle goddess, goddess of skill and industry (Athena Ergane, hence ergonomics)

Identified with: Olive, owl, goose (hence the 'Mother Goose' children's tales)

Temples, oracles and shrines: The Parthenon on the Athenian Acropolis, the temple of Athena Polias (Athena of the city) at Rhodes, the temple of the Capitoline Triad (Jupiter, Juno and Minerva) in Rome

Grey-eyed Athena, lady of wisdom and war.

She wove a portrait of herself, bearing a shield, and in her hand a lance ... there showing how she struck her spear into the fertile earth, from which a branch of olive appeared.

ATHENA AT THE LOOM: OVID *METAMORPHOSES* BOOK 6

Of all the great gods, Athena is the most reasonable, for she was born of reason. While the other gods represent blind forces of nature or ungovernable passions, Athena resides principally in the minds of humane, civilized beings. As a goddess, Athena represents logic and rationality, though in her human aspect she is also capable of partisanship and jealousy. But, like Hestia, Athena is always immune to Aphrodite.

Metis, the mother of Athena, was a daughter of Oceanus (see p. 23), and she embodied the concept of pure abstract thought. When she coupled with Zeus, it was realized that a child who inherited the power of abstract thought from Metis, and combined this with its practical application in Zeus, would possess the ability to rule the universe. However, this realization came too late for Zeus, as Metis was already pregnant. We have seen that, once created, life is divine, and therefore essentially indestructible (Chapter 2 *passim*). So Zeus stole his father's trick, and swallowed the child whole. Within Zeus, Athena migrated naturally to the seat of reason, the brain. There she proceeded to give her father a splitting headache. The 'splitting' bit of the headache is here quite literal, for Hephaestus worked out the cause of his stepfather's discomfort and whacked his head open with an axe. And from the forehead of Zeus emerged Athena, some say fully grown and already clad in armour, others say as a child who was raised by Triton, the son of Poseidon.

The birth of Athena, from a sixth-century BC vase painting.

Hephaestus and Athena have shared a bond ever since, she as a goddess of industry, he as the patron of craftsmen. Only Hephaestus dared to test how seriously Athena took her status as a maiden goddess, and did better than any other, human or divine, by getting as far as landing some of his semen on her thigh. Athena disdainfully wiped it off, and it fell to earth where it seeded the father of the

Athenians (or so claim the people of that city). No other god pushed his luck even that far, for as Athena Promachos the goddess is terrible in battle. She is also invincible in her Aegis, a gold-tasselled shield, or shield covering, or cuirass of goatskin fashioned for her by Hephaestus (and which even Zeus needed to borrow at critical moments). And although she is not vindictive (that would be unreasonable), Athena can be terribly persevering. Furthermore Nike (the goddess of victory, who is still earnestly courted by patrons of a certain brand of sports equipment) is always close to Athena, who never contemplates defeat. (In a separate tradition both Athena and Nike are children of the Titan Pallas, which is why one comes across references to both Athena Pallas and Athena Nike.)

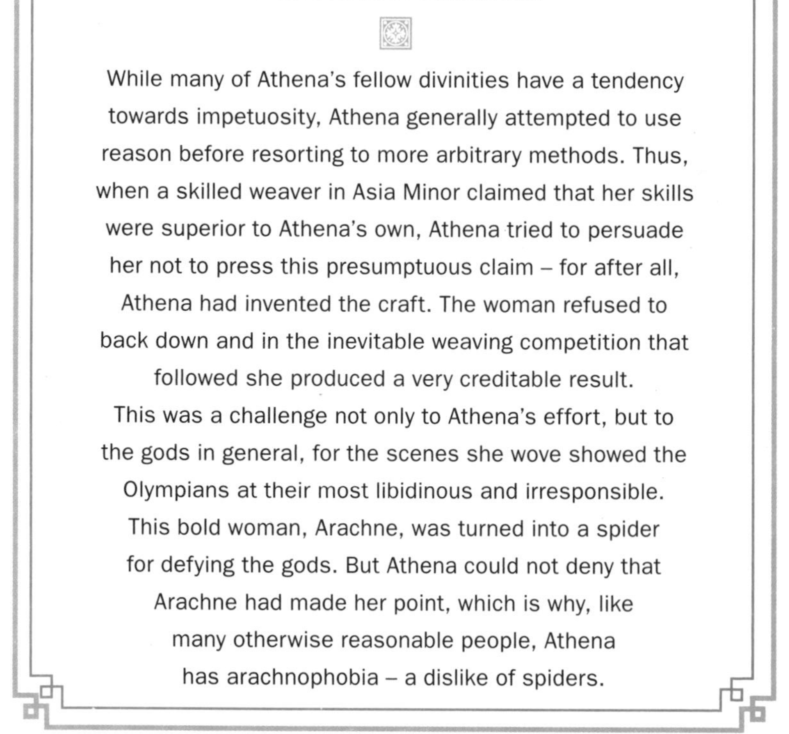

ATHENA AND ARACHNE

While many of Athena's fellow divinities have a tendency towards impetuosity, Athena generally attempted to use reason before resorting to more arbitrary methods. Thus, when a skilled weaver in Asia Minor claimed that her skills were superior to Athena's own, Athena tried to persuade her not to press this presumptuous claim – for after all, Athena had invented the craft. The woman refused to back down and in the inevitable weaving competition that followed she produced a very creditable result. This was a challenge not only to Athena's effort, but to the gods in general, for the scenes she wove showed the Olympians at their most libidinous and irresponsible. This bold woman, Arachne, was turned into a spider for defying the gods. But Athena could not deny that Arachne had made her point, which is why, like many otherwise reasonable people, Athena has arachnophobia – a dislike of spiders.

Athena became patroness of Athens when its people chose her gift of the olive over Poseidon's salty spring (see p. 68). Later, she helped the Athenians to grow other crops as well. She and the city have done well by each other, with Athens coming to symbolize the intellectual gifts that Greece gave to the world, and the Athenians raising the beautiful temple to Athena the Maiden Goddess (Athena Parthenos) on their acropolis.

LATER ART AND CULTURE:
ATHENA (MINERVA)

The contest with Arachne has long attracted artists. Velázquez depicted it in his famous *Las Hilanderas* ('The Spinners') of 1657. More generally, Athena has been depicted by Frans Floris (*Athena*, *c*. 1560), Paris Bordone (*Athena Scorning the Advances of Hephaestus* *c*. 1555–60), Gustav Klimt (*Pallas Athena*, 1898), and Jacques-Louis David (*The Combat of Mars and Minerva*, 1771).
In sculpture, one of the most remarkable depictions is that of Athena Parthenos in her re-created Parthenon in Nashville, Tennessee.

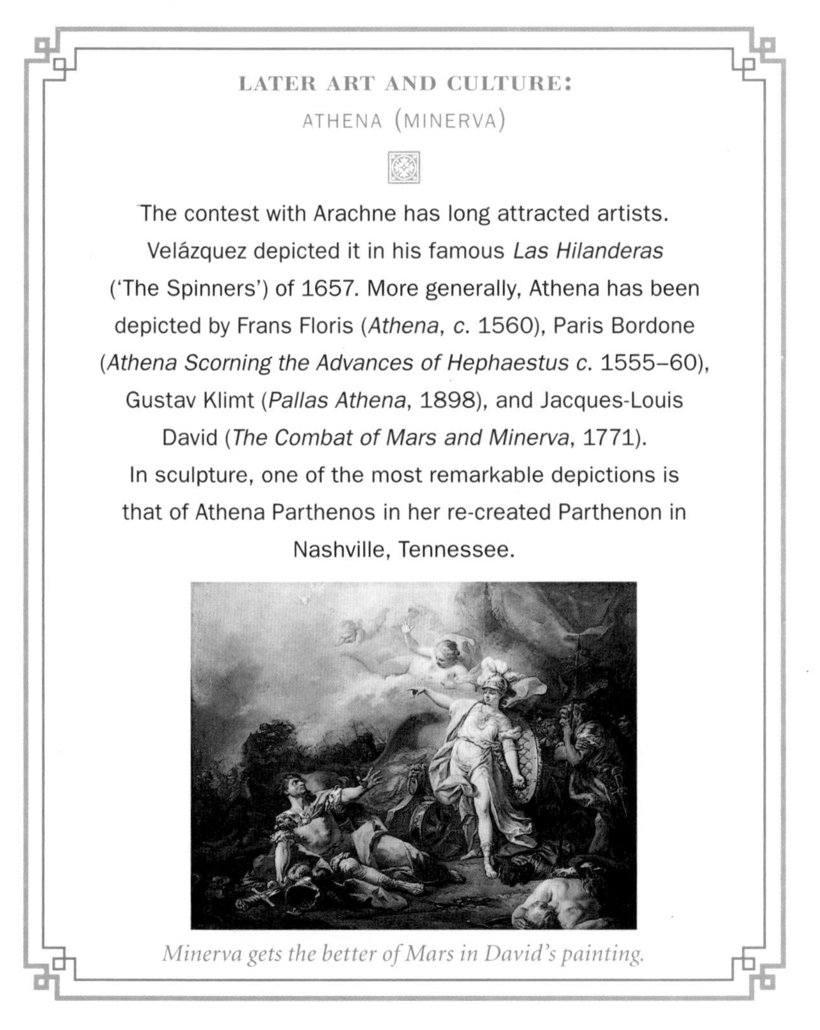

Minerva gets the better of Mars in David's painting.

Phoebus Apollo, the Shining God

Parents: Zeus (father), Leto (mother)

Spouse: None

Significant lovers: Sinope, Coronis, Marpessa, Hyacinth, Daphne

Children: Asclepius, Miletus, Linus

Primary aspect: God of prophecy

Minor aspect(s): God of music and healing, protector of flocks and new cities

Identified with: Eagle, snakes, crow, cicada, wolf, dolphin, lyre, laurel, number 7 (from his birth date)

Temples, oracles and shrines: The Oracle at Delphi, the temple of Apollo on the Palatine hill in Rome, the sacred island of Delos

Engraving of the Belvedere Apollo, a famed masterpiece of classical sculpture.

'The lyre and the curved bow shall be my dearest possessions,
and I will announce to mankind the unfailing will of Zeus.'
So said Phoebus, the long-haired god who shoots from afar.
And he began to walk the wide paths of the earth to
the wonder of all the goddesses.
HOMERIC HYMN TO APOLLO 2, 133–39

As described earlier (p. 62), Apollo was born on Delos, the twin of his sister Artemis, with whom he shared a love of archery and a talent for gruesomely disposing of those who offended him. In many ways Apollo is the most human of the gods, being both gifted and unfortunate, civilized yet capable of dark barbarism. The multiple sides to Apollo are also seen in his godly portfolio, which encompasses diverse aspects. He is the god of prophecy, and the patron of the arts, and though he is a god of healing, his arrows kill through disease.

When grown, Apollo and Artemis made it their business to retrace the footsteps of their mother as she fled Hera's wrath. Along the way, they demonstrated to those who had denied Leto sanctuary that there were worse things than Hera's displeasure – and those things included Apollo and Artemis. One who had insulted Leto on her travels was a dragon called Python (who later gave his name to a species of large snake). Apollo tracked Python to his lair, a cave in Mt Parnassus, and slew him there. Since Python had been in the habit of giving oracular responses from his cave, Apollo took over the job, and his oracle at Delphi on Parnassus soon became a major shrine. He obtained his first priests by intercepting a ship carrying holy men from Crete, and in the guise of a fish-like being he forced them to go to Delphi instead. The fish-like being remained after the spirit of the god left it, and received its name from the destination, becoming Delphinium – the dolphin.

Apollo viewed his job as patron of the arts very seriously. He took the Muses into his charge, and even today, many towns and cities have multiple shrines to Apollo in Odeons – originally temples where music and drama were celebrated.

APOLLO AND MARSYAS

Athena once took up playing the flute, but gave it up because it made her cheeks bulge out in an unseemly manner. The discarded instrument was found by a satyr called Marsyas who rapidly became proficient with it. In his hubris, Marsyas challenged Apollo, god of music, to a contest. Though both god and satyr played equally well, Apollo was judged the victor as he could both play holding his instrument upside down and accompany it with singing. Some bias has been suggested on the part of the judges, as these were the Muses who were subject to Apollo. The other judge, King Midas (see p. 105) registered a dissenting vote to the majority, and was rewarded by Apollo by having a pair of donkey's ears transplanted on to his skull. Marsyas suffered an even worse fate, as Apollo skinned him alive for his presumption – according to Herodotus, the flayed skin was still to be seen in his day near the River Catarraktes in Phrygia where the contest was alleged to have taken place.

Apollo in love

Daphne If Apollo was not lightly mocked, nor was Eros, another archer god. For criticizing the feeble arrows of the matchmaker, Apollo was shot through the heart by an arrow of Eros that was tipped with gold. This caused him to fall desperately in love with the nymph Daphne (Laurel). Yet Daphne had been shot with a lead-tipped arrow of Eros, which caused her to flee Apollo's advances until, unable to flee further, she had herself changed into the tree which now bears her name (bay laurel). Still Apollo would have her, using the wood for his lyre and his bow, while the leaves of the tree were used for the wreath which crowned the victors in competition – though, unlike Apollo, many of those victors have since been able to rest on their laurels.

Cassandra It seems Eros really took against Apollo, who continued to be unlucky in love. The Trojan woman Cassandra refused Apollo, even though he gave her the gift of prophecy. (The rejected Apollo amended the gift so that Cassandra would always speak the truth but no one would ever listen.)

Sinope This lady, after whom the city in Turkey was named, agreed to lie with Apollo if he first gave her whatever she wanted. It turned out that she wanted to remain a virgin. By some traditions she later relented, for her child, Syrus, is considered the founder of the Syrian race.

Marpessa This lady chose a fellow mortal rather than run the risks associated with a divine romance.

Coronis Though Apollo bedded this mortal, she wed another. Outraged, Apollo killed his lover, only to find she was pregnant with his child. He had to go to extraordinary lengths to save the child, who became Asclepius, the god of medicine (p. 115).

Hyacinth With males Apollo's luck was no better, for he loved a beautiful youth called Hyacinth. The flower of that name sprang from the blood shed when Apollo accidentally killed his love with a discus.

Et alii Other loves of Apollo have left their mark on the world. One, ***Cyrene***, founded a great city in ancient Libya, and a son by another romance, Miletus, was founder of a famous Greek city. Linus, child of Apollo and one of the Muses, has given his name to characters as diverse as the second Pope, a cartoon character and the founder of a well-known computer operating system. In recent years Eros has relented, allowing Apollo, as the eleventh spacecraft of that name, to conquer Selene, the moon.

LATER ART AND CULTURE:
APOLLO (PHOEBUS)

Apollo appears in many paintings, such as Lucas Cranach the Elder's *Apollo and Diana*, *c.* 1526, Titian's gruesome *The Flaying of Marsyas*, 1570–76, and the cultured Nicolas Poussin's *Apollo and the Muses at Parnassus*, 1630–31. His pursuit of Daphne has also interested artists, including Giovanni Battista Tiepolo (*Apollo Pursuing Daphne*, 1755/60), Robert Lefevre (*Daphne Fleeing from Apollo*, 1810), Gustave Moreau (*Apollo and the Nine Muses*, 1856) and J. W. Waterhouse (*Apollo and Daphne*, 1908).

Titian's graphic depiction of the flaying of Marsyas.

Apollo's musical dispute with Marsyas has inspired a lively musical piece from Johann Sebastian Bach entitled *Der Streit zwischen Phoebus und Pan*. And at the age of 11, Mozart made one of his first major musical forays with a piece entitled *Apollo et Hyacinthus*, 1767.

Artemis (Diana), Lady of the Beasts

Parents: Zeus (father), Leto (mother)

Spouse: None

Significant lovers: None

Children: None

Primary aspect: Goddess of all wild things

Minor aspect(s): Goddess of the hunt, also closely associated with Selene the moon and Hecate the witch goddess

Identified with: Deer, cypress, the moon

Temples, oracles and shrines: The temple of Artemis at Ephesus, the temple of Diana at Baiae, Italy, any wild meadow

Diana of the beasts, in a maidenly pose with her bow.

Fierce huntress, who delights in woodland combats: swift in the chase, dread mistress of the bow, wanderer by night, rejoicing in the meadows, tall and proud as a man, generous of mind, revered divinity, nurse of humankind; immortal yet earthly, bane of foul monsters. Blessed maiden, let the tree-crowned hills be your home.

ORPHIC HYMN TO ARTEMIS 36

In the Greek and Roman world, the hunt was a serious business. Much of the countryside was uncultivated and wild beasts were a threat to men and their crops alike. Hunting was sport, pest control and a meat supply combined, and almost everyone who lived in the countryside did a considerable amount of hunting as part of their daily activities. The risks involved were not inconsiderable. Apart from bears and boars (which substantially outmatched any single hunter), the chase itself had dangers, including the risk of excited individuals propelling sharp objects in the wrong direction. Unsurprisingly, hunters needed a divinity to look after them, and the job fell to Artemis, maiden goddess of all things wild.

Artemis and Apollo show Niobe that the gods are not lightly mocked.

Artemis was the elder twin of Apollo. As a child she asked her father Zeus that she might always remain a virgin, and roam the hills with her attendant nymphs and a pack of hunting dogs. Like Apollo, she took the bow as her weapon (hers was made of silver by the Cyclopes), and with Apollo, she avenged any insult to her mother.

One Niobe apparently had not heard of the pair's vendetta against those who had denied Leto sanctuary (see above), and she boasted that she was seven times superior to Leto as she had seven sons and seven daughters, while Leto had only one of each. A brisk bout of bowfire soon evened things up, and Niobe was left without children of either gender to boast of.

ARTEMIS AND ACTAEON

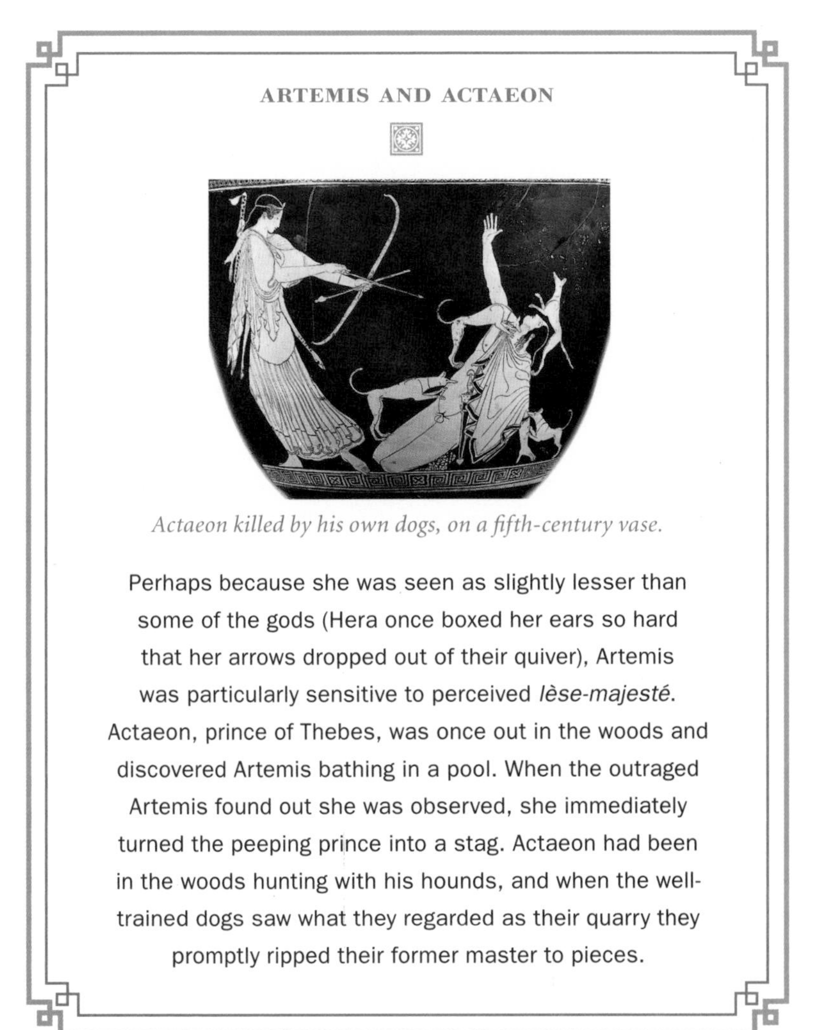

Actaeon killed by his own dogs, on a fifth-century vase.

Perhaps because she was seen as slightly lesser than some of the gods (Hera once boxed her ears so hard that her arrows dropped out of their quiver), Artemis was particularly sensitive to perceived *lèse-majesté*. Actaeon, prince of Thebes, was once out in the woods and discovered Artemis bathing in a pool. When the outraged Artemis found out she was observed, she immediately turned the peeping prince into a stag. Actaeon had been in the woods hunting with his hounds, and when the well-trained dogs saw what they regarded as their quarry they promptly ripped their former master to pieces.

All-star followers: the Pleiades, Callisto and Orion

Pleiades The companions of Artemis were seven sisters called the Pleiades. These ladies were less successful at retaining their virginity than their leader, and almost all had relationships with other gods – some less willingly than others. Maia, the eldest Pleiad, was mother to Hermes, while Electra, meaning 'bright', is still very much about on earth as she shares her name with amber ('electron' in Greek), which the ancients used to generate sparks of electricity.

Callisto As well as the promiscuous Pleiades, another favourite of Artemis, Callisto, was also seduced by Zeus. Afterwards Callisto was transformed into a bear. By whom is uncertain, though neither Artemis nor Hera were best pleased. Eventually, for her own protection, Zeus gave Callisto and her son shelter in the heavens, where they can still be seen nightly as Ursa Major and Ursa Minor. Today Callisto is also, like Zeus' fellow seducees Io, Europa and Ganymede, a moon of Jupiter.

Orion Artemis was both the protector of wild things and an enthusiastic huntress. Another of her companions was the mighty hunter Orion, who boasted of his intention to slay every wild thing on earth. This brought the two aspects of Artemis into jarring conflict, which was resolved when Orion was killed by a scorpion (responsibility for this death has been laid upon several different suspects, including Artemis herself). Orion had been another suitor of the Pleiades, and like Callisto and the Pleiades he ended in the heavens, where the three stars of his belt make him one of the most visible of constellations as he still pursues the seven stars of the Pleiades across the night sky.

In the Trojan War (see Chapter 8), Agamemnon, king of the Achaeans, gave multiple offence to Artemis, who was in any case (like her brother) a supporter of the Trojans. She tried to prevent the Greek ships from sailing by denying them a favourable wind until Agamemnon sacrificed his daughter Iphigenia. When Agamemnon showed his intention of going right ahead with the sacrifice, Artemis substituted a deer at the last moment and took Iphigenia into protective custody.

To the Romans, Artemis was Diana and her temple at Ephesus was one of the Seven Wonders of the World. From the isle of her birth Artemis was also known as Artemis of Delos, or simply as the feminine form of the island's name – Delia. The Roman rendering of Artemis as Diana remains a popular girl's name, though Phoebe (the feminine form of Apollo's name of Phoebus) is now less popular than it once was.

LATER ART AND CULTURE:
ARTEMIS (DIANA) AND ACTAEON

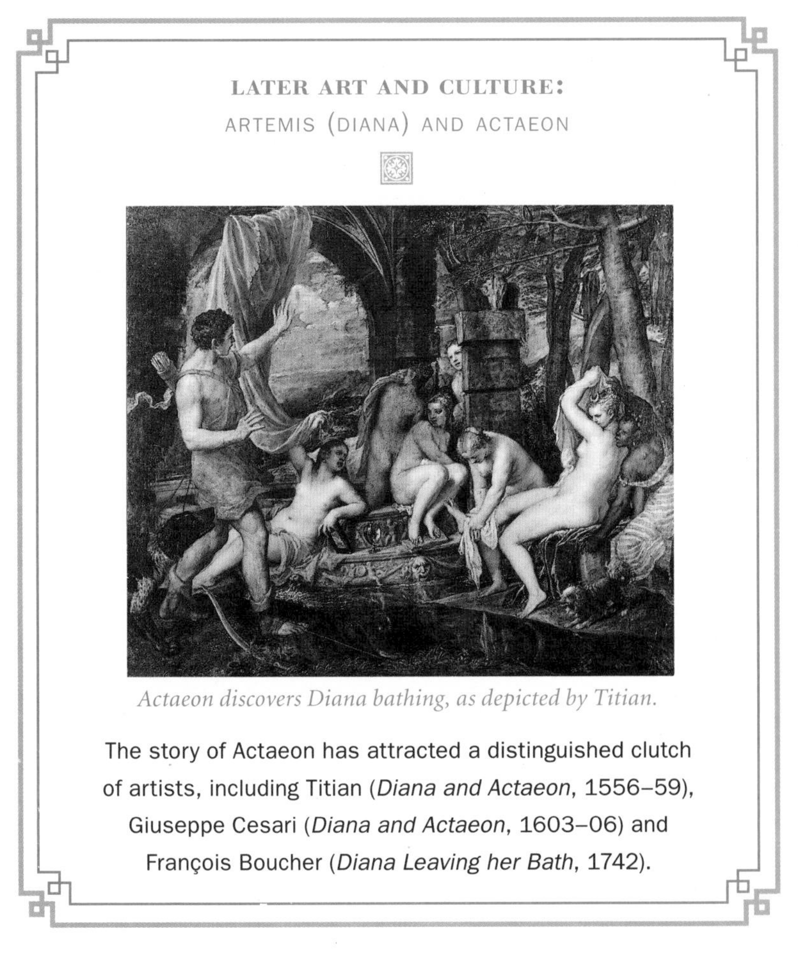

Actaeon discovers Diana bathing, as depicted by Titian.

The story of Actaeon has attracted a distinguished clutch of artists, including Titian (*Diana and Actaeon*, 1556–59), Giuseppe Cesari (*Diana and Actaeon*, 1603–06) and François Boucher (*Diana Leaving her Bath*, 1742).

Ares (Mars), God of Battle

Parents: Zeus (father), Hera (mother)

Spouse: None

Significant lovers: Aphrodite, Pyrene, Rhea Silva, Eos (the dawn)

Children: Deimos, Phobos, Cycnus, the Dragon of the Sparti, Diomedes, Ixion, Harmonia, Romulus and Remus

Primary aspect: God of battle

Minor aspect(s): None

Identified with: Spear, woodpecker, vulture, dog

Temples, oracles and shrines: The temple of Mars in the forum of Augustus, Rome, the temple of Ares in Athens, any battlefield

It may be that I am a henchman of the lord Ares,
but yet I am trained in the school of the muses
and serve them too

ARCHILOCHUS, MERCENARY AND POET,
SEVENTH CENTURY BC (FRAG 1)

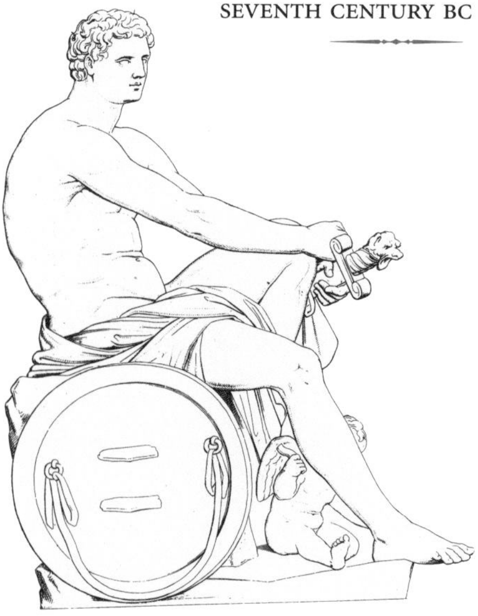

Mars, with a cherub at his feet; drawing of a statue from the Villa Ludovisi in Rome.

Ares and Athena are both battle gods, but whereas Athena represents cool strategy, Ares represents blind force and violence. This explains why, when the pair came to blows during the Trojan War, Athena comprehensively beat Ares on both occasions. Ares was supporting the Trojans, but he could as easily have supported the Achaeans, since for Ares, the battle and slaughter were important for themselves, rather than for who won afterwards. Unsurprisingly given this attitude, he was not particularly popular, either among gods or men. Even Zeus, who had fathered Ares with Hera, felt somewhat ambivalent about his offspring, who was more at home among the warlike and savage Thracians than the civilized folk of southern Greece.

Cadmus kills the water dragon, with Athena in the background.

The battle-prone Spartans, naturally enough, were fonder of Ares than most, and believed that they were descended from one of Ares' children. This child was a water dragon slain by the hero Cadmus. When the dragon's teeth were sown in the earth, from each grew a fully armed proto-Spartan. Cadmus made peace with Ares by marrying his daughter Harmonia, and founding the city of Thebes near the place where the water dragon was slain (and where, probably not coincidentally, there was a lake in prehistoric times).

Harmony seems a strange child for a god whose other children include Fear and Panic (p. 55), but by some accounts this gentler character is explained by the fact that Harmonia's mother was Aphrodite, who was strongly drawn to Ares. As will be seen (p. 97), Hephaestus, the husband of Aphrodite, took a dim view of the romance and went out of his way to humiliate the pair. Harmonia and Cadmus, incidentally, were the parents of that Semele whom Zeus inadvertently incinerated (p. 52). Eos, goddess of the dawn, was another lover of Ares, and Aphrodite jealously sentenced her always to be in love, though her lovers might vary.

Another odd conjunction of Ares is with justice. This link comes from another of his children, a daughter whom Ares saved from a son of Poseidon by killing the would-be rapist. In the first-ever murder trial, Ares successfully defended his actions to the other gods on a hill that would later be part of the city of Athens, and which was called the Areopagus after this occasion. Thereafter the Areopagus was where all Athenian murder trials were held, and where St Paul later made a famous speech denouncing 'pagan' gods such as Ares himself.

HERACLES WOUNDS ARES

Ares had a depraved son called Cycnus, whose hobby was the construction of a temple to his father from the skulls and other bones of travellers whom he had killed. He came unstuck when one traveller turned out to be Heracles. Ares, who had inherited his mother's hatred for Heracles, rushed to his son's assistance. Athena promptly appeared in Heracles' defence, and stopped Ares from striking Heracles while he was fully engaged with Cycnus. Warned of the threat, Heracles promptly wounded Ares in the thigh. The war god withdrew to Olympus to nurse his wounded thigh (and pride), while Heracles dispatched the bloodthirsty son without further hindrance.

Though the Greeks were distinctly ambivalent about their battle god, Ares found himself much more welcome in Rome, where he was rolled together with a variety of other war gods to become Mars. As Mars, he allegedly impregnated the Vestal Virgin and royal heir Rhea Silva to produce Rome's founders, Romulus and Remus. The emperor Augustus, though normally an admirer of the civilizing arts of Apollo, founded a temple to Mars in his newly built forum in Rome. He called it the Temple of Mars the Avenger, as he credited Mars with allowing him to overcome in battle the assassins of his adoptive father, Julius Caesar.

As Mars, Ares remains in the modern consciousness as the 'red planet', and also as the month in which the campaigning season habitually started – March. The word 'martial' still refers to matters military, and the verb 'to mar' refers to the effect of war on the landscape. And of course, the Greek hoplite shield with a spear behind remains the symbol for Mars and the male gender, just as the hand-mirror of Aphrodite serves the female.

Hephaestus (Vulcan), the Cunning Artificer

Parents: Hera (mother)

Spouse: Aphrodite

Significant lovers: Atthis, Aglaia, Athena (almost!)

Children: Pandora (creation), Erichthonius, Periphetes

Primary aspect: God of craftsmen

Minor aspect(s): Particularly god of blacksmiths, god of fire and volcanoes

Identified with: Hammer, anvil and tongs, axe

Temples, oracles and shrines: The Hephaestaion in Athens, the Isle of Lemnos (where the modern international airport is called 'Hephaestus'), the temple of Vulcan at Agrigentum, Sicily

Oh, Muses, sing in your clear voices of Hephaestus glorified for his inventions. With Athena the bright-eyed he showed men throughout the world how to use his wonderful gifts. For until they had learned the crafts of Hephaestus, men lived like wild beasts in the mountain caves.

HOMERIC HYMN TO HEPHAESTUS 2.1–7

Hephaestus was above all a blacksmith, and he had the same role on Olympus as blacksmiths are believed to have had in Archaic Greece. An outsider, Hephaestus was sometimes mocked, but was also secretly feared for his arcane skills. Like many blacksmiths in early Greece, Hephaestus was lame. This was because blacksmiths sometimes added arsenic while smelting copper ore so as to burn out sulphide impurities. Breathing in the fumes resulted in arsenicosis, which causes lameness. The Greeks themselves believed that the lameness of Hephaestus was through his being an imperfect attempt by Hera to produce a child by herself without involving her philandering husband. So disgusted was Hera with the result that she threw the infant from the heavens. He landed in the sea and was cared for by Thetis, the Nereid who was later to be the mother of Achilles.

Hephaestus with Thetis and the armour of Achilles.

Hephaestus was raised on the island of Lemnos, which became a cult centre for the god. Here, he learned to become a cunning blacksmith. He made, for example, the winged sandals of Hermes, and footwear for the other gods, including adamantine sandals for his mother Hera (which caused her to fall flat on her face when she tried walking in them). Hera either did not take the hint, or was unaware of the provenance of a golden throne that her despised son next sent to her. As soon as Hera sat on the throne, golden coils sprang out and locked her into place. Nor would Hephaestus release his mother until he was readmitted to Olympus and furthermore given the fair Aphrodite as a wife. Further concessions were averted by Dionysus, who got Hephaestus drunk and inveigled the key from him.

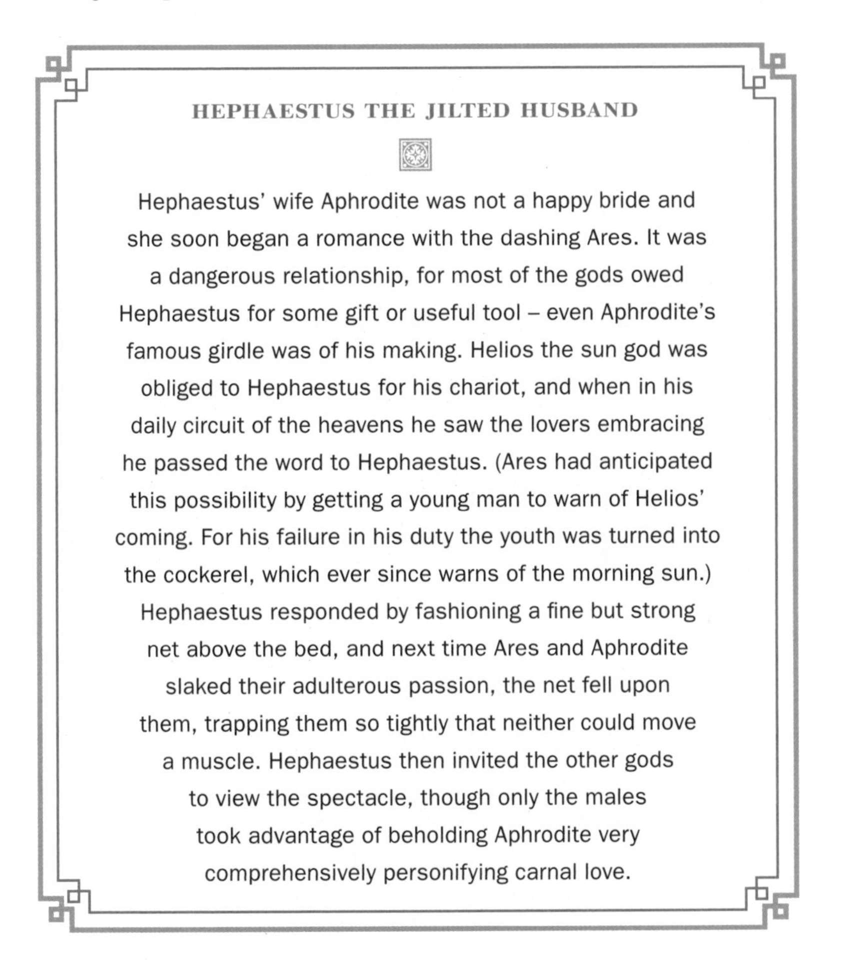

HEPHAESTUS THE JILTED HUSBAND

Hephaestus' wife Aphrodite was not a happy bride and she soon began a romance with the dashing Ares. It was a dangerous relationship, for most of the gods owed Hephaestus for some gift or useful tool – even Aphrodite's famous girdle was of his making. Helios the sun god was obliged to Hephaestus for his chariot, and when in his daily circuit of the heavens he saw the lovers embracing he passed the word to Hephaestus. (Ares had anticipated this possibility by getting a young man to warn of Helios' coming. For his failure in his duty the youth was turned into the cockerel, which ever since warns of the morning sun.) Hephaestus responded by fashioning a fine but strong net above the bed, and next time Ares and Aphrodite slaked their adulterous passion, the net fell upon them, trapping them so tightly that neither could move a muscle. Hephaestus then invited the other gods to view the spectacle, though only the males took advantage of beholding Aphrodite very comprehensively personifying carnal love.

Despite his usefulness in the heavens – it was Hephaestus who also created Pandora (p. 29) and the chain that bound Prometheus to his rock

(p. 27), and it was Hephaestus who wielded the axe that led to the birth of Athena (see above) – the blacksmith god was exiled once more.

This time his exile was for taking his mother's part in one of her frequent quarrels with her husband. Offended by Hera's constant persecution of Heracles, Zeus had prepared a painful punishment for his wife, and Hephaestus either protested strongly or (by some accounts) took physical measures to help. Literally thrown out of heaven, Hephaestus fell for an entire day. On earth he set up his forge under the constantly grumbling volcano of Mt Etna in Sicily. Here he produced wonders such as walking tripods and bronze mechanical men. The Romans said Etna would flare up whenever Venus (Aphrodite) was unfaithful to her exiled husband, though it should be noted that Hephaestus is also believed to have carried on a dalliance of his own with one of the three Charities, Aglaia (the Roman Charis).

To the Romans, Hephaestus was known as Vulcan, and the similarity of Vulcan and volcano suggests that Hephaestus took over some of the earlier attributes of a Roman fire god. Fish were an acceptable sacrifice to Vulcan, especially in his August festival of the Volcania, in which bonfires were lit. As he is a rational, solution-orientated god, it is no surprise to see that the alien 'Vulcans' in the long-running science fiction series *Star Trek* have the same attributes. Objects such as car tyres are made from rubber hardened with heat in a process known as vulcanization.

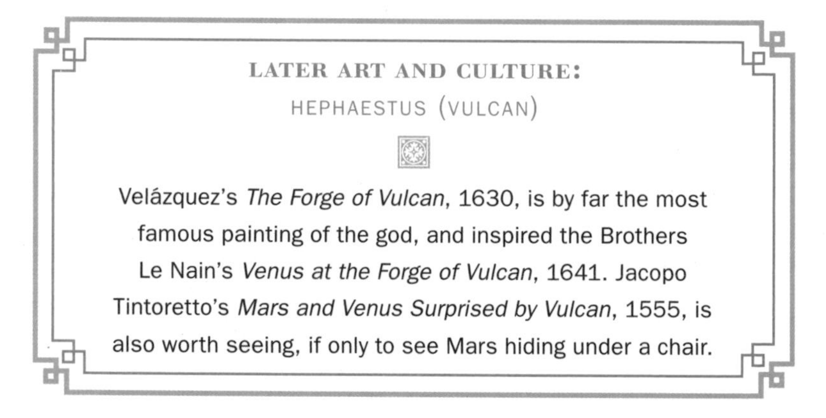

LATER ART AND CULTURE:
HEPHAESTUS (VULCAN)

Velázquez's *The Forge of Vulcan*, 1630, is by far the most famous painting of the god, and inspired the Brothers Le Nain's *Venus at the Forge of Vulcan*, 1641. Jacopo Tintoretto's *Mars and Venus Surprised by Vulcan*, 1555, is also worth seeing, if only to see Mars hiding under a chair.

Hermes (Mercury), the God at the Gate

Parents: Zeus (father), Maia (mother)

Spouse: None

Significant lovers: Dryope, Aphrodite

Children: Pan, Hermaphroditus, Autolycus, Priapus, Evander

Primary aspect: Messenger of the gods

Minor aspect(s): Bringer of dreams, god of athletes, travellers, liars, harlots, all who cross or transgress boundaries, god of insight (hence 'hermeneutics') and eloquence

Identified with: Caduceus, winged helmet, winged sandals, rooster and tortoise

Temples, oracles and shrines: The temple of Mercury at Pompeii, the temple of Hermes and Aphrodite on Samos

Gemstone depicting Mercury (whose gemstone is traditionally emerald).

Oh mighty Hermes ... Be not pitiless towards our prayers... the most human, the most generous of the gods, be favourable towards us.

SUPPLICATION TO HERMES IN ARISTOPHANES *PEACE* 385ff

The most raffish of the gods, Hermes extends his protection to harlots, thieves, conmen and all who push the boundaries of acceptable behaviour. For that is the true role of Mercury (as the Romans called him). He stands at the boundary, and helps all who cross over. So travellers setting out on a journey will pray for the god to guide them, and those embarking on the last and longest journey of all find Hermes waiting to conduct them safely to the underworld. With Persephone and the witch-queen Hecate (p. 118), Hermes is one of the few gods who travels unchallenged into Hades' dark realm, and for this reason it was he who first escorted the kidnapped Persephone back to the waiting Demeter.

Fallen gladiators were dragged from the arena through the 'gate of the dead' by an attendant dressed as Hermes in his Roman incarnation of Mercury.

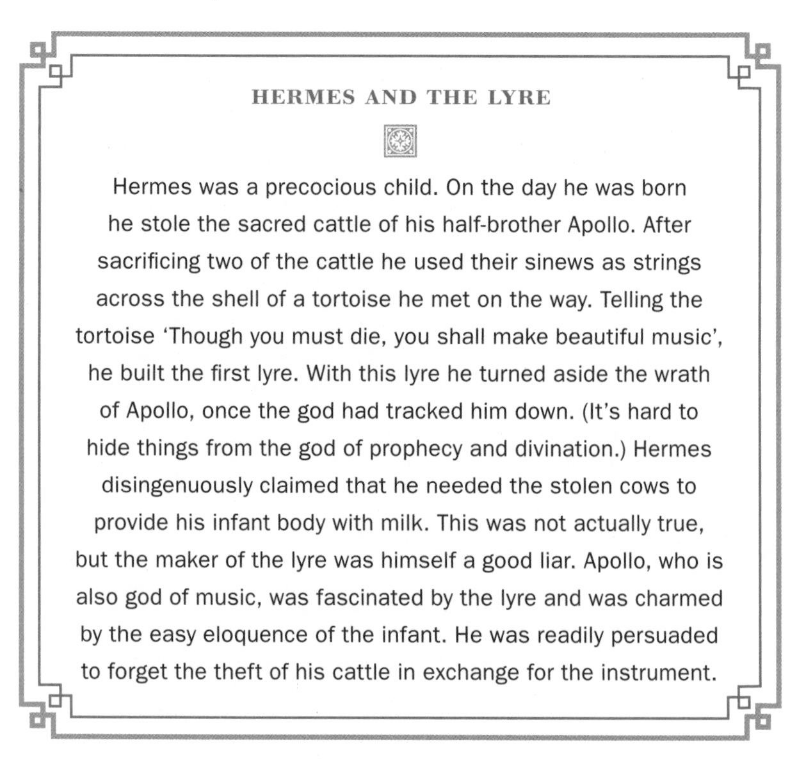

HERMES AND THE LYRE

Hermes was a precocious child. On the day he was born he stole the sacred cattle of his half-brother Apollo. After sacrificing two of the cattle he used their sinews as strings across the shell of a tortoise he met on the way. Telling the tortoise 'Though you must die, you shall make beautiful music', he built the first lyre. With this lyre he turned aside the wrath of Apollo, once the god had tracked him down. (It's hard to hide things from the god of prophecy and divination.) Hermes disingenuously claimed that he needed the stolen cows to provide his infant body with milk. This was not actually true, but the maker of the lyre was himself a good liar. Apollo, who is also god of music, was fascinated by the lyre and was charmed by the easy eloquence of the infant. He was readily persuaded to forget the theft of his cattle in exchange for the instrument.

From Apollo, Hermes received his golden staff, the caduceus. With this staff, Apollo also gave an extra aspect to Hermes, for the caduceus is a winged staff and bears two fighting serpents. This became Hermes' role – to be the ambassador between warring sides, the protector of embassies and diplomats, which fits in well with his aspect as the god of boundaries.

With winged sandals and winged helmet provided by Hephaestus, Hermes was not only able to travel freely between heaven, earth and the underworld, but also to do so with extraordinary swiftness. Unsurprisingly he became the messenger of the gods, a role that he still holds today as the symbol of several newspapers and communications companies, and also as the emblem of the Royal Signals Corps of the British Army. His caduceus, possibly through confusion with the snake and staff of Asclepius (p. 116), has become the symbol of several branches of the medical profession. The divine messages – called 'angelia' – have since found a life of their own as 'angels'. The role of messenger of the gods Hermes shared with Iris, the goddess of the rainbow, whom the Greeks often saw arching from sea to heaven and back to the land.

Almost by definition, Hermes was master of the chat-up line, and by some accounts he managed to father a child with Aphrodite, apparently without Hephaestus taking offence. This child was the fertility god Priapus (see p. 56), whose outstanding feature was his hugely erect phallus. The misuse of certain chemical remedies for male erectile dysfunction has in modern times led to a considerable increase in the once rare condition of priapism by which some unfortunate men have discovered that one can have too much of a good thing, and also have it for too long.

Another of Hermes' children, Hermaphroditus, was loved so deeply by the nymph Salamacis that the gods agreed to let them be combined into one body, the hermaphrodite, which had (and has) both male and female sexual characteristics. Another child of Hermes was the woodland god Pan (p. 109).

Just as the children of Hephaestus tended to be lame, so the children of Hermes inherited their father's light-fingered habits, cunning and easy charm. Thus it comes as no surprise that the son of Hermes called Autolycus, the prince of thieves, was grandfather to Odysseus, the most wily and persuasive of the Greeks.

As Mercury, Hermes became the modern planet – a recognition not of Mercury's closeness to Helios, the sun, but the speed with which he gets around him. Today some of Hermes' most recognizable aspects are in the field of fashion, where scarves and bags branded with his name are prized by dedicated followers. Someone with quick-changing moods is mercurial, and the smoothly flowing poisonous metal that bears his name is a reminder that dabbling with Mercury can lead you to the underworld.

LATER ART AND CULTURE:
HERMES (MERCURY)

Annibale Carracci painted *Mercury and Paris* in 1597–1600, and François Boucher *Mercury Confiding the Infant Bacchus to the Nymphs*, 1732–34. Velázquez's *Mercury and Argus*, 1659, was saved from a fire in 1734 by a quick-thinking workman who cut it from its frame as he fled the burning Alcazar palace where it was housed.

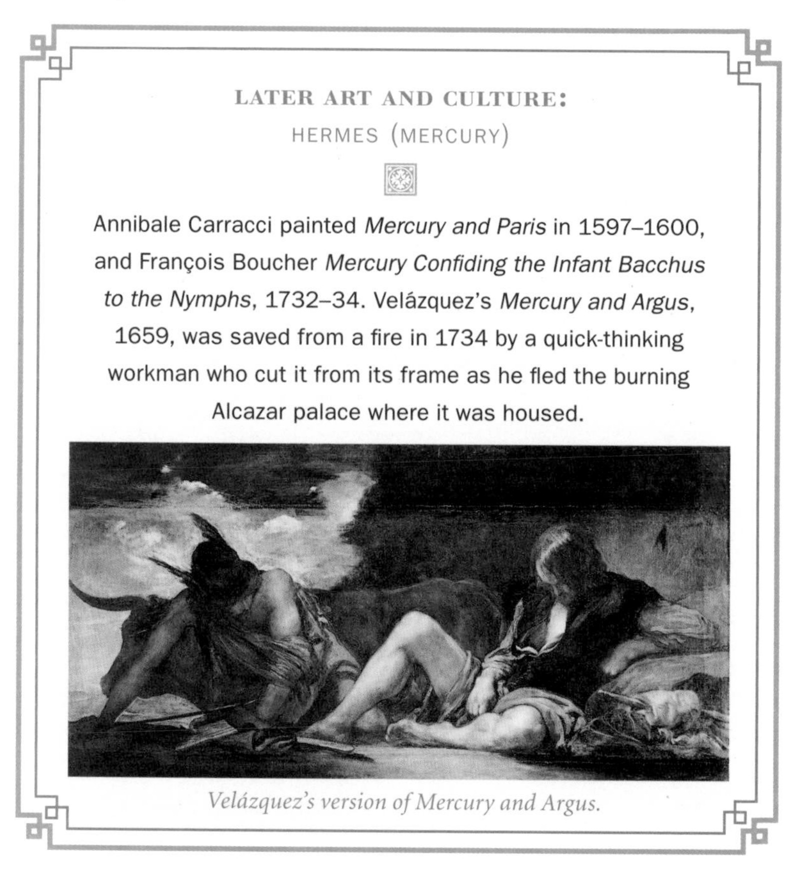

Velázquez's version of Mercury and Argus.

Dionysus (Bacchus), Thrice-born Party God

Parents: Zeus (father), Semele (mother)

Spouse: None

Significant lovers: Ariadne, Pallene

Children: Eurymedon

Primary aspect: God of wine

Minor aspect(s): Giver of charm, god of fellowship and freedom from care

Identified with: Grapes, the thyrsus, panthers

Temples, oracles and shrines: The temple of Dionysus beside the eponymous theatre in Athens, the temple of Bacchus at Baalbek (modern Lebanon), the temple of Dionysus at Pergamum

Dionysus as a symbol of rebirth on a third-century AD *Roman sarcophagus.*

'I am Dionysus, son of Zeus, born to him from Semele, Cadmus' daughter, delivered by a midwife of fire, the incandescence of Zeus.'

DIONYSUS INTRODUCES HIMSELF IN THE PROLOGUE TO THE *BACCHAE* OF EURIPIDES

Festivities, as anyone who has attended a family celebration will be familiar with, can often have a dark undercurrent, and too much wine will turn a wild party into a frenzied one. The Greeks and Romans knew this well, and Dionysus (Bacchus to the Romans) was a much more dangerous, complex and ambivalent figure than the jolly vine-crowned imbiber imagined by the modern era.

Multiple births

Dionysus had a strange birth and an equally strange upbringing.

Birth 1

We have already seen how his mother Semele was incinerated when exposed to the true nature of Zeus (p. 52). To save his unborn offspring, Zeus had hastily to pull the child from the remains of his mother's womb, and put him in a gash ripped in the god's own thigh.

Birth 2

Apparently a god's thigh made a good surrogate womb, for Dionysus was carried to term. But protecting the child from Hera's vindictive jealousy was not an easy task. By one story, the young Dionysus was disguised in the form of a kid goat.

Birth of Dionysus.

Birth 3

Hera saw through the disguise and arranged for some of the Titans to tear the child apart and eat him raw. Athena rescued the heart, and this bit of Dionysus was re-implanted in the womb and the god regrew. Dionysus was then brought up in the guise of a girl, and his images often had an androgynous appearance.

Hera managed to smite Dionysus again, this time with the madness with which the god is often associated. In a semi-demented state Dionysus wandered Asia Minor as far as the River Ganges, accompanied by various satyrs and Maenads. Maenads were literally 'the frenzied ones' – women who wore deerskins, handled live snakes and were reputed to tear apart animals in their ecstatic state and consume the flesh raw. Some ancients believed that by this act the Maenads did as the Titans had done with the kid, and ritually consumed their god – as also did anyone who partook of Dionysus through wine.

KING MIDAS

Midas was a king in Asia Minor, son of the man who gave the world the legendary Gordian knot. One day Midas found Silenus, the satyr who was friend and schoolteacher to Dionysus, passed out in the palace rose garden after a prolonged bout of communing with his god. Midas treated the stranger hospitably and entertained him for ten days and nights until Dionysus himself came in search of his lost follower. In reward for his kindly treatment of Silenus, Dionysus offered Midas one wish, and Midas famously asked that whatever he touched should turn to gold. Sadly Midas had paid little attention to drafting sub-clauses to his wish (a common error among those asking divine favours), and consequently *everything* he touched turned to gold. This included whatever he tried to eat or drink, and even, in one version of the myth, his daughter when he turned to her for comfort. Dionysus was finally persuaded to allow Midas to relinquish his baneful gift by washing in the River Pactolus, which became famous thereafter for its golden sands.

Cured of his madness by Rhea, Dionysus returned to Greece, where he had a hard time convincing people of his divinity – a tradition that even the ancients felt might reflect the reluctant acceptance of an Asiatic cult by the pre-classical peoples of Greece. Certainly there was much about Dionysus that was alien to the worship of other gods. His effeminate side (though the most frequently depicted of all gods, Dionysus is never shown with an erection, and he is often shown in female clothes), as well as the frenzy he inspired in his predominantly female worshippers caused considerable unease in the patriarchal and overtly macho cultures of Greece and Rome.

Frenzied Maenads tear apart an unfortunate (left), in the presence of Dionysus.

So disturbing did the Romans find the rites of Bacchus that these later caused a moral panic in the Republic, and hundreds of suspected Bacchic 'orgiasts' were arrested, and a good number executed. Even in later eras when festivals of Dionysus became standard features of life in many ancient cities, there was considerable reluctance to include the god in the standard Olympian pantheon, and many surviving 'canonical' lists do not do so.

Dionysus/Bacchus was inseparably linked with wine, especially the intoxication that it brings. The first man whom Dionysus taught to make wine was killed by his neighbours who thought he had poisoned them (as in a way he had – the 'toxic' in 'intoxication' is because alcohol is a mild poison). But no matter how later Greeks and Romans felt about Dionysus, they were not going to give up the god if it meant giving up his drink as well. So Dionysus came to represent festivity, the abandonment of cultural norms and the legitimizing of transgression. But he also represented unrestrained frenzy, uncontrolled passion, and while those in a state of Bacchic frenzy are never referred to as mad, Dionysus does inflict madness on those who offend him.

The symbol of Dionysus was the thyrsus, a staff wreathed with vines and topped with a pine cone. In case the phallic symbolism was missed by anyone (though Dionysian celebrations often featured phalluses lovingly carved with anatomical precision), the thyrsus was frequently shown in conjunction with its female counterpart, the wine-cup. Dionysus himself was often depicted riding a leopard, or in a chariot drawn by panthers.

Androgynous or not, Dionysus had many lovers, including Ariadne, whom he took up, according to some accounts, after she was abandoned by Theseus (see p. 171). Their son, the Argonaut Eurymedon, gave his name to the site of one of the major battles of the Peloponnesian War.

LATER ART AND CULTURE:
DIONYSUS (BACCHUS)

Bacchus the imbiber has proved more attractive to painters than the more complex Dionysus, and is well exemplified in the tippling infant of Giovanni Bellini's *The Infant Bacchus*, 1505–10. This theme is made even more explicit in Guido Reni's *Drinking Bacchus*, 1623. Titian gives a more mature (in every sense) treatment in *Bacchus and Ariadne*, 1520–23.

Titian shows Bacchus leaping from his chariot smitten by love at first sight.

Bacchus in stone is popular in gardens ancient and modern, the *Bacchus* in St Petersburg's Hermitage Museum being a good example of the genre. And in 1909 Jules Massenet even gave Bacchus his own opera.

Lesser Gods, Magical Creatures and Heroic Ancestors

There were dozens of gods in the Greek world, and thousands in the Roman, but most of these, including some major Roman divinities such as Janus, Mithras and Isis, do not feature largely in the world of myth. Of those who do appear, among the most common are the following.

Pan (Silvanus)

Pan in pursuit of a goatherd, by the Pan Painter.

Beloved son of Hermes, goat-footed, lover of music,
who wanders with the nymphs through the woodland meadows.
HOMERIC HYMN TO PAN 2ff

The mother of Pan was Dryope, a nymph who may have been one of the Pleiades (p. 90). Dryope had liaisons with several gods, including Hermes. Her child by Hermes was a hairy little baby with horns and goats' feet. So terrified was she at her first sight of the strange infant that Dryope ran away screaming, and Pan has always been able to induce that sudden unreasoning terror that is today called 'panic'.

Pan was adopted by woodland nymphs and ever after made the woods his home, with a preference for the tree-covered hills of Arcadia in southern Greece. He became the god of shepherds and goatherds, and so faithful were they to their god that he can still be recognized, complete with goats' legs and horns, in the Christian arch-enemy, the Devil. As a fertility god, Pan was relentless in his courtship of nymphs, one of whom, Syrinx, had herself changed into a reed-bed to elude him. Pan used those reeds to make the pipes with which his name is still associated, and with which he challenged (and lost to) Apollo in a music contest.

The Athenians later credited Pan with direct intervention in the battle of Marathon, and the runner Pheidippides (who sped to Athens with news of the victory, so that the long-distance race is still associated with his feat) recounted a conversation he claimed to have had with Pan while bearing an earlier message to the Spartans.

The Furies (Erinyes, Dirae)

The winged furies who inflict their torments
yet on the proud and overbearing.

QUINTUS SMYRNAEUS *THE FALL OF TROY* 5.520

Vengeance in the world of Greek mythology came in an abundance of forms. The Erinyes – 'the angry ones' – to give them their Greek name, were the Dirae to the Romans, and share their awful origins with the modern word 'dire'. Though Nyx and Hades are sometimes also given as possible parents, Hesiod insists that the Furies were, in a manner of speaking, sisters of Aphrodite, for they too were born of the blood of Uranus when he was castrated by Cronos. Perhaps as a result of this deed, the Furies took as their purpose in life the avenging of crimes by children against their parents, but soon added murder and breaches of hospitality to their portfolio, as well as blasphemy, sacrilege and other insults to the gods. The retaliation could take the form of madness or illness. Sometimes a whole community might suffer for not having taken action against an offender, in which case the illness could manifest itself as plague or crop failure, and the madness in an ill-conceived desire (for instance) to invade a large and well-armed neighbour. And yes, the modern 'fury' as insane rage comes from the name of these ladies.

Orestes confronts the Furies (panel from an ancient sarcophagus).

While an ill-treated parent could explicitly call down the Furies upon a child, it seems that the Furies picked up on offences against the gods by default. There were three Furies – Allecto, Tisiphone and Megaira. Though the playwright Aeschylus saw them as hideous snaky monsters, the Furies are generally depicted as serious young women in black mourning clothes, although when on a case they changed into short maiden dresses with knee-high hunting boots and armed themselves with whips.

Nemesis

You, the child of Nyx [Night], and the Furies
who avenge the blind dead and those who do
wrong by day, now hear me!

AESCHYLUS *EUMENIDES* 321ff

The goddess none can escape, the relentless daughter of Nyx (Night), had a somewhat broader operating brief than the Furies. She was seen as something of a balancing principle, a counter to that most capricious of goddesses, Tyche, or good fortune. Where Tyche bestowed her favours upon the undeserving, Nemesis would follow relentlessly behind and inevitably inflict a corresponding misfortune. She particularly set her sights on those afflicted with hubris, or overweening pride. In the words of the modern proverb: pride goes before a fall. The ancients expected the fall to be a push by Nemesis – probably over the nearest precipice.

For example, there was a beautiful young man who was loved by Echo, the nymph who was condemned to repeat everything she heard (p. 65). The youth was totally uninterested in the maiden, and he rejected her so forcefully that she pined away to nothing but her voice. Enter Nemesis, who cursed the young man so that he fell utterly in love with his own reflection when he saw he saw it in a pool. Unable to tear himself away, Narcissus wasted away at the water's edge. He left behind his narcissistic personality for later psychologists to study, and the flower of the same name. The spirit of Narcissus is said to remain on the banks of the River Styx, passionately inspecting its reflection in the waters. The Romans called Nemesis Fortuna, and even today many Italians still regard her with deep respect.

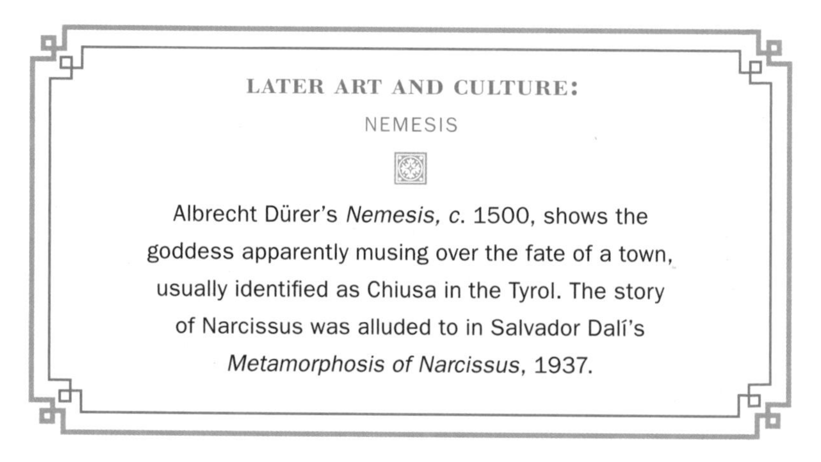

LATER ART AND CULTURE:

NEMESIS

Albrecht Dürer's *Nemesis, c.* 1500, shows the goddess apparently musing over the fate of a town, usually identified as Chiusa in the Tyrol. The story of Narcissus was alluded to in Salvador Dalí's *Metamorphosis of Narcissus*, 1937.

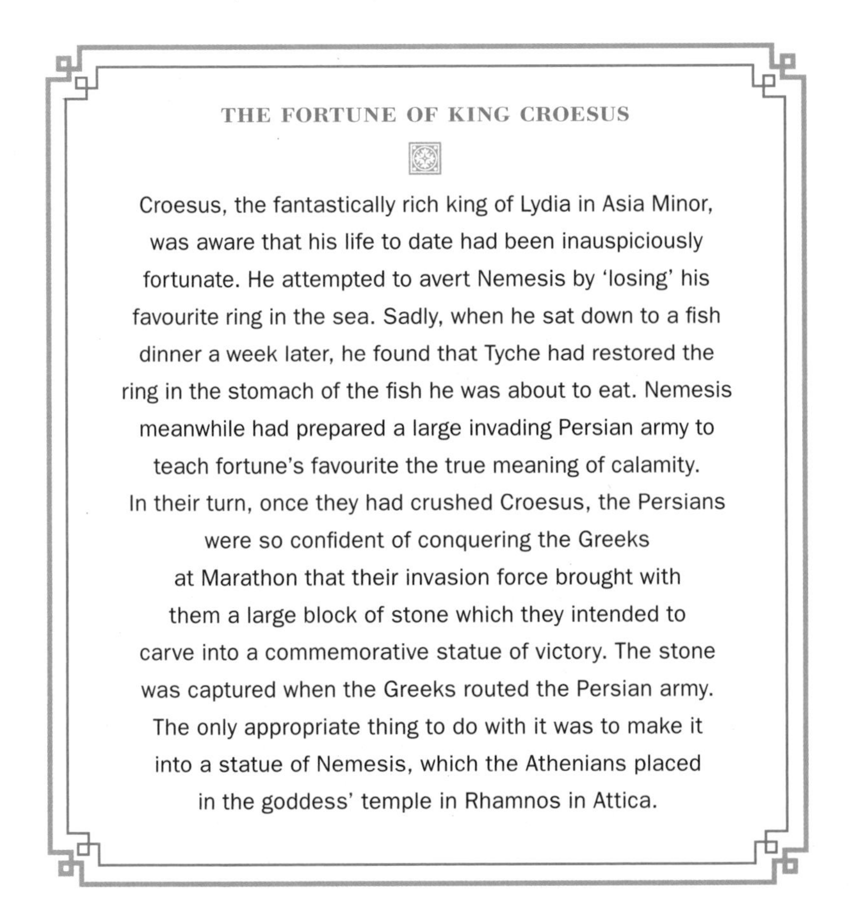

THE FORTUNE OF KING CROESUS

Croesus, the fantastically rich king of Lydia in Asia Minor, was aware that his life to date had been inauspiciously fortunate. He attempted to avert Nemesis by 'losing' his favourite ring in the sea. Sadly, when he sat down to a fish dinner a week later, he found that Tyche had restored the ring in the stomach of the fish he was about to eat. Nemesis meanwhile had prepared a large invading Persian army to teach fortune's favourite the true meaning of calamity. In their turn, once they had crushed Croesus, the Persians were so confident of conquering the Greeks at Marathon that their invasion force brought with them a large block of stone which they intended to carve into a commemorative statue of victory. The stone was captured when the Greeks routed the Persian army. The only appropriate thing to do with it was to make it into a statue of Nemesis, which the Athenians placed in the goddess' temple in Rhamnos in Attica.

Nemesis was also involved in the (eventual) downfall of the large and successful city of Troy. In one version of the legend, Nemesis was courted by Zeus, but she changed into a variety of shapes to try to evade the god's attentions. When Nemesis turned into a goose, her swain became a swan and in that guise won her heart. Their child was conceived as an egg, which hatched out Helen, the most beautiful of mortal women. In this version of the story, Helen, daughter of Nemesis, was adopted by a woman called Leda. However, in the more common version, Zeus repeated his trick of seduction by swan with Leda, and thus conceived Helen.

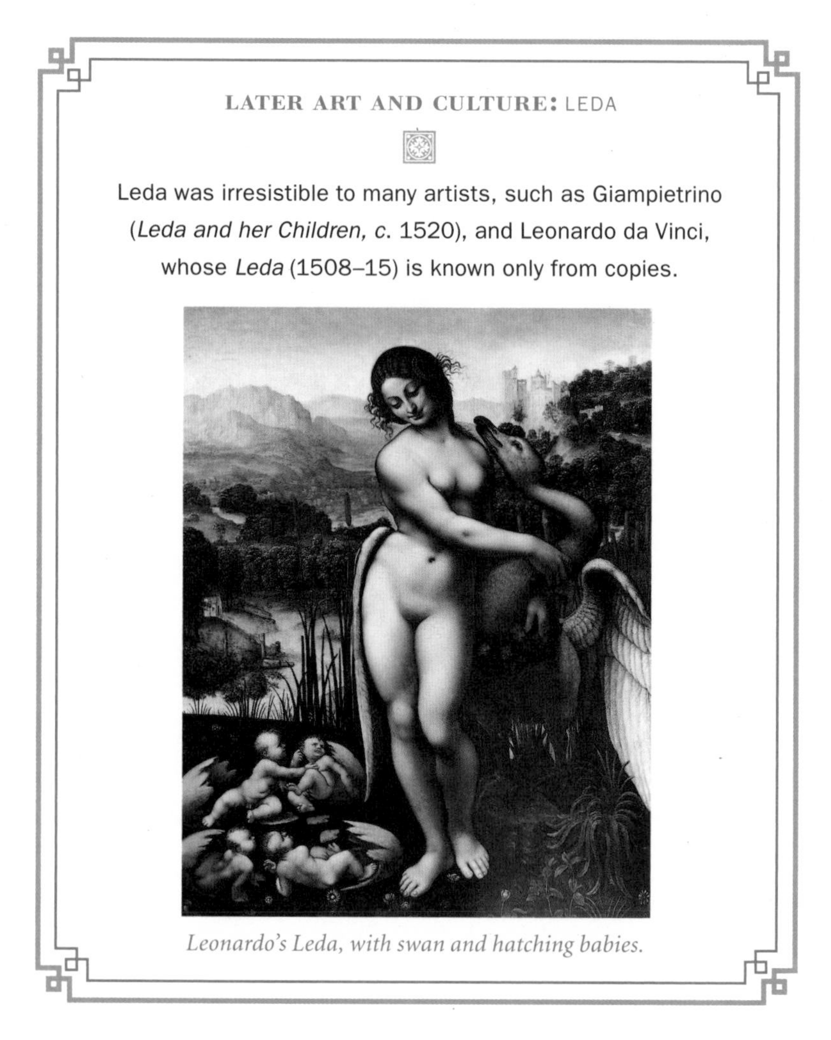

LATER ART AND CULTURE: LEDA

Leda was irresistible to many artists, such as Giampietrino (*Leda and her Children, c.* 1520), and Leonardo da Vinci, whose *Leda* (1508–15) is known only from copies.

Leonardo's Leda, with swan and hatching babies.

The Beaver and Lots of Sweetness

Helen of Troy had two brothers. Though twins, the pair had different fathers, one human, the other Zeus. This meant that one brother, Castor (literally 'Beaver'), was mortal, but the other, Polydeuces ('multiple sweetness'), was not. Known together as the Dioscuri, the brothers were involved in most of the heroic high jinks of their era.

They sailed with Jason's Argonauts (p. 136), took part in the Calydonian Boar hunt (p. 144) and joined in the attack on Athens when their sister was kidnapped by Theseus (p. 173). A feud with another pair of brothers over brides led to their undoing, and ultimately to the death of Castor. But in an exemplary instance of brotherly love, Polydeuces offered to surrender half his immortality to his brother, so the pair alternated daily between Olympus and Hades.

As Castor and Pollux, the twins were revered battle gods of the Romans, who dedicated one of the major temples in the Roman Forum to their worship.

Those born between 21 May and 21 June will have a special bond with the Dioscuri, who make up the astrological sign of Gemini – the twins.

The Charities (Graces)

As we have seen (p. 61) there were three Charities: Aglaia (Brightness), Euphrosyne (Festivity) and Thalia (Cheerfulness). They were handmaidens and companions of Aphrodite, who would join them in their dances. The Charities (known to the Romans as the Graces) wove the gown of Aphrodite, and comforted and pampered her on the isle of Paphos, where she had fled after being humiliated by Hephaestus (p. 97). The parentage and the names of the Charities vary according to different sources, and sometimes they number more or less than three, but they always symbolize gentleness, good humour and fun. The Charities were naturally party people, and the ancients often evoked their presence at the start of banquets and dinner parties.

Asclepius

O Asclepius, grown son of Apollo, gladly accept this hair,
well-praised, which Caesar's best boy gives you.

STATIUS *SILVAE* 3.4

Asclepius – engraving of a gemstone.

In the most common version of the myth, Asclepius was the child of Apollo and a mortal woman called Coronis (p. 85). Coronis made the major error of jilting the love-blighted Apollo, and added insult to injury by preferring a mortal to the god. Apollo duly smote his faithless lover, discovering too late that she was pregnant with his child.

Snatched from his mother's funeral pyre, Asclepius was raised by the gentle centaur Chiron (see below). Apollo was a god of healing, and Asclepius followed his father into that profession. He was helped by Athena, who gave him gifts with which he was able to effect miraculous cures – indeed, even raise people from the dead. This caused considerable ructions in heaven, for Hades hated it when people left his realm without permission. Consequently, the lord of the underworld made representations to his brother Zeus who agreed that Asclepius was usurping the powers of his betters, and blasted him to Tartarus with a thunderbolt. Aggrieved, but unable to strike directly at his father, Apollo wreaked his vengeance on the Cyclops who had made the thunderbolt. This infuriated Zeus still further, and only the pleading of Apollo's mother, Leto, mitigated his punishment.

It was believed that Asclepius made his escape from Tartarus disguised as a snake, and in that guise taught healing to men. This is why the serpent and staff have become the symbol of the medical profession. Meditrina, one of Asclepius' daughters, may have given her name to the profession, while following the dictates of another daughter, Hygieia, remains the most effective way of avoiding Meditrina's practitioners. We can but pray that a third daughter, Panacea, who cures all, might also make a reappearance soon.

It was traditional for Roman slaves deemed too ill for treatment to be left at the temple of Asclepius on his sacred isle on the Tiber (there is a hospital there still today). The emperor Claudius decreed that all who recovered should be freed.

The Muses

The Muses were the daughters of Zeus and Mnemosyne, and as companions of Apollo they assisted humans in different fields of artistic endeavour. Their number varies between one, three and nine, and although their place of residence is usually Mt Helicon in Boeotia, they are associated with wells and springs in many other places as well, most notably Delphi and Parnassus, the haunts of their leader Apollo. It was customary to ask the assistance of the appropriate Muse for inspiration, and give thanks for a successful production. Each of the nine was associated with a specific area of artistic performance.

Calliope – epic poetry
Clio – history
Euterpe – music and lyric poetry
Terpsichore – lyric and dance
Erato – lyric poetry, especially love and erotic poetry
Melpomene – tragic drama
Thalia – comedy
Polyhymnia – mime and sacred poetry (choral song)
Urania – astronomy

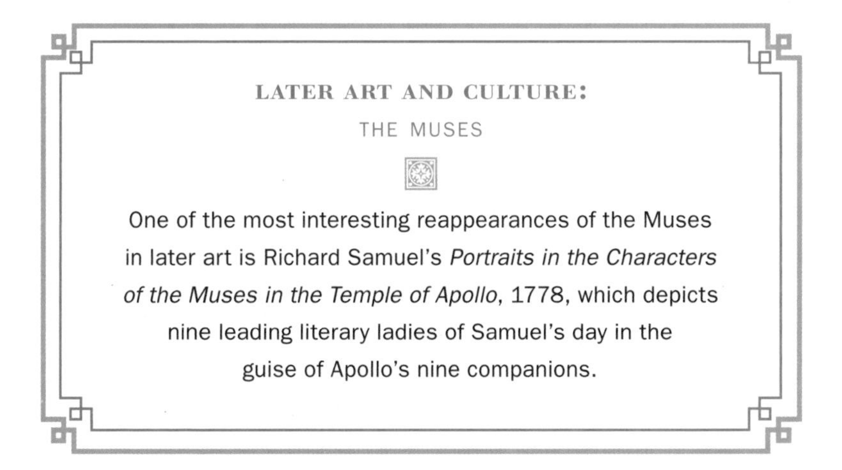

LATER ART AND CULTURE:
THE MUSES

One of the most interesting reappearances of the Muses in later art is Richard Samuel's *Portraits in the Characters of the Muses in the Temple of Apollo*, 1778, which depicts nine leading literary ladies of Samuel's day in the guise of Apollo's nine companions.

Hecate

Torch-bearing Hecate, holy daughter
of the deep-bosomed night.

BACCHYLIDES FRAG 1B

Triple Hecate of the crossroads; Roman copy of a Greek original.

Hecate assisted Demeter in her hunt for Persephone (p. 74), carrying torches to continue the search through the night. When Persephone was located in the court of Hades, Hecate found the underworld to her taste and remained to become one of the infernal gods. Such was the character of Hecate that even those accustomed to occasionally bizarre conduct on the part of their gods found her somewhat unsettling. To Hecate fell the supervision of religious rites, purifications and expiations, so she was often found mediating between mortals and dark forces such as the Furies or Nemesis as they relentlessly pursued wrongdoers.

Shrines to Hecate were found at crossroads. Crossroads have long been a favoured site for the summoning of demons and the meeting of witches (and are where murderers and suicides were buried in Britain until the 19th century), so it is appropriate that Hecate was the mistress of the former and patron of the latter.

Although some, such as necromancers and those casting spells and curses, sacrificed to Hecate for what she could do, the average Greek and Roman sacrificed to Hecate for what she would not do, or in the hope that the goddess would order the various malign beings over which she had power to cease blighting the appellants' lives.

Hecate was generally accompanied on her nocturnal travels by the Trojan queen Hecuba, who had taken gruesome revenge on the killer of one of her sons after the fall of her city, and whom Hecate had transformed into a black dog (p. 192). Another familiar was a black polecat who had once been a witch. Hecate herself could take the triple form of horse, dog and lion, and she may have appeared as such at her crossroad shrines, with the human form facing in the fourth direction.

It was traditional to lay certain foods – honey was a favourite – at the crossroads during the full moon as a sacrifice to Hecate, where the poor gratefully consumed it on her behalf.

Eris (Discordia)

There is Eris, the one who incites the evils of war and butchery. She is brutal and unloved by all, but sometimes through necessity, or because the immortal gods will it so, it happens that humans yet seek to honour her harsh ways.

HESIOD *WORKS AND DAYS* 11ff

Eris was among the grim brood of Nyx, the Night. However, so capable and enthusiastic was she in her role as goddess of strife and discord that many called her the sister of Ares. Eris was the goddess of contention, whether that contention ended in a family spat or a full-blown international war. There was also another aspect to Eris, in that she was the goddess who promoted a spirit of competition and rivalry, and this could have positive effects. So a poor and lazy man, says Hesiod, might gaze at the rich fields of his neighbour and be encouraged by Eris to get off his backside and make something of his own fields. Or Eris could encourage him to assemble a group of friends and try to seize the neighbour's fields in the name of equitable distribution. All was grist to her mill.

A FUTILE LABOUR OF HERACLES

Aesop tells a fable in which Heracles was going through a mountain pass when he beheld what appeared to be an apple lying on the ground. Idly he swung his club at it, and to his surprise not only was the apple unsmashed by the blow, but it even appeared somewhat more robust than before. Never a man to step back from a challenge, Heracles proceeded to give the apple several hearty whacks from the club which had previously slain monsters and caused the earth itself to tremble. The apple thrived lustily on the abuse. Heracles was not the subtlest of thinkers, but when the apple had grown to the point that it blocked his way, it dawned on him that he had better stop hitting it. Athena, who always had a soft spot for the muscle-bound demigod, appeared to explain that the apple was manifested by Eris, and if you leave a cause for contention alone, it stays small, but the more you agitate it, the faster, and bigger, it grows.

Homer remarked that Eris starts as a little thing, but by encouraging bitterness on either side, she can grow 'until her head strikes the heavens'. By general agreement, the masterstroke of Eris was her response to not being invited to the wedding of Thetis (p. 178). Thetis the sea-nymph was a friend and helper to many of the gods, and all came gladly to attend her wedding to a mortal called Peleus. Not altogether unexpectedly, Eris was somehow left off the guest list – after all, who wants Strife at a wedding? Unable to enter the feast, Eris lobbed in an apple inscribed 'to the fairest' while carefully not saying who this was. Aphrodite, Hera and Athena each claimed the apple, and hundreds were to die beside the walls of Troy before the issue was resolved.

Satyrs (Fauns)

Satyrs at play, in a red-figure fifth-century vase painting.

Humans shared the world of myth with many other intelligent species. We have already met nymphs, Nereids and Titans, all of whom were to some degree divine. However, two other species – satyrs and centaurs – were on a par with humans, or even somewhat lower (though there were exceptions who far outclassed the average mortal).

As the woodland companions of Dionysus and nymphs, it comes as no surprise to discover that satyrs were enthusiastically dedicated to wine, women and song. (In fact, 'satyriasis' is the modern medical term for those who suffer from excessive and uncontrollable sexual desires – in women the equivalent condition is known as 'nymphomania'.)

The ancients believed that the satyrs' surrender to sensuality was a major moral failing. Nevertheless, since the species managed to enjoy life to a greater degree than most humans, the ancients had grudgingly to admit that perhaps the satyrs were on to something (apart from passing nymphs).

There were different types of satyr – though by definition all were male. Young satyrs were Satyriskoi, and the ancient, horse-tailed variety were called the Seleni (see Silenus, the companion of

Dionysus – p. 105) though these gradually lost their equine qualities with the evolution of myth and became conflated with the caprine goat-footed creatures who are properly called 'Panes'. Despite their decadent lifestyles, all satyrs enjoyed robust health, though they had a tendency to go bald early, which accentuated the knobbly horns on their heads. Fauns were technically a different species, but even the ancients soon abandoned the distinction. (Nor are fauns related to fawns, as the latter get their name from Old English.)

Silenus at his most satyrical, in the interior of a drinking cup.

Satyrs were respected for having stood by Dionysus in his madness, and the satyr plays at the Athenian festivals are not to be confused with modern satirical plays ('satire' has a different etymology). The raffish Hermes also enjoyed their company.

Exceptional satyrs included the musical Marsyas (p. 84) and Crotos, whose skill as a drummer made him a friend of the Muses. Oenophiles (wine lovers) are invited to raise a glass to Leneus, the ancient satyr who became the patron of wine-makers, and another glass, and another, and another and another to Silenus, the satyr who has become patron of drunken excess.

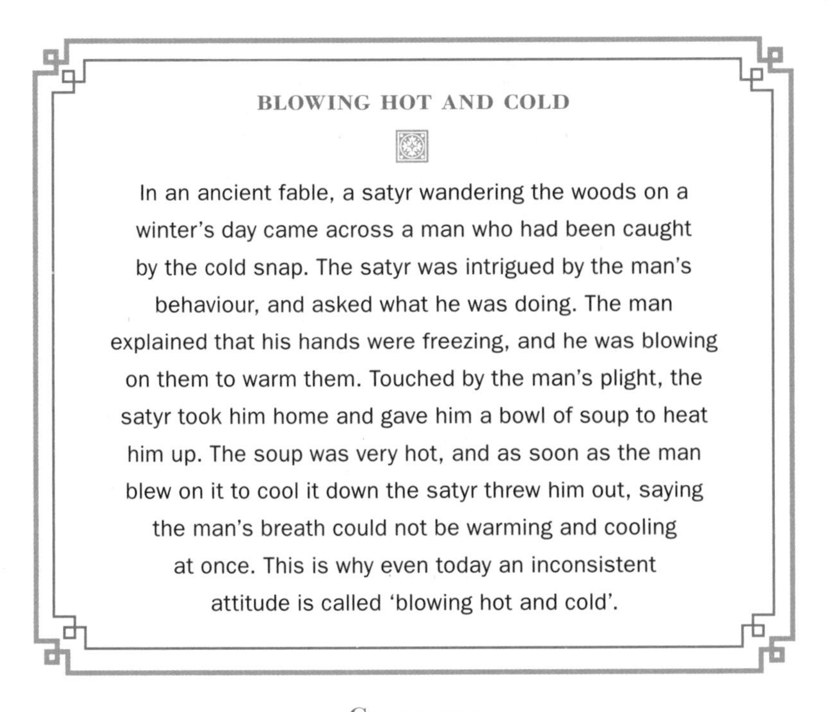

BLOWING HOT AND COLD

In an ancient fable, a satyr wandering the woods on a winter's day came across a man who had been caught by the cold snap. The satyr was intrigued by the man's behaviour, and asked what he was doing. The man explained that his hands were freezing, and he was blowing on them to warm them. Touched by the man's plight, the satyr took him home and gave him a bowl of soup to heat him up. The soup was very hot, and as soon as the man blew on it to cool it down the satyr threw him out, saying the man's breath could not be warming and cooling at once. This is why even today an inconsistent attitude is called 'blowing hot and cold'.

Centaurs

Ixion, son of Ares, was a generally bad lot. He killed his father-in-law – and on being forgiven by Zeus, he went on to conceive a passion for his own grandmother, Hera. Zeus suspected that Ixion was up to no good, and shaped a cloud into Nephele, a being who exactly resembled Hera. Ixion's lustful assault on Nephele resulted in him being eternally tied to a fiery wheel (the wheel was embodied by a nymph called Iinx, whose wheel was also used by enchanters, which is the origin of the modern jinx). The rape also resulted in Nephele becoming pregnant, and when her waters broke, the resultant shower of rain produced the centaurs.

Centaurs were found on the borders of the civilized world, and though intelligent they were born of violent lust and easily lost their self-control – like satyrs, they were swayed by their passions. Unlike satyrs, centaurs were powerful creatures, and a passionate centaur

Cupid riding on a centaur, Roman copy of a Greek original.

was extremely dangerous. Caenis, the woman whom Poseidon transformed into an invulnerable male warrior (p. 68), met his/her end when the centaurs pounded him/her into the earth with the trunks of pine trees. Attempts by humans to befriend the centaurs invariably foundered on the rock of unreason that was at the core of the centaur character. Pirithous, a Thessalian king, invited the centaurs to attend his wedding. The centaurs promptly got drunk and made an assault on the bride and her female attendants, and the wedding became a pitched battle. This is described by Ovid at his excitable and gory best.

... falling backwards, [he died], his feet drumming the blood-drenched ground. Blood fountained, both from his mouth and
his wound, mixed in part with brain-matter and wine.
His brothers, alike in their natures, were inflamed by his death,
and stirred each other to action, bellowing in unison: 'To arms!
To arms!' They were made berserk by wine, and, in that

opening battle, cups, delicate jars and round basins,
all the things designed for the feast, now were sent
flying or employed as weapons of war and death.
OVID *METAMORPHOSES* 12.220ff

Even a wise and civilized centaur such as Pholus was a dangerous friend, for when he entertained Heracles in his cave the scent of the wine was enough to stir the other centaurs into a dangerous fury. The hero calmed matters in the way that he knew best – by killing every centaur in sight. This included Pholus, who accidentally got a poisoned arrow in his foot, but was rewarded for his well-intentioned but disastrous hospitality by a berth in the constellation of Centaurus (of which Alpha Centauri is the closest star to our own in the galaxy).

Chiron, the tutor of Achilles, was another 'good' centaur, as he was of different stock, being a child of Cronos and a nymph. Nevertheless, Chiron contributed to Achilles' savage nature by feeding him warm blood from his kills. Chiron was interested in medicine (hence the name of the medicinal plant centaury). Despite this, he had no remedy for the agony he suffered when struck by an arrow tipped with the Hydra's poison (yet again, the arrow courtesy of Heracles), and voluntarily gave up his immortality to be placed among the stars. Though officially connected with the constellation Centaurus, Chiron's association with archery has led to the constellation of Sagittarius (the archer) being commonly depicted as a centaur.

Reliefs from the Parthenon of centaurs clashing with humans.

6

Heroes and their Quests

I sing of arms and the man.
OPENING LINE OF VIRGIL'S *AENEID*

Before the time of Homer, a hero was simply someone able to afford a full panoply of armour and ideally a chariot as well. But after the likes of Heracles and Perseus had entered classical mythology, a hero was a semi-divine figure who conversed with the gods on a regular basis and who, with the gods' help, achieved superhuman feats. (It is because it makes one feel capable of such achievements that a dangerously addictive opiate is called 'heroin'.) Heroic feats usually ended with a monster dead, and the earth that bit more orderly and safer for humanity. While there were hundreds of minor myths featuring heroes great and small, most of these myths were sub-plots related to the events recounted in the following chapters.

The Basic Heroic Quest

A hero's lot was to reach some distant thing and either kill it or bring it home – or both in the case of Perseus (see below). The path to the hero's destination was often blocked by obstacles that could only be overcome with divine help and the hero's native wit. Frequently the hero started with a major disadvantage such as a malign destiny, or a deeply antagonistic goddess (in the case of heroic children of Zeus, the latter could be taken as read, thanks to Hera). Though the heroes of myth sometimes met sticky ends, they shared a common consolation with heroes of all times and places – they generally got the girl.

Essentially, the heroic quest went through the following stages:

Part 1

Origins Commoners need not apply. The great heroes of myth are noble, or even semi-divine. Jason, leader of the Argonauts, may have been of royal birth, but others such as Heracles, son of Zeus, were positively slumming in his company.

Part 2

Malign destiny A hero is born with the cosmic dice weighted against him. Since attempting to avoid one's destiny is invariably futile, most heroes concentrate on sharing the pain with as many deserving victims as possible.

Part 3

Into bondage Our hero somehow ends up in the power of a nasty king who sends him on a carefully contrived …

Part 4

… Suicide mission

Part 5

Assistance While contemplating his task, our hero obtains heroic implements and assistants, divine or otherwise.

Part 6

The journey Our hero proceeds to his destiny, generally leaving a trail of corpses along the way. With Heracles, the combination of vindictive goddess and club-happy hero made the carnage particularly intense.

Part 7

Doing the deed This was the sometimes stirring, sometimes anti-climactic moment when the mission was accomplished.

Part 8

Getting home See Part 6. With extra corpses.

Part 9

Aftermath The hero returns, usually having picked up female company. This is often the point where the nasty king dies messily.

Perseus: Getting a Head

The son of rich-haired Danae, the horseman Perseus ...
with his winged sandals and black-sheathed sword.

HESIOD *THE SHIELD OF HERACLES* L.215

Perseus flees with the head of Medusa, with Athena in attendance.

Origins Son of Danae, of the line of Danaus (p. 37), grandson of King Acrisius and son of Zeus, king of the gods.

Malign destiny Perseus was fated to kill his grandfather, which led to Acrisius trying to make sure his daughter never conceived a child. He failed when Zeus penetrated her chamber as a shower of radiant gold.

Into bondage After being exiled with his mother, Perseus grew up under King Polydectes, who decided to marry his mother. Polydectes levied a tax of horses on Perseus, which he knew the hero could not pay.

Suicide mission Perseus must find Medusa the Gorgon, kill her and bring back the head in lieu of the unpaid horse tax.

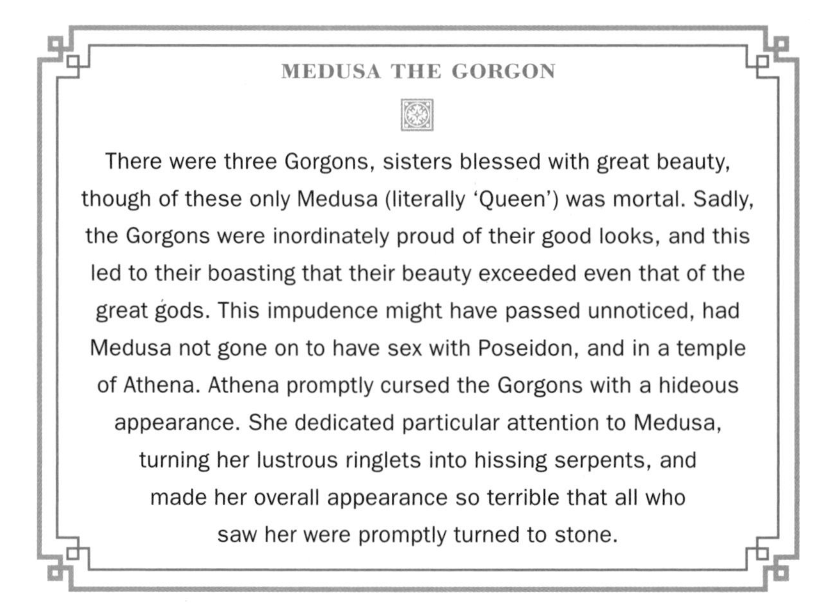

MEDUSA THE GORGON

There were three Gorgons, sisters blessed with great beauty, though of these only Medusa (literally 'Queen') was mortal. Sadly, the Gorgons were inordinately proud of their good looks, and this led to their boasting that their beauty exceeded even that of the great gods. This impudence might have passed unnoticed, had Medusa not gone on to have sex with Poseidon, and in a temple of Athena. Athena promptly cursed the Gorgons with a hideous appearance. She dedicated particular attention to Medusa, turning her lustrous ringlets into hissing serpents, and made her overall appearance so terrible that all who saw her were promptly turned to stone.

Assistance An adamantine sword and bronze shield from Hermes (who also lent his winged sandals), advice on how to find Medusa from Athena and a cap of invisibility from some friendly nymphs.

The journey Perseus was guided to a cave with three hags who knew the Gorgon's whereabouts. These three women had but one eye and one tooth between them. In what was far from his finest moment, Perseus intercepted the eye being passed from hand to hand and terrorized the old ladies into giving him the information he wanted. On leaving he dropped the eye into a nearby lake.

Doing the deed Made invisible by the cap and using the shield as a mirror so that he did not look directly at Medusa, Perseus severed the head and fled with his winged sandals while the other Gorgons were still trying to work out what had happened.

Getting home After a stopover in Egypt, Perseus happened upon Andromeda chained to a rock for consumption by a sea monster. (This was because Cassiopeia, Andromeda's mother, had offended the gods with boasts of her 'divine' beauty.) Perseus killed the monster, married Andromeda and petrified her former fiancé and his retinue with Medusa's head when they objected.

Aftermath King Polydectes was also petrified, and Danae saved from wedlock. Perseus inadvertently lobbed a mis-thrown discus at his grandfather during a sporting event, killing him as scheduled by prophecy. Unusually for an ancient myth, Perseus and Andromeda lived happily ever after.

Footnotes The Gorgon's head was often painted on the shield of Athenian hoplites, perhaps in the hope that it would afford the same protection as the original head, which ended up on the impenetrable Aegis of Athena.

Perses, a son of Perseus, went east to become ancestor to the Persian nation. On their deaths Perseus, Andromeda and Cassiopeia were transported to the heavens. Andromeda is an entire galaxy, while Perseus is but a constellation. The star Beta Per in his constellation represents the Gorgon's head, so it may not be advisable to stare at it too long.

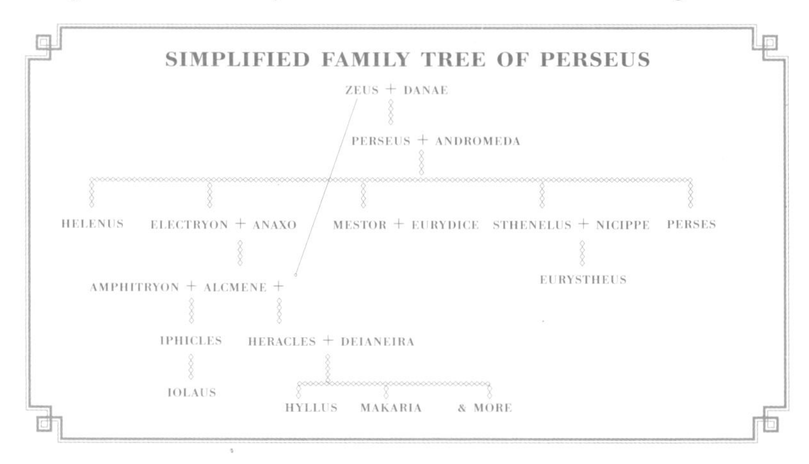

LATER ART AND CULTURE:

PERSEUS AND MEDUSA

As well as the downright sensuous, e.g. Titian's *Danae Receiving the Shower of Gold,* 1553, the violence and eroticism of the Perseus legend has proved irresistible for many artists. In the field of sculpture, these include Benvenuto Cellini's *Perseus With the Head of Medusa,* 1545–54, and Antonio Canova's *Perseus with the Head of the Gorgon Medusa,* first shown in 1801 (the origin of both of these last may be a Roman fresco in Villa San Marco at Stabiae in Italy).

Canova's Perseus holding the head of Medusa.

In painting, we find *Medusa* by Caravaggio (who liked the theme so much he did two in the late sixteenth century), and *The Head of Medusa,* 1617–18, in a joint work by Jan Brueghel the Elder and Peter Paul Rubens.

LATER ART AND CULTURE:

PERSEUS AND ANDROMEDA

The story of Andromeda, meanwhile, allowed artists to express sadomasochism as high culture, and many leapt at the opportunity, including Rubens (*Andromeda*, 1638), Pierre Mignard (*Perseus and Andromeda*, 1679), Theodore Chasseriau (*Andromeda Chained to the Rock by the Nereids*, 1840), Giorgio Vasari (*Perseus and Andromeda*, 1570–72), Gustave Doré (*Andromeda*, 1869) and Edward Poynter (*Andromeda*, 1869).

Poynter's Andromeda chained to a rock.

(Oddly enough, although nothing in the legend says Andromeda was chained naked, post-classical artists insist the lady must always be so, perhaps because her garments might have got stuck in the monster's teeth.) In sculpture, we find depictions by Daniel Chester French (*Andromeda*, 1929 – naked), and Pierre Puget (*Perseus and Andromeda*, 1678–84 – practically naked). In opera, in 1781 Anton Zimmermann produced his *Andromeda und Perseus*.

Bellerophon: The Lycian Air Force

The fearsome Chimera … the warrior Amazons …
the most valiant men of Lycia … Bellerophon killed them all.
HOMER *ILIAD* 6.179–90

Origins His father was Glaucus, king of Corinth, and he was a grandson of Sisyphus. Originally a dashing young fellow called Hipponous, our hero killed a man called Bellerus (Bellerophon means 'killer of Bellerus') and was exiled to Argos.

BELLEROPHON'S GRANDFATHER

A master of cunning, Sisyphus was the founder of the Isthmian Games (which were still celebrated by Corinth in Roman times). He gained his parched kingdom a valuable spring, the Pirene, by telling the river god Asopus where Zeus had taken his daughter with ravishment in mind. Zeus had Sisyphus thrown into Tartarus as a result, but the tricky Sisyphus escaped. As a clever ruse he ordered his wife to leave his corpse unburied and unhonoured on his death – which she did. In the underworld Sisyphus persuaded Hades to let him return to punish his wife's mistreatment of his corpse, and by reneging on his parole, managed to live a very long and happy second lifetime, in the course of which he fathered Glaucus, the future king of Corinth and the father of Bellerophon.
Hades was revenged when his errant guest died a second time. He was condemned to push a gigantic stone uphill. The task had no end, for just before the stone reached the top it would roll away, and the task would have to be done again. In the modern era any fruitless or endless task is called a 'Sisyphean labour'.

Malign destiny None.

Into bondage In Argos, Bellerophon won the heart of Queen Antira. This was bad news, as Antira was already married to the local king. When Bellerophon spurned Antira's advances, she falsely accused him of rape.

Suicide mission This was to perform various deeds in Lycia (in Asia Minor), but mainly to slay the Chimera. A child of terrifying Typhon (p. 21), this was a fire-breathing horror which had the forequarters of a lion, the middle of a she-goat and the tail of a snake (for which reason 'chimera' is modern medical shorthand for any transgenic animal).

Assistance The winged horse Pegasus (and his lesser-known brother, Chrysaor, father of Geryon – see p. 156) was the fruit of the illicit affair between Medusa and Poseidon (see p. 129). When Medusa's blood, still fertile with Poseidon's seed, leaked to the ground, it created Pegasus, for Poseidon was also of course a horse god. Pegasus flew to Greece, and where he landed on Mt Parnassus a spring leapt from his hoof prints. This was the Hippocrene, the font of inspiration for many a poet.

When Bellerophon appealed to Athena for assistance she gave him a magic harness, with which he tamed Pegasus.

The journey Uneventful, though Bellerophon had been sent with a note for his new host, the king of Lycia, that instructed that Bellerophon be killed on arrival. Fortunately the host did not read the note until later.

Doing the deed Bellerophon used a lead spear, which he thrust down the Chimera's throat. When the Chimera breathed fire, it melted the spear and the monster choked to death.

Getting home Bellerophon remained in Lycia. By now aware that he was supposed to kill his guest, the king sent Pegasus and Bellerophon against a series of enemies, but the pair triumphed every time. Finally, the king abandoned his malign intentions, confessed all, and allowed Bellerophon to marry his daughter.

Aftermath Bellerophon grew restless with peace and prosperity, and became arrogant. Eventually he tried to ascend to Olympus on Pegasus. Zeus sent a gadfly to sting Pegasus, who bucked violently, and Bellerophon fell. He was crippled, disfigured and far from home: 'hated by the gods, he wandered that plain alone, eating his heart out and avoiding the ways of men' (Homer *Iliad* 6.200). Since he died in exile, it is fitting that the *Bellerophon* was one of the ships that took Napoleon Bonaparte to his exile on St Helena.

Footnotes Pegasus was mortal, and on his death became a constellation. He remains one of the most durable symbols of classical myth and has appeared on a host of products. Indeed, this text was written on a computer manufactured by a company that was called Pegasus before the first three letters were dropped from the name.

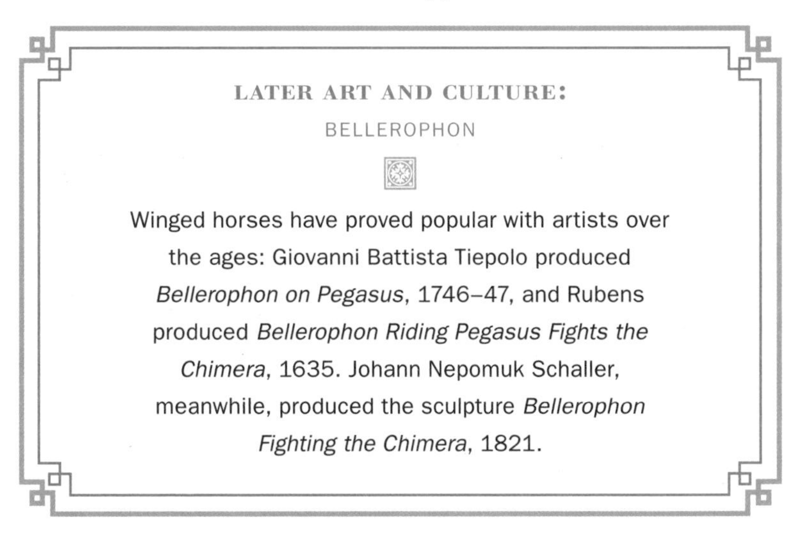

LATER ART AND CULTURE:

BELLEROPHON

Winged horses have proved popular with artists over the ages: Giovanni Battista Tiepolo produced *Bellerophon on Pegasus*, 1746–47, and Rubens produced *Bellerophon Riding Pegasus Fights the Chimera*, 1635. Johann Nepomuk Schaller, meanwhile, produced the sculpture *Bellerophon Fighting the Chimera*, 1821.

Jason: Going for Gold

For Phrixus orders us to proceed to the halls
of Aeëtes' palace ...
and carry off the deep-fleeced
hide of the ram,
on which he escaped over the sea.
PINDAR, *FOURTH PYTHIAN ODE* 285

Origins Son of minor Thessalian royalty. Owing to a complex mix-up he was raised by the centaur Chiron.

Malign destiny The malign destiny was that of King Pelias, against whom Hera had a grudge. Pelias was warned to beware of a 'man with one sandal'.

Into bondage Jason's error was to turn up improperly shod (having lost a sandal in a river) at the court of the murderous but justifiably paranoid tyrant.

Suicide mission Bring the Golden Fleece back to Thessaly. The origins of the Golden Fleece lie with Nephele (p. 123), who married the first king of Thessaly and had two children, Helle and Phrixus. The Thessalian king was polygamous and had a second wife, the daughter of Cadmus and Harmonia (p. 93), who was fiercely jealous of the children. This wife contrived to sabotage the kingdom's harvest by parching the seed grains.

When the king sent to Delphi to find out what had happened, she bribed the messengers to report that all would be well if Nephele's children were sacrificed to the gods. Nephele got word of the plan, and used her divine connections to get a magical ram from Hermes. The children fled east on the ram, though Helle fell off during the crossing between Europe and Asia and drowned in the waters, which are called the Hellespont after this occasion. Phrixus arrived safely in Colchis on the shores of the Black Sea, where he sacrificed the ram to the gods and nailed its golden fleece to a tree. It was subsequently guarded by a dragon.

The ram became the constellation of Aries (Latin for ram). Aries rising signified to farmers that it was time to sow their grain. Sowing earlier results in the grain becoming parched, which was how the entire episode came about – or at least so says Pseudo-Hyginus in his *Astronomica* (Book 2).

Assistance Jason gathered a band of adventurers (including Orpheus the musician, two sons of Hermes, the son of Pelias, the Dioscuri, and the superhero Heracles – see below). He then built a ship – the *Argo* – to Athena's instructions. As the ship's prow was built from one of the sacred oaks of the oracle of Zeus at Dodona, the ship itself was sentient, and not shy about expressing its opinions.

The journey

1. A pause at the isle of Lemnos, where the women had killed their menfolk and were living alone. These ladies welcomed the boatload of heroes with what may politely be called 'open arms'. Jason had several children with the queen, Hypsipyle.

2. A stop at the Hellespont, where King Cyzicus attacked the crew. Attacking a boatload of heroes was always a mistake, triply so if the crew included Heracles. Cyzicus was buried by the town, which took his name and became a considerable city in ancient times.

3. Sundry obstacles, including floating rocks that crushed any ship that sailed between them. The Argonauts were guided by the blind seer Phineas, whom they saved from the Harpies. Later, the music of Orpheus took the crew unscathed past the dreaded Sirens (p. 138).

HARPIES AND SIRENS

Iris, the beautiful messenger of the gods had two (or three) vile sisters, the Harpies. 'Harpyiae' means 'snatchers', and that is what these creatures did, swooping on the food of their victims and snatching it away before it could be eaten. What was left was so polluted with their rank smell that it could not be eaten anyway. Their feathers were steely as armour and their faces pale with hunger. They tormented Phineas the seer until driven off by the Argonauts and took shelter on an island where Aeneas later ran into them on his way to Italy.

Harpies on a Greek vase from the seventh century BC.

The Sirens were maidens who failed to protect Persephone and were transformed into bird-like creatures. They stayed mainly in the islands around southern Italy and lured sailors to their deaths with beautiful songs. The catch was that if a siren failed to get her man, she perished. So the Argonauts wiped out the entire eastern branch when the siren song failed to match that of Orpheus. Later, Odysseus also withstood their charms, leading to further deaths. Sirens have become more cacophonous since their modern namesakes were fitted to nineteenth-century steamboats; a 'siren song' still refers to a seductive, but best-avoided, offer.

Somewhat the worse for wear, Jason emerges from the dragon.

Doing the deed The fleece was in the care of King Aeëtes (the brother of Pasiphae – see p. 153), who promised to hand it over as soon as Jason did a bit of ploughing and seeding. The bulls that were to pull the plough were the brazen-footed, man-killing variety, and the seeds were dragon's teeth that instantly sprouted homicidal armed men.

However, Jason had caught the eye of Aeëtes' daughter, the very (very) formidable witch Medea. Medea drugged the bulls and advised Jason to throw stones at the armed men as they sprang up, so that they killed each other in the brawl that followed. The dragon guarding the fleece attempted to swallow Jason, but Medea made the beast give up its meal forthwith.

Getting home Aeëtes set sail in pursuit when the *Argo* left with the fleece, but Medea had brought along her little brother for just this eventuality. By chopping up the unfortunate lad and dropping chunks overboard at regular intervals, she forced her father to abandon the chase so as to retrieve enough of the body for burial. For Medea's horrible crime, the Argonauts needed to be purified by the witch Circe (see p. 204).

Aftermath Medea persuaded the daughters of King Pelias that they could bring their father youth and eternal life by cutting him into mincemeat and boiling the bits. When Pelias did not return from the soup, Jason and Medea were exiled.

After living in Corinth for ten years, Jason divorced Medea to marry the Corinthian princess Glauce (a descendant of Sisyphus – p. 133). Medea gave Jason's new wife a spectacular wedding dress, which burst into flame when the bride put it on (a case where the bride truly did look radiant). The intense heat killed both Glauce and her father. After the killing of her children by Jason, Medea fled to Athens in a chariot drawn by dragons.

This left Jason a broken man, sitting in the shadow of his beloved *Argo*, dreaming of past glories. But the ship had become decrepit, and the rotted prow dropped on Jason and killed him.

The story of Medea was another hit for the ancient Greek playwright Euripides. Pliny the Elder says the 'Temple of Argive Juno' in Etruria was reputed to have been founded by Jason – if the Argonaut, this suggests that he made a huge and otherwise unrecorded detour.

Medea the witch-queen prepares to depart as Glauce (centre) ignites.

LATER ART AND CULTURE:

JASON AND MEDEA

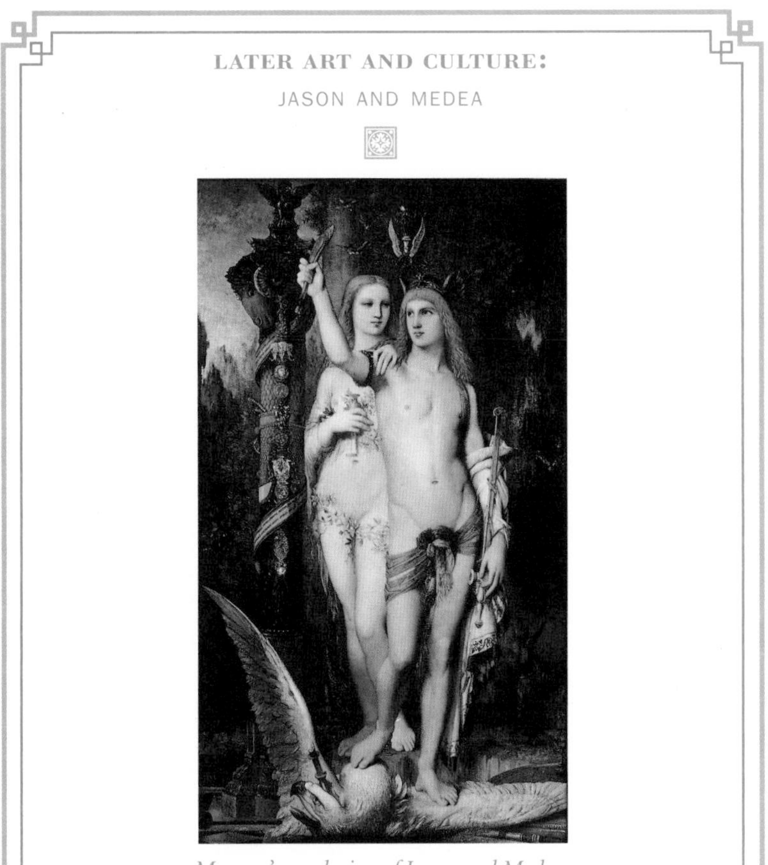

Moreau's rendering of Jason and Medea.

Unsurprisingly Medea has been a popular subject for artists, and has somewhat stolen the show from Jason in later art. In painting she has been depicted by Gustave Moreau (*Jason and Medea*, 1862), Frederick Sandys (*Medea*, 1866–68), J. W. Waterhouse (*Jason and Medea*, 1907), Bernard Safran (*Medea*, 1964), and Eugène Delacroix (*Medea*, 1862). *Medea* is also an opera of 1693 by Marc-Antoine Charpentier.

Psyche and Cupid

This everyday tale of girl meets boy-god, girl loses boy-god, girl gets boy-god is a late addition to the mythological corpus, and appears in one of the only two surviving novels from ancient Rome, the *Golden Ass* of Apuleius.

Origins Uncertain (Psyche is Greek for 'soul'), but daughter of a king, and of exceptional (and therefore perilous) beauty.

Malign destiny The envious wrath of Venus (this is a Roman myth, so Aphrodite is Venus).

Into bondage Sent by Venus to sabotage Psyche's love life, Cupid fell in love with the girl himself, and she, of course, with him. He carried her to a palace where Psyche had everything but the sight of her husband, whom she was forbidden to see. When she broke the rules and looked at her husband, Cupid fled, leaving Psyche at Venus' mercy.

Suicide missions Venus ordained that to reclaim Cupid, Psyche must perform an ever more lethal series of tasks:

- sorting a huge basket of mixed grains (accomplished by sympathetic ants)
- getting wool from golden, but murderously vicious sheep (accomplished with help from a friendly river god)
- getting water from an inaccessible cliff-side spring guarded by venomous serpents (done by a helpful eagle)
- going to the underworld, and returning with a gift from Persephone (which Psyche gamely attempted, but failed at the last, falling into an eternal sleep).

Getting home Cupid, who had forgiven Psyche, awakened her. He had considerable bargaining power, since if he went on strike neither human nor animal would feel any urge to reproduce, and he used this power to force a council of the gods, at which Jupiter (Zeus, but we're still in ancient Rome) himself decreed that Psyche should marry Cupid and that by drinking ambrosia, Psyche should become immortal.

Aftermath This is a case where the lovers literally did live happily ever after, with emphasis on the 'ever'. The child of Cupid and Psyche is Voluptas, the goddess of sensual delights.

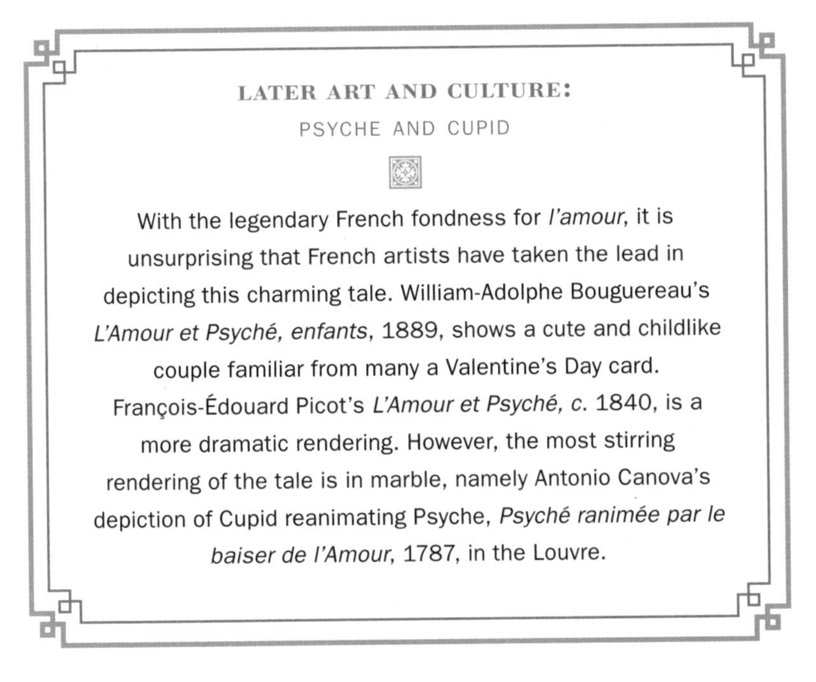

LATER ART AND CULTURE:

PSYCHE AND CUPID

With the legendary French fondness for *l'amour*, it is unsurprising that French artists have taken the lead in depicting this charming tale. William-Adolphe Bouguereau's *L'Amour et Psyché, enfants*, 1889, shows a cute and childlike couple familiar from many a Valentine's Day card. François-Édouard Picot's *L'Amour et Psyché, c.* 1840, is a more dramatic rendering. However, the most stirring rendering of the tale is in marble, namely Antonio Canova's depiction of Cupid reanimating Psyche, *Psyché ranimée par le baiser de l'Amour*, 1787, in the Louvre.

Atalanta – Trials of a Heroine

Perhaps thou may'st have heard a virgin's name,
Who still in swiftness swiftest youths o'ercame?

OVID *METAMORPHOSES* BOOK 10
(TRANS. JOHN DRYDEN)

Origins Atalanta's father wanted a boy. So disappointed was he when his wife bore him a daughter that he left the child to die in the wilds of Arcadia. However, in a sort of prequel to the story of Romulus and Remus, Atalanta was adopted by a wild animal. In her case she was suckled by a she-bear until some hunters happened by and took over the task of rearing the wild child.

The hunters did an exceptional job, as Atalanta turned out to be a great runner, wrestler and archer as well as an exceptional beauty. She defeated the father of Achilles in a wrestling match, and casually slew two centaurs who tried to rape her. She was among those who volunteered to accompany Jason on the *Argo*, but Jason declined her offer, wisely considering the effect this tomboy beauty would have on his testosterone-laden crew.

Malign destiny When irresistible beauty meets an immoveable commitment to virginity, something has to give …

The task Atalanta set her own mission in life – she was determined to remain a virgin at all costs. Given her exceptional abilities and beauty this was no easy task, as the entire male population of Greece took her attitude as a challenge. But matters were made even more complicated by Aphrodite, goddess of love, who generally seems to have regarded virginity as a personal affront, but especially so when stridently expressed by a beautiful maiden.

Obstacles The next bit of unrestrained piggery that Atalanta had to face was not of the male chauvinistic variety, but a huge, rampaging wild boar. This creature had been inflicted on the region of Calydon in Greece by Artemis as punishment after the king had forgotten to sacrifice to her. With his countryside being torn apart at a great rate, the king appealed for all the heroes of the land to join in a massive boar hunt. Several recent Argonauts took up the challenge, and thus ended up adventuring alongside Atalanta after all. One of these Argonauts was a handsome young prince called Meleager.

Atalanta was instrumental in slaying the boar, as it was her arrow that mortally wounded the beast. However, some of the other hunters were reluctant to award the prize – the boar's skin – to a mere woman. Meleager was determined that Atalanta should have the skin. The matter became a major controversy that pitted Meleager against his uncles, and resulted in the deaths of both the uncles and, indirectly, of Meleager too.

The ancient travel writer Pausanias records a spring in southern Greece, which was believed to have gushed from a rock that Atalanta struck with her spear.

MELEAGER AND THE FATES

One day in Meleager's infancy, as the baby was lying by the fire, the three Fates appeared and the child's mother heard them discussing his future. Two of the Fates, Clotho and Lachesis, had prepared a noble future for the infant, but Atropos, who cuts the threads of human lives, sadly looked at a log on the fire, and said 'He will die as soon this branch is burned up'.

As soon as the Fates vanished, the mother hastily pulled the flaming log from the fire, extinguished it and locked it securely away. Meleager grew up to enjoy the happy future the other two Fates had predicted. However, Meleager came into conflict with his relatives, and ended by slaying his uncles in battle. Infuriated by the death of her brothers, the mother pulled out the log she had stored for so many years, and threw it on the fire, although after Meleager's death she was so remorseful that she hanged herself. Other relatives of Meleager's went on to play major parts in later myth – including a sister, Deianeira, who married (and inadvertently killed) Heracles (p. 159) and a nephew, Diomedes, who was a mighty warrior in the Trojan War (p. 184).

Doing the deed Atalanta thereafter was more disillusioned with the male gender than ever. She was, however, reconciled with her father, who desired her to marry. Atalanta agreed, on one condition: instead of her suitors pursuing her, she would pursue them – with a weapon. The contest would be a footrace, with Atalanta's hand and virginity as the prize. However, anyone who failed to stay ahead of Atalanta would be killed when the fleet-footed huntress caught up.

Atalanta was very attractive, but she was also very fast, and soon an impressive number of heads adorned the side of the racetrack, struck from the necks of their lovelorn owners.

Aphrodite decided it was time to intervene directly. Her instrument was a young man called Hippomenes, whom she equipped with three irresistible golden apples. As the pair sprinted along, Hippomenes let fall a golden apple every time he heard Atalanta closing in on him. Atalanta stopped each time to gather the apple, both because she could not resist the attractive fruit and because she thought she had the measure of her opponent. It may well be that Aphrodite had weighted the dice even more firmly in the young man's favour, for as will be seen, Atalanta was strongly attracted to her quarry.

In any case, Atalanta was second over the finish line. She had lost her race, but had gained three heavenly apples and a rather delectable spouse.

Aftermath Regrettably, Hippomenes decided to give thanks for his victory to Zeus, which irked Aphrodite considerably. Consequently, she goaded the young couple into a state of such overwhelming lust that they buckled down to having sex then and there, defiling the sacred temple of Zeus in the process. Zeus could not overlook such an affront to his dignity, and he turned the newlyweds into lion and lioness. Atalanta was an innocent victim in all this, but it is uncertain whether she objected to being turned into a powerful huntress, who with her mate thereafter roamed carefree in the wild hills of Arcadia.

LATER ART AND CULTURE:

ATALANTA

Atalanta proved particularly popular with Baroque artists, including Guido Reni (the splendid *Atalanta and Hippomenes*, *c.* 1612), Charles Le Brun (*Atalanta and Meleager, c.* 1658) and Rubens (*The Hunt of Meleager and Atalanta*, early 1630s). Pierre Lepautre's *Atalanta*, 1703, is a copy of an antique sculpture, and she makes a guest appearance in Handel's opera *Serse* of 1738.

Atalanta stoops to pick up the golden apples in a painting by Reni.

The Golden Age of Mythology

The Heroic Age may have reached its climax in the Trojan War (Chapter 8), but the greatest heroes and some of the richest and best-developed myths are found in the generation preceding this all-consuming event. Both Greeks and Romans acknowledged that Heracles (Hercules to the Romans) was the greatest of heroes, but they did not pretend that this deeply flawed character was anything other than a thuggish bully who was as safe to be around as nitro-glycerine in a cocktail shaker. Theseus was not a great deal better, but almost all the myths of this era touch at least tangentially on these characters, who accounted for a substantial tally of monsters (human and otherwise), and so made the world a safer place.

Heracles: Ace of Clubs

The tales of mighty Heracles have filled the world,
and overcome Juno's hatred.
OVID *METAMORPHOSES* 9.140

Origins Heracles was the son of Zeus and Alcmene, a beautiful descendant of Perseus. Zeus appeared to Alcmene in the guise of her husband, Amphitryon; and just to confuse matters, Amphitryon actually *did* father a son with Alcmene at about the same time, so that Heracles was born with a twin brother, Iphicles, in a case of what modern medics might call 'heteropaternal (monotheic) superfecundation' ('a very productive pregnancy involving two fathers, one of whom is a god').

Heracles was allegedly born in Thebes, which is why many Theban hoplites later painted the club of Heracles on their shields.

Heracles with his traditional lionskin and club; Greek vase c. 480 BC.

Malign destiny Heracles was vehemently and passionately loathed by Hera. To put it mildly.

Into bondage Driven mad by Hera, Heracles slew his own children. To be purified he had to complete twelve tasks for King Eurystheus (the famous Labours of Heracles), another descendant of Perseus who saw Heracles as a rival for the throne. The original agreement was for ten tasks. However, as will be seen below, the tricksy Eurystheus extended the tasks to twelve by displaying a twisted genius for manipulating contract law which would have made his fortune in a later era.

Assistance The guidance of Athena, and a bow from Apollo.

Suicide missions The Twelve Labours, as follows:

I The Nemean Lion

Although invulnerable even to the arrows of Apollo, the lion proved susceptible to Heracles' favoured hit-them-very-hard-on-the-head approach (even though this particular head was so solid it broke

Heracles' club). Heracles then used the beast's own claws to cut off its near-invulnerable hide, and thus equipped himself with a flexible skin of armour with which he was thenceforth almost invariably clad. Those born in mid- to late summer have reason to remember this occasion, as Zeus placed the lion in the heavens as the constellation and zodiacal sign of Leo.

II The Hydra

Every time a head was cut off this serpent-like child of Typhon (see p. 21), two more grew in its place. Indeed, 'a hydra-headed problem' is still used in the modern era to describe any issue that is made worse by efforts to resolve it. As additional handicaps, the Hydra's venom was of supernatural potency (and this venom was to get Heracles in the end, as will be seen), and Hera contributed a giant crab to assist the serpent by snapping at Heracles' feet.

Heracles gets ahead in his combat with the multi-headed Hydra.

Heracles overcame this beast with the help of his nephew Iolaus. Every time Heracles lopped off a head, Iolaus cauterized the stump so it could not grow back. The final head was immortal, and so had to be buried deep under a massive rock on the road to Elaeus, where it probably lives yet. However, because Heracles received unauthorized assistance from his nephew, Eurystheus ruled a technical foul and declared this labour invalid. Nevertheless, the labour was not in vain, for henceforth Heracles' arrows were tipped with Hydra poison.

The crab was literally a footnote in the main battle. Heracles stamped it to pieces under a mighty sandal, and the dread crustacean took its place with Leo to become the zodiacal sign of Cancer. The Hydra, too, became a constellation.

III The Ceryneian Hind

This was Taygete (one of the Pleiades –see p. 90), whom her friend Artemis had transformed into a deer with golden antlers to escape the oversexed attentions of Zeus. Heracles captured her alive in a net. Apollo and Artemis made him release his prize, but Heracles had, however briefly, captured the hind, and therefore carried out Labour III to the letter.

IV The Erymanthian Boar

Eurystheus decided to keep Heracles going against his natural inclination, and bring back another creature alive – this time a huge boar that was ravaging Arcadia. With helpful advice from Chiron the centaur, our hero managed to capture the boar by tricking it into charging a deep snowdrift.

A wild boar hunt, as shown on a Roman sarcophagus.

Interlude While Eurystheus was researching further lethal tasks, Heracles was allowed a vacation, during which he joined the Argonauts, and slew sundry unnatural fauna, including the eagle that was eating Prometheus' liver (he freed Prometheus at the same time – though some accounts say the entire incident happened later).

V The Augean Stables

Eurystheus attempted to demoralize Heracles with an impossible yet demeaning task – to clean the Augean stables. These stables belonged to King Augeas of Elis in the Peloponnese, and housed his huge herd of cattle. Over the years, chronic understaffing had left the stables a massive, reeking complex of buildings semi-submerged in cow dung. King Augeas happily accepted Heracles' offer to clean up (and still today undertaking any apparently impossible, complex and messy job is called 'cleaning the Augean stables'), and offered a tenth of his herds if the stables were pristine by the day's end.

Heracles promptly diverted a nearby river through the stables, and this did the job for him. Augeas refused to pay, and to add insult to injury, Eurystheus ruled the task invalid as Heracles had accepted an offer of payment.

VI The Stymphalian Birds

These foul creatures were ruining crops in Arcadia with their droppings. Their feathers were bronze, and tipped with poison, and the birds shed them on anyone who ventured into the trees to try to kill them.

Athena and Hephaestus worked together (as they often did), he to produce a huge bronze cymbal, and she to advise the hero to strike it against a nearby mountain. When the birds flew up in panic, Heracles proved that bronze feathers could not stop the arrows of Apollo tipped with the poison of the Hydra.

Heracles shooting down the Stymphalian birds.

VII The Cretan Bull

King Minos (p. 44) was beloved of the gods. He once proved that whatever he prayed for would be granted, for when sacrificing on a beach he prayed to Poseidon for a suitable victim. Immediately there came a bull from the sea, a beast of such spectacular beauty that Minos decided to risk the wrath of Poseidon and substitute another bull in the sacrifice. Poseidon teamed up with Aphrodite for his retaliation, as Pasiphae, the wife of Minos, had been lackadaisical in her sacrifices to the goddess.

Mastering the Cretan bull.

Aphrodite inflicted Pasiphae with an unnatural lust for the bull. This lust Pasiphae slaked with the help of Daedalus, the palace inventor-in-residence, who constructed a wooden heifer for the deranged lady to conceal herself within. Regrettably, the affair resulted in a pregnancy, and the child was a very bad-tempered creature with a bull's head. Minos was quick to draw the appropriate conclusions. Daedalus was imprisoned, and the bull was turned loose to become a general menace. The child became known as the Minotaur – of whom more anon.

For his seventh task, Heracles had to collect this bull and bring it to Eurystheus, which the hero did with minimal fuss.

VIII The Mares of Diomedes

The next task sent Heracles to Thrace to collect some horses. Thrace was a distant, savage and barbaric land, and the owner of the horses, King Diomedes, was even by Thracian standards a particularly savage and barbaric character with an army to match. And the horses were man-eaters.

Heracles gets the better of a man-eating mare.

On the positive side, Heracles was allowed to round up some volunteers to help with this task. Heracles and his band defeated the army of Diomedes, and the hero was pleasantly surprised to find that once the king had been fed to his own horses, the beasts became remarkably docile.

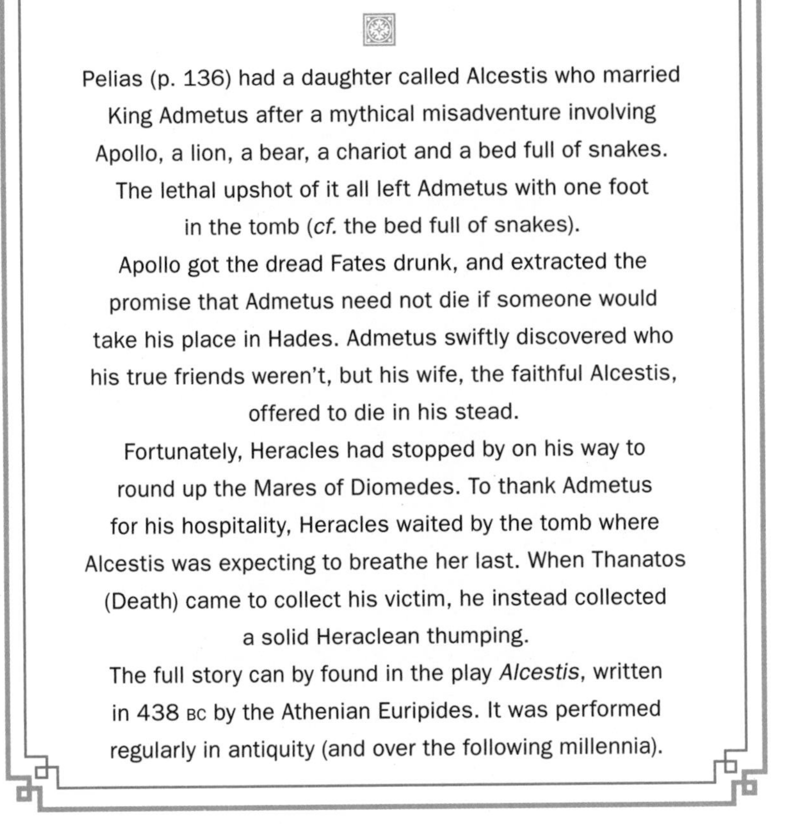

HOW HERACLES SAVED ALCESTIS

Pelias (p. 136) had a daughter called Alcestis who married King Admetus after a mythical misadventure involving Apollo, a lion, a bear, a chariot and a bed full of snakes. The lethal upshot of it all left Admetus with one foot in the tomb (*cf.* the bed full of snakes).

Apollo got the dread Fates drunk, and extracted the promise that Admetus need not die if someone would take his place in Hades. Admetus swiftly discovered who his true friends weren't, but his wife, the faithful Alcestis, offered to die in his stead.

Fortunately, Heracles had stopped by on his way to round up the Mares of Diomedes. To thank Admetus for his hospitality, Heracles waited by the tomb where Alcestis was expecting to breathe her last. When Thanatos (Death) came to collect his victim, he instead collected a solid Heraclean thumping.

The full story can by found in the play *Alcestis*, written in 438 BC by the Athenian Euripides. It was performed regularly in antiquity (and over the following millennia).

IX The Girdle of the Amazon Queen

Eurystheus next sent Heracles to get the girdle of the Amazon queen Hippolyta as a present for his daughter. Heracles left his habitual trail of corpses on his way to Hippolyta, including some sons of King Minos slaughtered on the isle of Paros. He was again accompanied by a trusty band of companions (including Theseus – see below). On arrival, Heracles found that his sweaty charisma was sufficient to charm the belt off Hippolyta. However, Hera told the warrior women that Heracles was kidnapping their queen. The hero responded to the impending crisis by promptly killing Hippolyta (to be on the safe side) and escaped with the girdle.

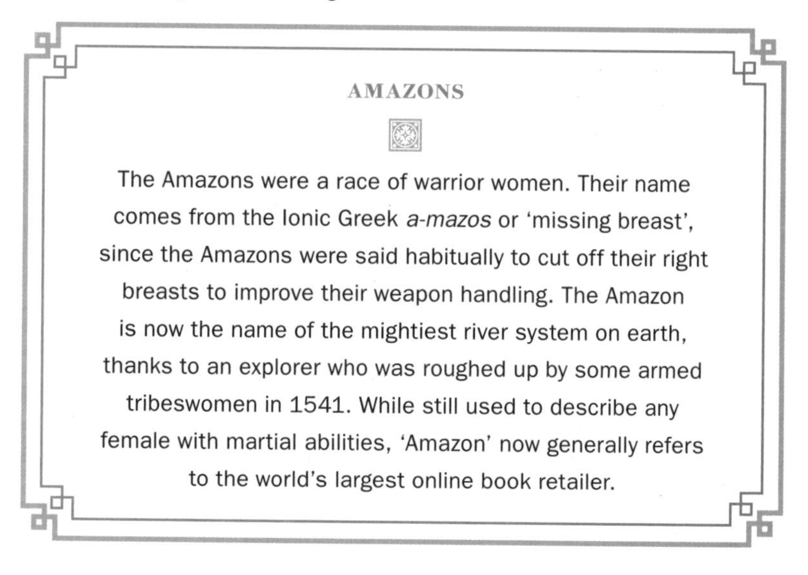

AMAZONS

The Amazons were a race of warrior women. Their name comes from the Ionic Greek *a-mazos* or 'missing breast', since the Amazons were said habitually to cut off their right breasts to improve their weapon handling. The Amazon is now the name of the mightiest river system on earth, thanks to an explorer who was roughed up by some armed tribeswomen in 1541. While still used to describe any female with martial abilities, 'Amazon' now generally refers to the world's largest online book retailer.

X The Cattle of Geryon

Omitting a host of minor myths, Heracles essentially went to the far west of the world, killed Geryon, his herdsman and his dog, and then stole his cattle. The outward journey took Heracles through Libya and the Iberian Peninsula. The return trip left corpses across Italy and around the shores of the Black Sea. Here, a woman with the lower body of a snake stole some of his cattle, but Heracles nevertheless slept with her, and as a result fathered the Scythian race.

On crossing from North Africa to Europe, Heracles noted that the strait was dominated by a large and unstable mountain. He tidied this up by splitting the mountain in two, and putting one part on each side of the strait. In ancient times these half-mountains were called the 'Pillars of Heracles' – the European 'pillar' is today called Gibraltar.

XI The Golden Apples of the Hesperides

These were given by Gaia to Hera as a wedding present (see p. 64), and few people knew where they were. Heracles obtained the information from the minor sea god Nereus (by force, naturally). Acting on a tip provided by Prometheus (by some accounts it was now that he killed the eagle and freed the Titan), Heracles went to see Atlas, another of the Titans. The apples were guarded by a hundred-headed serpent and the Hesperides, daughters of Atlas. In return for Heracles holding up the sky for him (Athena helped), Atlas went to persuade his daughters to hand over the apples (Atlas had to be tricked into taking up the sky again on his return). To make the entire enterprise literally fruitless, the apples were too sacred for the mortal Eurystheus to own, so Athena put them back again.

While on this quest Heracles is said to have stolen and sacrificed an ox on the island of Rhodes. He ate the beast while the owner stood nearby impotently swearing at him. Thereafter, sacrifices to Heracles in Rhodes were traditionally accompanied by similar expletives.

XII The Capture of Cerberus

Heracles now had to play 'fetch' with the mighty three-headed hound that guarded the portals of the underworld (p. 42). Helped by Hermes, who naturally knew the way, and accompanied by Athena, Heracles made his ungentle journey to Hades, beating up

Cerberus taken for a walk by Heracles, while minor deities look on.

Charon and Hades himself in the process. (Some say that in defeating Hades he became assured of immortality when his allotted time on earth was done.) While in the underworld, Heracles found his friend Theseus imprisoned there, and promptly freed him.

In the end Persephone let Heracles borrow Cerberus on condition that he captured the hound barehanded, and brought him back in good condition. So Heracles simply picked up the fearsome guardian of Hades on his way out, slung the doubtless confused animal over one shoulder, and proceeded back to the world of mortals. The way to Eurystheus was somewhat more corpse-ridden than usual, as Cerberus was a particularly deadly beast (for example, the poisonous plant aconite sprang up wherever Cerberus dribbled saliva, and he salivated a lot). Heracles finished his labours by putting Cerberus back where he belonged, to general relief all round.

Aftermath Freed from his thrall to Eurystheus, Heracles was soon in trouble again. He killed a young man, possibly because he had again gone mad (alternatively, he may have gone mad as a result of the killing). He sought advice on purification from Delphi, and threatened to wreck the place when this was not forthcoming. Eventually Apollo himself had to stop Heracles, and a nasty fight ensued, which only ended when Zeus blasted his squabbling sons apart with a thunderbolt.

Heracles was put back in bondage, this time to Queen Omphale of Lydia. After she had employed Heracles to mop up the general riff-raff of the kingdom, she put the hero in a dress and set him to weaving while she posed in his lionskin with his club. Apparently Heracles bore no grudges for his treatment, and by some accounts, he and Omphale became lovers.

His own man once more, Heracles spent the next few years revenging himself on those who had impeded him on his Twelve Labours. In the course of a series of bloodstained escapades around the Mediterranean he found time to establish Priam as king of Troy, take part in a battle between gods and Giants, and establish the Olympic games.

Deianeira handing Heracles the fatal tunic.

He also married a woman called Deianeira, as he had promised a friend whom he met in the underworld. This proved his undoing.

In the course of his various escapades Heracles had done much to make centaurs practically extinct, and a survivor called Nessus was somewhat bitter that Heracles had wiped out his clan en route to capturing the Erymanthian Boar. Nessus attempted to kidnap Deianeira, but was felled by a Hydra-poison-tipped arrow from Heracles. With his dying breath Nessus told Deianeira that a vial of his blood would keep Heracles faithful to her forever.

Some years later Deianeira felt threatened by a younger rival, so she poured the vial over Heracles' tunic. This vial contained not only the blood of Nessus but also the hideous poison of the Hydra, which immediately made its effect felt. Heracles ripped off his tunic at once (taking huge chunks of corrupted flesh with it), but it was too late. Calmly the hero built his own funeral pyre, and died. Zeus claimed the shade of his errant son and took him to Olympus to join the gods. Finally reconciled with his stepmother Hera, Heracles took as a wife Hebe, goddess of youth.

The funeral pyre of Heracles was erected above the pass at Thermopylae where the hero's supposed descendant, Leonidas, was later to fight off the Persians with his 300 heroes.

Death by Heracles

An abbreviated list in roughly chronological order of those incidentally slain by the hero in the course of his adventures:

Two snakes Sent by Hera in an attempt to snuff out Heracles as an infant. Heracles assumed they were toys and throttled them while playing.

Linus Music teacher of Heracles; for chastising his pupil he was brained by Heracles with his own lyre.

The Lion of Cithaeron For slaying this beast, the king of Thespis rewarded Heracles with a night of passion with his daughters. In what is sometimes called the 'first labour of Heracles' the hero impregnated each of the girls in a single night. All fifty of them.

Thersimachus, Creontidas, Deicoon Children of Heracles slain by him in a fit of madness.

The children of Iphicles Also killed while Heracles was deranged (Iphicles was the half-brother of Heracles – see p. 148).

Pholus the centaur, and Chiron the centaur, and Nessus the centaur, and Nessus' tribe of centaurs, and Eurytion the centaur – in fact, mythology does not record a single centaur who survived meeting Heracles.

The Gegeneis Giants in Asia Minor (while Heracles was on the *Argo*).

Calais and Zetes Two of the Argonauts.

Augeas He of the stables. Augeas got away with his double-dealing for a time, but Heracles knew how to hold a grudge.

Laomedon, king of Troy Heracles killed a monster for him. As the hero had to fight his way out of the beast after it had swallowed him, Heracles was unhappy when Laomedon refused to pay the agreed fee.

Sarpedon of Thrace A son of Poseidon, killed for being rude to Heracles.

King Eryx of Sicily A son of Aphrodite, killed by Heracles in a wrestling match.

Alcyoneus A giant who flung a stone at Heracles so hard that he was killed by the rebound.

Busiris, king of Egypt He tried to sacrifice Heracles to his gods.

Antaeus A son of Gaia who gained strength every time he was flung to the ground. Heracles took him on at wrestling, lifted him into the air and killed him there.

Emathion A son of Eos and Tithonus (p. 41), who tried to prevent Heracles taking the Golden Apples.

Iphitus A young prince slain in yet another fit of madness.

Eurypylus, king of Cos He and his men attacked Heracles on his travels.

King Neleus of Pylos For refusing to purify Heracles for an earlier killing.

Eunomus A boy who spilled wine when serving Heracles at table.

Cycnus A deranged son of Ares who was trying to build a temple of skulls. Heracles forcibly declined an invitation to contribute his own (p. 94).

Eurytus A king who refused to hand over his daughter as a concubine for Heracles.

Lichas Who inadvertently gave Heracles his poisoned tunic.

LATER ART AND CULTURE:
HERACLES (HERCULES)

Heracles has inspired artists ancient and modern. Annibale Carracci's *The Choice of Hercules, c.* 1596, shows the young hero choosing between hardship and heroism or an easy life of pleasure. Francisco de Zurbaran offers a dramatic depiction of *Hercules and Cerberus* (*c.* 1636), while Rubens in his *The Drunken Hercules, c.* 1611, shows the hero in a less-than-virtuous condition. And François Lemoyne in *Hercules and Omphale*, 1724, shows a lavishly decadent hero thoroughly enjoying his bondage. The sculptor Baccio Bandinelli, meanwhile, produced *Hercules and Cacus*, 1524–34. The centuries have seen *Heracles*, the Euripidean play in ancient Athens, *Hercules* the opera, presented by Handel at the King's Theatre in London in 1745, and *Hercules* the animated movie by Disney in 1997 (in this last, possibly by coincidence, some details are correct). The Twelve Labours have also given rise to a wealth of artworks. Rubens produced a memorable painting of *Hercules Strangling the Nemean Lion* (*c.* 1639), the Hydra proved irresistible for Gustave Moreau (*Hercules and the Lernaean Hydra, c.* 1876) and Antonio Pollaiuolo (*Hercules and the Hydra, c.* 1470), and Moreau also painted *Diomedes Devoured by his Horses* (1865). The sixteenth-century Flemish artist Frans Floris painted a series of the Labours, but these are now lost. Hippolyta appears in Shakespeare's *A Midsummer Night's Dream*, and Angelica Kauffmann painted *Death of Alcestis* (1790).

Oedipus: A Complex Tale

Should I never have come to shed
My father's blood, and share my mother's bed
The monstrous son of a womb defiled
Husband of my father's wife and yet her child
Was any man afflicted as I, Oedipus?
SOPHOCLES *OEDIPUS THE KING* 1.1665ff

No hero ever managed to avoid his predestined fate, but one can hardly blame Oedipus for making the attempt, since he was doomed to slay his father and marry his mother.

Origins Oedipus was the son of King Laius of Thebes and his queen, Jocasta. When told by the oracle at Delphi that his son would kill him, Laius bound the infant's feet together and drove a stake through them. This swelled the tortured infant's feet ('Oedipus' means 'swollen foot'). Dissatisfied with this preventive measure, Laius told a shepherd to kill the boy. Instead the shepherd passed the child to another shepherd who had heard that the king of Corinth was looking to adopt a child for his barren wife, Merope. Years later Oedipus, now a young man, came to Delphi, where the oracle repeated the prophecy that Oedipus would kill his father and marry his mother.

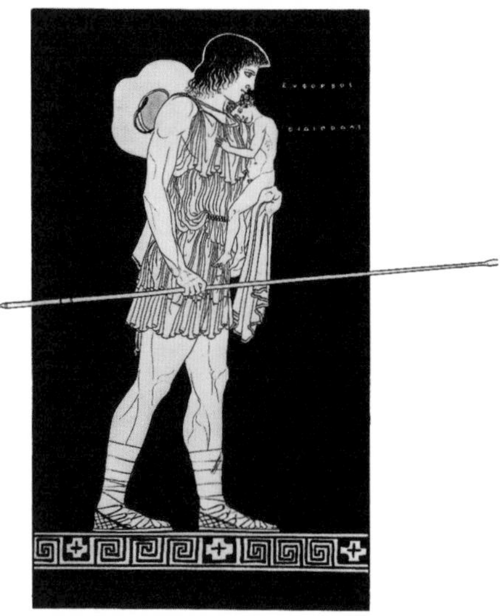

A shepherd with the baby Oedipus.

Malign destiny Determined to escape his destiny, Oedipus decided not to return to what he thought was his native city of Corinth, and instead went to Thebes. Along the way, he had an argument with an arrogant man in a chariot as to who should give way on the road, and when the man in the chariot pushed Oedipus aside and rode over his foot, the young prince slew the charioteer with a javelin. Arriving in Thebes, Oedipus discovered the city in turmoil. A monstrous creature with the head of a woman and body of a lion – a Sphinx – was killing travellers outside the city. When King Laius had set off to ask the oracle at Delphi what could be done, he had been slain by a person or persons unknown on the road.

Oedipus and the Sphinx on a fifth-century BC drinking cup.

Doing the deed Oedipus decided that he would make amends for his earlier road rage by destroying the Sphinx. He knew that the monster asked travellers a riddle and only ate them if they could not answer correctly. If it did receive a correct answer, the creature was bound to kill itself, so the game was not without risk for both participants. The riddle was: 'It walks on four legs in the morning, two in the day, and three in the evening. What is it?' Perhaps his swollen foot had given the hero sensitivity in this field, for he answered that the subject of the riddle was a man, who crawls as a baby, then walks upright on two legs until he takes up a stick in the evening of his days. Defeated, the Sphinx threw itself off a cliff. Oedipus returned in triumph to Thebes where the delighted populace proposed that the young prince should marry the recently widowed queen, Jocasta, and take over the leadership of the city.

Aftermath All went well for several years. Oedipus and Queen Jocasta had several children including Antigone, a daughter who was herself the basis of several myths and a dramatic play by Sophocles of Athens. Then a messenger came from Corinth announcing the death of the king, and asking Oedipus to take up the governance of that city. Oedipus explained about the risk of marrying his mother Merope and received the far-from-reassuring news that he was an adopted child. Queen Jocasta was the first to join the dots and reach the correct conclusion. She quietly withdrew and hanged herself. Oedipus, almost out of his mind with guilt and grief, blinded himself on discovering her body. He exiled himself from Thebes, and eventually died in Attica under the protection of Theseus, who was king of Athens at the time.

And there actually is a motive in the story of King Oedipus which explains the verdict of this inner voice. His fate moves us only because it might have been our own, because the oracle laid upon us before our birth the very curse which rested upon him. It may be that we were all destined to direct our first sexual impulses toward our mothers, and our first impulses of hatred and violence toward our fathers; our dreams convince us that we were. King Oedipus, who slew his father Laius and wedded his mother Jocasta, is nothing more or less than a wish-fulfilment – the fulfilment of the wish of our childhood.

SIGMUND FREUD COMES UP WITH THE OEDIPUS COMPLEX IN *THE INTERPRETATION OF DREAMS*, 1899

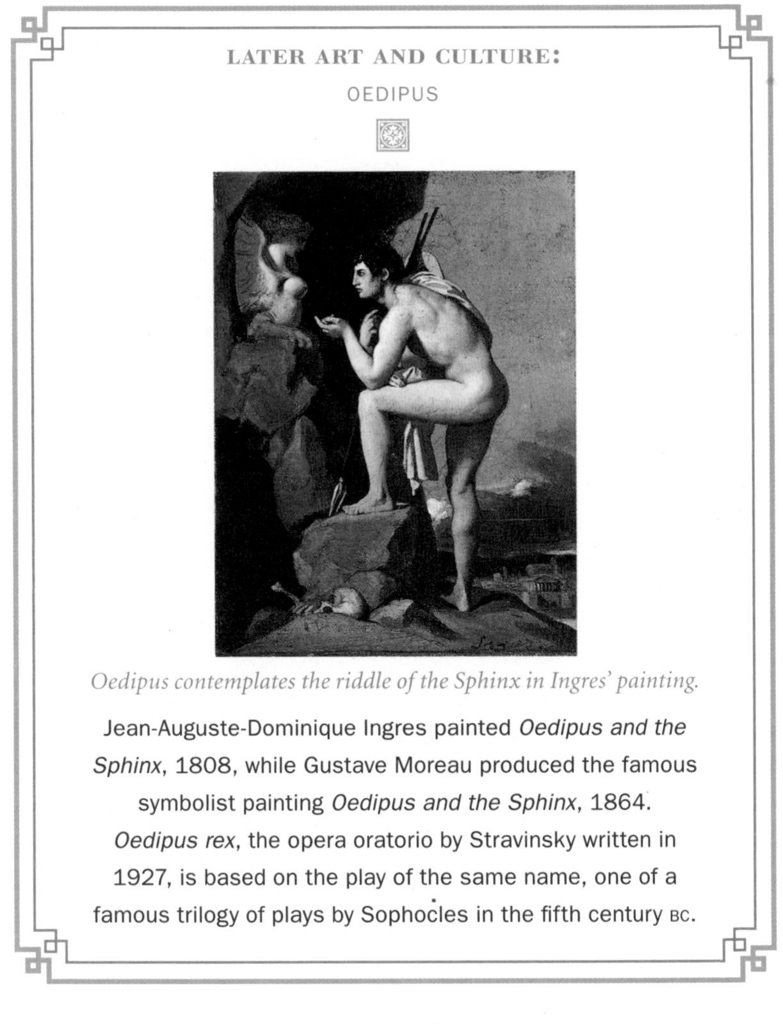

LATER ART AND CULTURE:
OEDIPUS

Oedipus contemplates the riddle of the Sphinx in Ingres' painting.

Jean-Auguste-Dominique Ingres painted *Oedipus and the Sphinx*, 1808, while Gustave Moreau produced the famous symbolist painting *Oedipus and the Sphinx*, 1864. *Oedipus rex*, the opera oratorio by Stravinsky written in 1927, is based on the play of the same name, one of a famous trilogy of plays by Sophocles in the fifth century BC.

Theseus: The Love Rat

The most savage-tempered beasts have shown themselves more mild and gentle than you have been to me. Never could I have trusted myself to more faithless hands.

OVID *ARIADNE ABANDONED BY THESEUS* 1ff

Even more than the Thebans claimed Heracles as their own, the Athenians considered Theseus their special hero. Theseus was the king who united all Attica under one rule, but the Athenian choice of Theseus as their iconic hero is particularly appropriate because, like most Athenian males, Theseus was something of a chauvinist – even by contemporary Greek standards.

Origins Aethra, the mother of Theseus, slept with Poseidon and Aegeus, king of Athens, in the same night and produced a single child who combined the qualities of human and divine.

Aegeus was returning to Athens when he impregnated Aethra in the small city of Troezen. He stayed with the lady long enough to ascertain she was pregnant, and then buried his sword and sandals beneath a large rock, telling the girl that when her son was strong enough to lift the rock, he should go to Athens. (Since Aegeus had taken up with the redoubtable Medea after she left Jason – see p. 140 – it was probably wise to keep Aethra and son out sight until the boy was grown.)

When he duly retrieved the items from under the rock, Theseus chose to take the land route to Athens instead of a short sea trip across the Saronic Gulf. This was bad news for a series of malefactors along the route, as young Theseus was determined to emulate his hero Heracles and slay all obstacles in his path. They included:

Periphetes A son of Hephaestus who carried a powerful staff, with which he hammered passing travellers into the ground, thus profaning Epidaurus, sacred to Asclepius. Theseus killed 'the clubber' (as he was named) and took the staff, with which he was generally identified thereafter.

Sinis Also called 'the pine-bender', as he used his great strength to bend pines. After having attached a traveller to two bent pines he would let go, causing pines and traveller to fly apart. He was not the only person able to do this, as Theseus demonstrated on Sinis himself. Theseus then impregnated the daughter of Sinis and went on his way.

Theseus and Athena (centre) on an Athenian drinking cup.

The Crommyon Sow This destructive creature was a child of Typhon, or (by other accounts) the other self of a robber queen. Theseus went out of his way to hunt down and kill her.

Sciron A thug who met travellers on a narrow cliff path and forced them to wash his feet. As they finished the job he kicked the unfortunates into the sea far below. He was himself tossed off the cliff when he confronted Theseus.

Cercyon As he neared Athens, Theseus met the king of Eleusis, who challenged strangers to a wrestling match, with the loser's life as the forfeit. Cercyon lost.

Procrustes Sometimes seen as the forefather of the modern hotel trade, Procrustes had one bed that fitted everyone, whether they liked it or not. The tall were cut to fit, and the short stretched on a rack until they measured up. In the words of Theseus' biographer Plutarch, the hero made Procrustes 'suffer the justice of his own injustice' and lie in the bed he had made. The adjective 'Procrustean' survives today to describe forced conformity to an arbitrary standard.

Theseus arrived in Athens with tales of his deeds preceding him. Aegeus was preoccupied with a power struggle with the sons of Pallas, his rival for the throne, but the witch-queen Medea recognized her husband's son at once. She persuaded Aegeus that the stranger was a threat, and that he should be invited to a banquet and poisoned. However, at the last moment Aegeus recognized the sword that Theseus carried, and knocked the poisoned chalice from his hands.

There followed a reckoning with Medea (who was exiled) and the sons of Pallas (defeated in battle) and also the killing of the bull of Marathon. This was Pasiphae's former boyfriend, retrieved by Heracles and released by Eurystheus (p. 153). The bull was making life unbearable on the plain of Marathon (where the Athenians later memorably defeated the invading Persians) and had already killed a son of Minos. Once he had slain the bull, Theseus discovered he had further business with its son.

Theseus in action against his various opponents.

This came about because the sons of Minos had little luck in Attica. Another son of Minos and Pasiphae had been unjustly slain by the sons of Pallas, and the outraged gods and equally outraged Minos threatened to turn the land about Athens into a wasteland unless recompense was made. Therefore every year seven maids and seven youths had to be sent to Crete in tribute, where they were sacrificed to the Minotaur, the bull-headed son of Pasiphae.

DAEDALUS AND ICARUS

Daedalus the inventor was exiled from Athens for murder (out of envy he had killed Perdix, the inventor of the saw). He made his way to Crete, where he created the fake heifer for Pasiphae and the labyrinth for Minos to hold the product of her passion. Imprisoned by Minos, Daedalus made his escape by constructing wings for himself and his son Icarus. Daedalus warned his son not to fly too high, but young Icarus gloried in the sensation of flying. He flew so high that the radiance of the sun melted the wax that secured the feathers to the wings, and sent the boy plummeting to his death. (Heracles, en route to pick up the cattle of Geryon, found the body and buried it.) Daedalus made his way to Italy, and the vengeful Minos was killed when he followed in search of his scapegrace inventor. One has sincerely to hope that the modern Icarus does not fall to earth – it is an asteroid almost a mile wide which swings past earth every thirty years or so, missing us by about four million miles. Such 'near-earth' asteroids are nicknamed 'doomsday rocks': the modern Icarus would equal 33,000 Hiroshimas were it to hit our planet.

LATER ART AND CULTURE

Icarus has become a symbol of the fate of the over-exuberant, and thus popular with artists. Carlo Saraceni's *Fall of Icarus*, painted in 1600, shows the moment of the fall, while Herbert Draper's *The Lament for Icarus, c.* 1898, shows the aftermath.

Ariadne betrayed Theseus volunteered to be among the seven youths sent to Crete, but first he sacrificed to Apollo and Aphrodite, asking for their favour. What happened next is highly confused as multiple versions of the tale exist, but in all accounts the sacrifice to Aphrodite yielded substantial dividends, and Ariadne, a royal princess of Crete, was smitten with the handsome young Theseus.

She gave the hero a sword and a ball of string. The latter was perhaps the more crucial, as so cunning was the Labyrinth of Daedalus that it has given its name to all labyrinths since. No one had found their way out before, and all who entered had either perished of fear and hunger or had fallen victim to the monstrous Minotaur who prowled the corridors. Theseus slew the beast and followed the thread back to the waiting Ariadne, and the pair fled by boat to Athens.

However, in matters of romance Theseus was the archetypal cheat. He dumped the pregnant Ariadne on the isle of Naxos, where she won the heart of the god Dionysus. Ariadne died in childbirth. Dionysus had intended to marry her – which led to her being slain by Artemis in some versions of the story – so instead Dionysus placed her wedding wreath in the sky as the Corona Borealis. (Ariadne has recently been attempting to retrieve this wreath in her modern incarnation as the main launch rocket for the European space programme.)

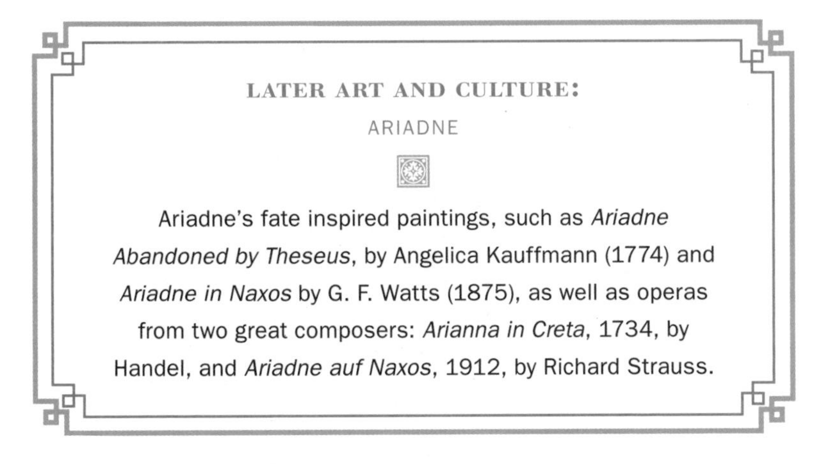

LATER ART AND CULTURE:

ARIADNE

Ariadne's fate inspired paintings, such as *Ariadne Abandoned by Theseus*, by Angelica Kauffmann (1774) and *Ariadne in Naxos* by G. F. Watts (1875), as well as operas from two great composers: *Arianna in Creta*, 1734, by Handel, and *Ariadne auf Naxos*, 1912, by Richard Strauss.

The death of Aegeus King Aegeus was aware that Theseus might be going to his death when he set off to slay the Minotaur. The ship that carried the young Athenians to their fate customarily had black sails, and in order to know as soon as possible the outcome, Aegeus ordered Theseus to change the sails to white if he was coming home alive. Theseus forgot, and when Aegeus saw the ominous black sails from his lookout on Cape Sounion, he leapt from the cliffs to his death.

The Athenians treasured the 'ship of Theseus', which they claimed was still preserved into classical times. By then all the original wood had rotted away and been replaced, leading to much debate by philosophers as to whether it was still the same ship.

The battle with the Amazons – a common theme in Athenian art.

Antiope slain The story of how Theseus met the Amazon Antiope has many versions. In one of the most common, Theseus accompanied Heracles on his mission to obtain the girdle of Queen Hippolyta of the Amazons (p. 155), and made Antiope his prisoner. He brought Antiope back to Athens, and as she was a high-ranking Amazon, the rest of the tribe followed to win her back. They fought a pitched battle with the Greeks in the middle of Athens in the course of which Antiope was killed. She left Theseus with a son called Hippolytus.

Phaedra doomed Theseus married Phaedra, another daughter of Minos, who appears not to have learned from Ariadne's experience. Despite the hero's past record, the pair were a happy couple until Hippolytus professed himself a devoted follower of Artemis and a life-long virgin. Aphrodite promptly resumed her feud with the family of Minos and inflicted Phaedra with the same lust for her stepson as her mother had had for the bull from the sea. The outcome was tragic. Hippolytus rejected Phaedra with horror, and she hanged herself. Her suicide note claimed an attempted rape by Hippolytus, and an indignant Theseus called on his father Poseidon to destroy his allegedly incestuous son, which he did.

Helen abducted Being without wife and son, Theseus was persuaded into a harebrained adventure by his friend, the reckless Pirithous. The pair decided that their next wives would be daughters of Zeus. First they went to Sparta and abducted the young Helen, who was already famous for her beauty although only twelve years old. Helen was kept securely in Troezen while the pair embarked on their quest for their next victim.

Hundreds of years later in the Peloponnesian War, the Spartans almost annually ravaged the lands of Attica, but they always spared the area of Dekeleia, where the locals had helped the Spartans reclaim their princess.

Persephone unraped Pirithous had decided that none other than Persephone would be his wife, and Theseus and Pirithous went to Hades to get her. The Lord of the Dead was grimly amused, for he immediately understood the reason for the visit of the foolhardy pair. Pretending to greet them, he offered chairs that immediately wiped the memories of those who sat in them. Theseus was eventually rescued by his friend Heracles who was in Hades to borrow Cerberus (p. 157), but Pirithous sits in his chair yet.

Female victims (continued by Plutarch)

There are other stories about 'marriages' of Theseus which neither start honourably, nor end well, but these have not come to the attention of dramatists. For instance, he is said to have kidnapped Anaxo, a maiden of Troezen, and after slaying Sinis and Cercyon he raped their daughters; also he married Periboea, the mother of Ajax, and Phereboea afterwards, and Iope, the daughter of Iphicles; and was passionate for Aegle, the daughter of Panopeus …

PLUTARCH *THESEUS* 29

Aftermath Theseus returned to the upper world to find that his kidnapping of Helen had sparked war between Sparta and Athens, just as Helen's later kidnapping would spark war between Greece and Troy. The Athenians were doing very badly, and were less than pleased to see Theseus who had caused all the trouble and then vanished. Theseus was exiled to the island of Skyros, where the king saw him as a threat to his rule and had the hero killed.

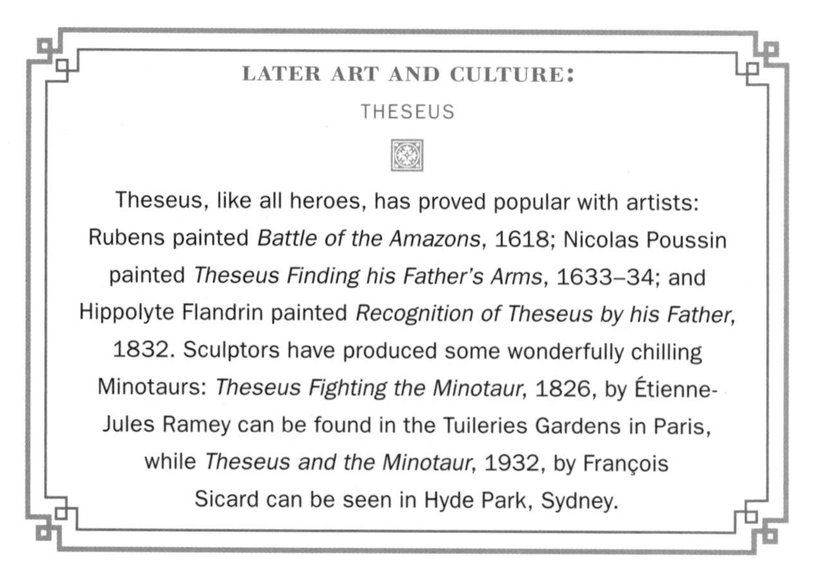

LATER ART AND CULTURE:

THESEUS

Theseus, like all heroes, has proved popular with artists: Rubens painted *Battle of the Amazons*, 1618; Nicolas Poussin painted *Theseus Finding his Father's Arms*, 1633–34; and Hippolyte Flandrin painted *Recognition of Theseus by his Father*, 1832. Sculptors have produced some wonderfully chilling Minotaurs: *Theseus Fighting the Minotaur*, 1826, by Étienne-Jules Ramey can be found in the Tuileries Gardens in Paris, while *Theseus and the Minotaur*, 1932, by François Sicard can be seen in Hyde Park, Sydney.

8

The Trojan War

The Trojan War makes riveting reading. It has the iconic Helen of Troy (H.O.T) seduced and abducted, it has Greeks versus Trojans, bravery and brutality, heroes and villains aplenty, and the famous Wooden Horse. For centuries, Troy was considered a city of legend, more imaginary than Arthur's Camelot. It took Heinrich Schliemann in the nineteenth century to establish that Troy was real, its remnants a large mound in northwest Turkey known as Hissarlik. Excavations show Hissarlik is in fact multiple cities, each built on top of the ruins of its predecessor. So which level is the Troy of Paris and Hector? Schliemann, an accomplished self-publicist, tried hard to prove that it should be the level in which he discovered his famous 'Priam's Treasure'. Inconveniently, this turned out to be over a millennium too early to fit the circumstances of the story. Archaeologists now say that the most likely candidate is the mundanely labelled level VIIa, where they have unearthed evidence of violent destruction and a huge fire.

Seven against Thebes

The light which had spread above the last shoots of the house of Oedipus is brought low in its turn into the blood-splattered dust … by folly in speech, and frenzy in the heart.

SOPHOCLES *ANTIGONE* L.600ff

The tragic heroine Antigone awaits the judgment of Creon.

The Trojan War had a lively warm-up in the war of the Seven against Thebes, which was for some years the largest war ever fought in the Greek peninsula. The origin of the war lay with the sons of Oedipus, Polynices and Eteocles. With their incestuous father exiled to Colonus near Athens, they were trying hard to pretend he had never existed. An embittered Oedipus cursed the pair neither to live in nor rule over his old kingdom of Thebes.

Polynices and Eteocles weren't prepared to take their father's word for this, no matter how colourfully expressed. After all, Thebes was one of the largest and richest kingdoms of Greece. So, ignoring their father's prophecy that they were doomed to slay each other, the brothers agreed to rule the kingdom by taking turns of one year each. The younger, Eteocles, took first turn, and promptly declared himself sole king, claiming – as have many others since – 'If we must do wrong, doing wrong to gain power is the best reason.'

Polynices fled to Argos, where he forged a coalition of the willing to support his claim to Thebes. The magnificent Seven of the coalition were led by Adrastus, king of Argos. Amphiaraus, a cousin of Helen (of Troy) was a reluctant coalition member, because as a seer, he knew that six of the Seven were doomed (Adrastus would emerge as the sole survivor, saved by the speed of his horse Arion, a gift of Heracles). In the end Zeus did the honours personally for Amphiaraus with a thunderbolt. Another thunderbolt casualty was the hero Capaneus, smitten even as he scaled the walls of Thebes, a victim of his own hubris, since he had claimed that not even Zeus could stop him. Eteoclus, son of another Argive king, died in the fighting, as did his fellow hero Hippomedon. Parthenopaeus, a son of Atalanta (p. 143) and friend of a son of Heracles, was crushed by a rock hurled from the walls. The mighty Tydeus was a son of the king who had organized Atalanta's Calydonian boar hunt. When ambushed, Tydeus single-handedly killed fifty of his attackers before perishing (possibly from exhaustion). The son of Tydeus was Diomedes, whom aficionados generally rate with Achilles and Ajax as one of the greatest Greek warriors at Troy.

Finally, there was Polynices. He ended the war as his father Oedipus had predicted by dying with his brother when the pair met in hand-to-hand combat.

Antigone, the sister of Polynices, insisted on burying her brother even though Creon, who had taken over as king of Thebes, decreed that Polynices should be left unburied. For her pains, Antigone too was buried, alive, in a small underground chamber. Her fate thereafter is disputed. (Both Sophocles and Euripides wrote plays on the topic in ancient Athens.) In one version she kills herself just before her beloved Haemon arrives to rescue her – a theme that Shakespeare later adapted for the tragic ending of his *Romeo and Juliet*.

The Judgment of Paris

Great woes ... were set in motion when Hermes ...
brought to the glen of [Mount] Ida the three goddesses,
a lovely team beneath a lovely yoke, helmeted for the fray,
in hateful strife for the prize of beauty.

EURIPIDES *ANDROMACHE* 1.270ff

Just as the war of the Seven set the scene for the Trojan War among the Greeks, the aftermath of the wedding of Thetis aligned the various factions on Olympus. Thetis, it will be recalled, was the Nereid who befriended Hephaestus (see p. 96) and Dionysus in their times of trouble. Both Poseidon and Zeus contemplated seducing Thetis (or raping her – the pair never seem to have worked out the difference). Poseidon stopped as soon as he learned that the son of Thetis was fated to be greater than his father. The sea god took care not to pass on the prophecy to his brother, and Thetis was just about to be seduced by Zeus when the libidinous god was providentially warned off by Prometheus, whom Heracles had just freed.

It was decided to give Thetis a relatively unassuming husband, the still very distinguished former Argonaut and Calydonian Boar hunter Peleus, a friend of Chiron the centaur. Everyone liked Thetis, and, as we saw above, all the gods turned up for the wedding, even Eris (Strife) who was not invited (p. 120). Eris responded to her exclusion by lobbing a golden apple into the wedding feast that bore the inscription 'for the fairest'. Athena, Hera and Aphrodite each immediately claimed the apple, rather ungraciously overlooking the fact that Thetis was herself stunningly beautiful, and anyway, she *was* the bride.

Zeus delegated arbitration to Paris, a son of Priam of Troy, who had shown his impartiality before. Though fair, the three goddesses did not play that way. Each attempted to bribe Paris with her speciality. Hera offered dominion over Europe and Asia, but Paris ignored this, and also Athena's suggestion that she give

Paris about to make two powerful enemies with his judgment.

him wisdom. Aphrodite could call on mighty Eros, who conquers all, and Aphrodite offered Paris the love of the most beautiful woman on earth. Paris accepted, and thereafter the jealous wrath of Hera and Athena doomed Paris, his family and his city.

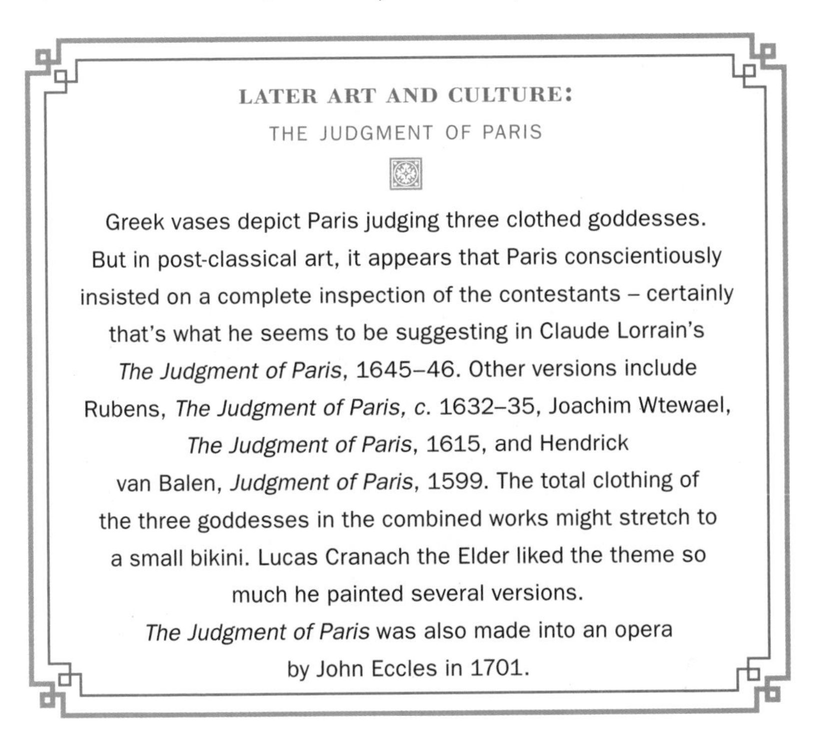

LATER ART AND CULTURE:

THE JUDGMENT OF PARIS

Greek vases depict Paris judging three clothed goddesses. But in post-classical art, it appears that Paris conscientiously insisted on a complete inspection of the contestants – certainly that's what he seems to be suggesting in Claude Lorrain's *The Judgment of Paris*, 1645–46. Other versions include Rubens, *The Judgment of Paris, c.* 1632–35, Joachim Wtewael, *The Judgment of Paris*, 1615, and Hendrick van Balen, *Judgment of Paris*, 1599. The total clothing of the three goddesses in the combined works might stretch to a small bikini. Lucas Cranach the Elder liked the theme so much he painted several versions.

The Judgment of Paris was also made into an opera by John Eccles in 1701.

The Siege of Troy

When it comes to abducting women, they say it is a villain who does it, but a fool who makes a fuss about it. Men of sense don't care about that kind of women, since they could never be carried off if they didn't want to be. … And yet the Greeks, for a single Spartan wench, got a huge armed force together, invaded Asia and destroyed the domains of Priam.

HERODOTUS *HISTORY* 1.4

Both modern archaeology and classical myth agree that Troy had undergone severe damage several times since its founding, though the ancient writers suggested that gods, monsters and Heracles had done the job while the moderns opt for marauding tribes or Hittite armies. However, after considerable renovation – including walls rebuilt by Apollo and Poseidon – Troy at the time of the rape of Helen was a formidable nut to crack.

It is a popular misconception that Homer's *Iliad* tells the story of the Trojan War. In fact, it relates the incidents that occurred during a (decidedly action-packed) fortnight some nine years into the war. What follows here is a capsule summary of that war, followed by a longer description of the *dramatis personae*.

1 Preliminaries to a Siege

Paris went to Sparta to pick up his payment from Aphrodite. He was not at all concerned that Helen was already married to King Menelaus. While the king was away at a funeral, Paris simply decamped with Helen and a good part of Menelaus' treasure. Menelaus did not take this well. Because of Helen's exceptional beauty, she had been courted by all the great men of Greece, who swore that they would unite to protect the honour of whomever eventually won the lady's heart. This oath (known as the Pact of Tyndareus, after Helen's stepfather) effectively united the people of Greece into a National Achaean Treaty Organization, and this swung into action on news of the abduction.

After some difficulty in locating Troy, the Greeks eventually sent Menelaus and the eloquent Odysseus to demand Helen and reparations. King Priam of Troy refused. The walls of his city had been built by gods and were unassailable. So he defied the Greeks to do their worst.

2 The Greeks Arrive

Getting their fleet to Troy was not easy, and when the Greeks finally arrived, they discovered that Troy had allies on the mainland of Asia

Minor, including the Amazons. The early part of the war involved cutting the Trojans off from their supplies. However, Troy itself was well stocked, and the Greeks were forced to become part-time farmers to keep their army in the field for year after year.

3 Battle and Prophecy

After nine long years things were not much nearer a conclusion. A host of heroes had fallen (as partly described in the *Iliad*), and even a few gods had had more than their pride injured. The Greeks captured a prophet who reported that they could never win because the gods had set conditions for victory that the Greeks had not fulfilled. In order to triumph, the Greeks must:

- get the son of the (now deceased) Achilles to fight on their side
- use the bow of Heracles
- obtain the Palladium – an antique statue of Athena currently in Trojan possession
- bring the remains of Pelops (p. 75) to the war.

4 Finale

The Trojan horse as depicted 2,800 years ago on the island of Mykonos.

The Greeks industriously brought their war operation into compliance with the divine terms for victory. Then Odysseus, the only Greek who had grasped that warfare involved more than poking sharp objects into people, came up with a cunning plan to get behind the Trojan walls. The Greeks pretended to withdraw, leaving behind the famous Trojan horse

– which was in fact a Greek horse (though admittedly *for* the Trojans). This massive wooden sculpture (allegedly a sacrifice to Poseidon) was taken into Troy, its hollow interior packed with an elite team of Greek commandos. These emerged from the horse after dark and Troy's gates were opened. Thereupon, the Greek army expended ten years of frustration in a single night. Few Trojans escaped.

Leading Dramatis Personae of the War

Zeus

Zeus was enamoured of his young cupbearer, Ganymede, who was a Trojan. He was therefore a pro-Trojan neutral in the war, and did his best to keep the gods from interfering. Not everyone paid much attention to him.

The Greeks (also known as the Hellenes, Achaeans and Danaids)

In order of seniority:

Gods

Poseidon

He helped Apollo build the walls of Troy, but the Trojan king of the time refused to pay him. After that Poseidon hated the Trojans, and was never much inclined to listen to Zeus anyway. He personally took part in the fighting for a while after his grandson was killed.

Athena

Naturally pro-Greek by inclination, she also of course had a special grudge against Paris. A little-remembered attribute of Athena is that as Athena Promachos – Athena of the battleline – the lady was a war goddess and an expert general and strategist. She was generous with her advice, and twice brutally beat up Ares when he interfered on the Trojan side.

Hera

Pro-Greek for much the same reason as Athena. She was also the patron of Argos/Mycenae, the leading Greek nation in the war. In Book Four of the *Iliad*, Zeus accuses her of wishing 'to enter the gates and long walls [of Troy] and devour Priam raw, and also Priam's sons and all the Trojans, and so assuage your anger'.

Hephaestus

Generally took Athena's lead, not least because of his unrequited love for the maiden goddess, and his dislike of his wife Aphrodite, who took the Trojan side. Hera was his mother, and the craftsman god was a loyal son. Also he was susceptible to the charms of Thetis.

Thetis

She was determined to make her son Achilles immortal, and so fed him on ambrosia and at night tucked him into the embers of the fire to burn away his mortality. Her outraged husband Peleus forbade the practice when he discovered it. (Since he had already lost five other sons to the roasting process, one wonders why it took so long for the penny to drop.) In a sulk, Thetis abandoned husband and son, and returned to the sea. But she continued to advise Achilles while he was fighting at Troy.

Kings

Agamemnon

'A dark heart filled with anger', is how Homer describes King Agamemnon in Book One of the *Iliad*. The grandson of Pelops and the brother of Menelaus, he married Clytemnestra, the sister of Helen. As king of Mycenae, the leading Greek state of the time, he led the war effort against Troy. He was ruthless, amoral and a generally nasty piece of work, even by the low standards of his contemporaries. His name means 'most resolute'. (A warship of that name, *HMS Agamemnon*, played a distinguished part in the battle of Trafalgar in 1805.)

Menelaus

King of Sparta. Wanted his wife back. But above he all wanted the head of Paris on a plate.

Odysseus (Ulysses)

Always I see you, son of Laertes, seeking an opportunity to go one up against your enemies.

ATHENA TO ODYSSEUS, SOPHOCLES *AJAX* 1.1

Odysseus was king of Ithaca, and reputed by some to be a son of the cunning, twice-lived Sisyphus (p. 133). He was deeply reluctant to go to war and abandon his beloved Penelope, and feigned madness. When the trick was discovered by one Palamedes, he made sure Palamedes later came to a sticky end. Odysseus left his son in the care of a Greek called Mentor, who has since given his name to that role.

Diomedes

In war your prowess is beyond question, and in council you excel all who are of your own years

NESTOR TO DIOMEDES, *ILIAD* 9.50

The hero of choice for the knowledgeable mythologist, Diomedes, king of Argos, was a favourite of Athena, and he wounded both Ares and Aphrodite when the pair tried physically to intervene in the combat. On meeting an old friend on the Trojan side, he stopped fighting for a chat and to exchange armour. He helped Odysseus steal the Palladium, which was one of the victory conditions for the Greeks (see above), and he was one of the fifty warriors who hid inside the wooden horse.

Heroes

Achilles

The bulwark of the Achaeans, the violent child
of dark-haired Thetis of the sea.
PINDAR 5 *PAEAN FOR THE DELPHIANS*

Achilles seated at leisure; a line drawing of a vase painting

Deciding to make her son invulnerable if she could not make him immortal, Thetis dunked the boy in the River Styx as a parting gift. She could not touch the water herself, so the part where she held the baby was Achilles' weak spot – in fact, his Achilles heel. An attempt to keep Achilles from Troy by disguising him as a girl failed, and the hero went on to distinguish himself and die in the war. He was proud, cruel and arrogant to the point of stupidity. In short, he was the perfect archetype for the Greeks at Troy.

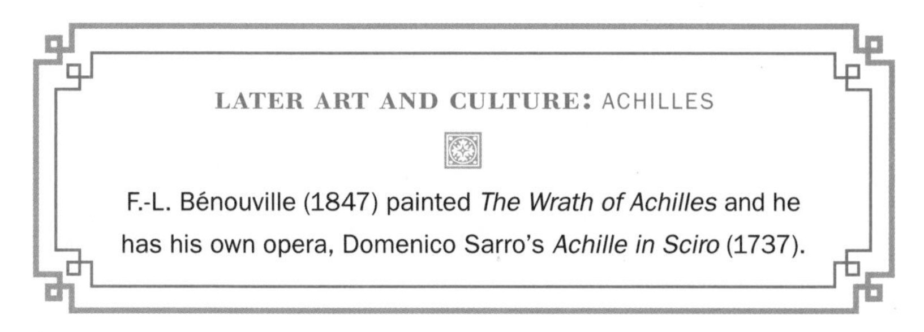

LATER ART AND CULTURE: ACHILLES

F.-L. Bénouville (1847) painted *The Wrath of Achilles* and he has his own opera, Domenico Sarro's *Achille in Sciro* (1737).

Ajax

That wayward one of the ill-boding name.

SOPHOCLES *AJAX* L.1080

The grandson of Heracles, Ajax (also known as Aias) seldom harboured an evil thought about anyone, mainly because thinking caused him pain and wasted time better spent in hitting people. His one initiative was planning an attack on his own side, from spite at not being given the armour of the slain Achilles. Athena sent him mad and he attacked a herd of cattle instead (an event which inspired the moving *Ajax* of Sophocles). Afterwards he committed suicide.

Achilles and Ajax gambling at dice, on a vase by Exekias.

Thirsites

An antihero. He was of ignoble birth, bald and bandy-legged. He constantly mocked the pretensions of his 'betters' and correctly described the antics of Agamemnon and Achilles as childish squabbling. He was knocked about by Odysseus for suggesting the Greeks should pack it all in and go home, and finally killed when he made fun of Achilles once too often.

Stentor

A Greek herald who had the voice of fifty men. Deserving of mention as a loud announcement may even today be given in a stentorian voice.

Women

Last because, apart from the uxorious Odysseus, this was where they came in the considerations of the participants in the war.

Iphigenia

Eldest daughter of Agamemnon. The Greek fleet was becalmed at Aulis – by several accounts because of the impiety of Agamemnon towards Artemis. Discovering that sacrificing Iphigenia would speed up the fleet, the king sent for his daughter on the pretence that she was to marry Achilles. The sacrifice worked, though by some accounts Artemis substituted a hind at the last moment and took Iphigenia to be her priestess.

Briseis

An orphan taken in by Achilles (she became an orphan after he had killed her parents and the rest of her family). She served as Achilles' concubine until Agamemnon lost his bedmate and demanded Briseis as a replacement. Achilles responded by going on strike, refusing to leave his quarters and join in the fighting.

The Trojans

The vigour of the Trojan defence has led to the saying 'to work like a Trojan'; and it was perhaps the impenetrability of the Trojan walls that inspired the naming of the family-planning device which is how Trojans are best known in North America. It is therefore appropriate that the foremost divine champion of the Trojans was Aphrodite.

Gods

Aphrodite

The goddess of love was prepared to stand by Paris, and anyway had a dispute with Menelaus about the non-delivery of some cattle the king had promised as a sacrifice in exchange for winning Helen's hand.

Ares

Not so much pro-Trojan as pro-Aphrodite, Ares considered the entire war as a huge sparkly present laid on for his personal enjoyment. However, when he got carried away and joined in the fighting he was wounded by Diomedes (with Athena's help). He immediately fled, thereafter to supervise the slaughter from a safe distance.

Apollo

Completing the pro-Trojan faction at the top of the alphabet, Apollo seems to have supported the Trojans simply because the conduct of the Greeks offended his civilized sensibilities. It did not help that almost the first action of Achilles on disembarking was to kill Tenes, one of Apollo's sons. The last straw came when the Greeks kidnapped the daughter of one of his priests, and Apollo responded by smiting the entire Greek camp with a pestilence.

The Trojan Royal Family

Priam

Old sire, we have heard how of old time you
were blessed ... of all people, men say,
none exceeded you in wealth or in sons.
ACHILLES TO PRIAM, *ILLIAD* BK 24

Priam begs for Hector's body, here shown lying beneath Achilles' couch.

As the last survivor of the ruling house, Priam became king of Troy when Heracles wrecked the place and killed the rest of his family. By the time of the Trojan War, Priam was a very old man who had some fifty children with a number of wives. Until his fateful decision to stand up to the Greeks he had ruled well and wisely. He had the unenviable task of going to Achilles to plead for the body of his son, Hector, and he was in his turn killed by Neoptolemus, son of Achilles.

Hector

How we marvel at noble Hector, the spearman
and bold man of war!

HOMER *ILIAD* BK 5

Greatest of the Trojan warriors, Hector is depicted as honest, kindly and a ferocious fighter. With the help of Apollo he slew Patroclus, the friend of Achilles who wore the hero's armour to encourage the Greeks while Achilles was sulking. Achilles was very annoyed about this.

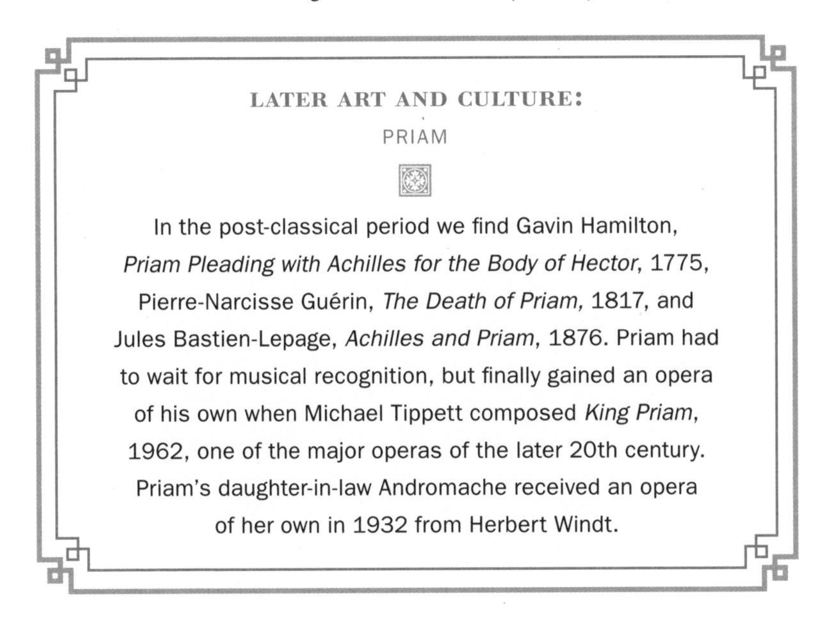

LATER ART AND CULTURE:

PRIAM

In the post-classical period we find Gavin Hamilton, *Priam Pleading with Achilles for the Body of Hector*, 1775, Pierre-Narcisse Guérin, *The Death of Priam*, 1817, and Jules Bastien-Lepage, *Achilles and Priam*, 1876. Priam had to wait for musical recognition, but finally gained an opera of his own when Michael Tippett composed *King Priam*, 1962, one of the major operas of the later 20th century. Priam's daughter-in-law Andromache received an opera of her own in 1932 from Herbert Windt.

Paris

You woman-mad deceiver, I wish you had never been born, or died unwed ... in your heart there is neither strength nor courage.

HECTOR TO PARIS, HOMER *ILIAD* BK 3

The love of Paris for Helen would have been more romantic had the man not been an adulterer – he was married to a river nymph called Oenone when he abducted Helen – a thief and a coward who initially shrank back into the ranks at the sight of Menelaus. Homer refers to him as 'hated by all, even as is dark death'. It was he who slew Achilles by shooting his heel with a poisoned arrow. When Paris was dying (shot in his turn by an arrow from the bow of Heracles) Oenone could have healed him, but declined to do so.

Heroes

Aeneas

He, whom the Trojan people honoured like a god

HOMER *ILIAD* 11.58

A son of Aphrodite by a mortal, Aeneas was of a different branch of Trojan royalty. He came close to being killed by Diomedes, but was rescued by Apollo. Poseidon, aware of the hero's importance in future events, did the same when Aeneas was in mortal peril from Achilles.

Penthesileia

In women too dwells the spirit of battle.

SOPHOCLES *ELECTRA* 1242

A daughter of Ares, Penthesileia had been purified after a murder by Priam and had come to repay her debt. With a dozen other Amazons she wreaked havoc among the Greeks until slain by Achilles, who regretted his action as soon as he stripped her armour and beheld her beauty.

Memnon

A prince of Ethiopia, and a son of Eos and Tithonus (p. 41), Memnon had armour forged by Hephaestus, which made him formidable on the battlefield until he met Achilles. At this point Achilles had lost his own armour to Hector when it was stripped from the body of Patroclus, so Thetis had persuaded Hephaestus to provide another set. With divine armour on both sides, Achilles won the duel, but a few hours later he was shot in the heel by Paris who used a poisoned arrow to finish off the hero.

Women

Helen

Whom we have met already too many times to need introduction. Christopher Marlowe's *Doctor Faustus*, performed from 1594 on, shows that the lady aged well over the millennia:

Was this the face that launched a thousand ships,
And burnt the topless towers of Ilium?
Sweet Helen, make me immortal with a kiss....
Here will I dwell, for heaven is in these lips,
And all is dross that is not Helena.

Alternatively:

Misbegotten child of the enduring curse, of envy,
murder and death, and all the plagues of earth!

ANDROMACHE'S VIEWPOINT,
EURIPIDES *TROJAN WOMEN* 769

Hecuba

The foremost of the wives of Priam, she gave her husband nineteen children, many of whom – including Hector – were mown down by Achilles outside Troy. She lived through the ghastly sack of the city, and while enslaved in Greece took gruesome revenge in kind on the slayer of one of her favourite sons. She was then transformed into a black dog with fiery eyes and became a companion of the witch goddess Hecate.

Cassandra

The most beautiful of the daughters of Priam, Cassandra rejected the advances of Apollo, and so was cursed to see the future but never be believed. She unavailingly warned the Trojans not to let Paris go to Greece, pleaded with them not to let the Trojan horse into the city, and when taken as a slave into the household of Agamemnon, unsuccessfully warned the king of his impending doom. For this reason anyone who prophesies misfortune to an unheeding world is called a Cassandra.

Andromache

Wife of Hector, she firmly disliked Helen and had a presentiment of the coming doom of her husband and children. She herself survived the war, and after a brutal period as the concubine of Achilles' son Neoptolemus, she married another Trojan survivor and with her son later founded the city of Pergamum in Asia Minor.

Key Episodes in the Iliad of Homer

While nothing can replace reading Homer's masterpiece (preferably in archaic Greek), some short extracts may serve to give something of the flavour of the whole. Those below are taken wholesale from the *Illiad*, and try to recapture some of the swashbuckling spirit of the original.

Chryseis is captured

Book 1 1.1–21 The Achaeans duly distributed the booty, and decided that the lovely Chryseis should be the concubine of King Agamem-

The tragic farewell of Hector and Andromache.

non. But then Chryses, priest of Apollo, came to the ships of the Achaeans to obtain his daughter's freedom. He brought with him a great ransom, but more importantly he carried in his hand the sceptre of Apollo, wrapped with a supplicant's wreath.

Agamemnon loses Chryseis and takes the concubine of Achilles, as the hero complains

1.375ff All the Achaeans were unanimously in favour of respecting the priest and accepting the ransom. But not Agamemnon, who fiercely rebuffed him and sent him away. So the priest went in anger to Apollo, who loved him dearly. The god heard his prayer and fired his deadly arrows at the Argives, and the corpses lay thick on one another, as the arrows flew among the host of the Achaeans.... And now the Achaeans are taking the girl in a ship back to Chryses, and sending gifts of sacrifice to the god. But the heralds have just taken from my tent the daughter of Briseus, whom the Achaeans had awarded to myself [and are giving her to Agamemnon to replace the girl he had lost].

The war proceeds without Achilles, who goes on strike after losing his girl, and even the gods get involved – here Athena takes on Ares

Book 5 5.840ff Pallas Athena took the whip and reins [of the chariot], and drove straight at Ares who was in the act of stripping the armour of mighty Periphas, son of Ochesius and bravest of the Aetolians. Athena wore the helmet of Hades, so Ares could not see her. However, he did see Diomedes, and went right at him abandoning the corpse of Periphas. As they closed in combat Ares unleashed his bronze spear ... confident he had thus put paid to the hero, but Athena batted the spear aside making it fly harmlessly over the chariot. Diomedes threw his spear in reply, and Athena made sure it went into the pit of Ares' stomach. Ares bellowed as loudly as nine or ten thousand men [and fled].

The combat between Trojans and Achaeans was now left to rage unhindered, and the tide of war surged to and fro over the plain.

The Greeks beg Achilles to help

Book 9 9.222 We are facing calamity, and without your help we might well lose the fleet. The Trojans and their allies have camped right beside our ships and our ramparts. They imagine that nothing can now stop them from attacking our ships. Zeus aids them with his thunderbolts and Hector, in all his glory, rages like a berserker ... Up, then, and late though it be, save the sons of the Achaeans who quail before the fury of the Trojans. ... Save the Danaans from destruction!

Achilles replies

9.307ff Agamemnon, the dog, can't even look me in the face. I have nothing to say to him and want nothing to do with him. He has wronged me and lied to me and I won't be fooled again. Since Zeus has made him mad, he can live with the mess he has made. I spit on his presents, and do not give a damn about the man himself. He can offer ten, twenty times what he is offering, or everything he has or will ever have, he can promise me the wealth of Orchomenos or of Egyptian Thebes, ... But I will be avenged, nevertheless, for the bitter wrong he has done me, and I will not move.

Patroclus rallies the Greeks in the armour of his friend Achilles, but loses a duel with Hector

Book 16 16.790ff As the life ebbed from him Patroclus gasped, 'Boast if you want, Hector. Zeus, the son of Cronos, and Apollo have given you the victory. It was they who won this bout and took the armour from my shoulders. Twenty mortals like you I could have slain with my spear … Now listen well, and take my words to heart. You have not much longer to live. Nemesis and Death are closing in fast on you, and they will bring you down by the hand of Achilles.'

Hector meets Achilles

Book 22 22.260ff Like a soaring eagle which swoops from the clouds down on to a lamb or timid hare, Hector swung his sword and leapt at Achilles. Mad with fury, Achilles rushed to meet him … and bright as the evening star that outshines all others through the still night, so burned the spear in his right hand, eager for the death of noble Hector … Achilles struck as Hector advanced on him, and his spear went right through his neck … Achilles stood over him saying 'Hector, did you think you could get away with killing Patroclus, just because I was not with him? You fool, I was at the ships, not gone, and you awakened a far more dangerous foe in me. Patroclus the Achaeans shall send off with a noble funeral, while with you the dogs and vultures can do what they want.'

Priam comes in person to beg for Hector's body and Achilles relents

Book 24 24.570ff They took the ransom for Hector's body but left two good cloaks and a body covering for Achilles to wrap Hector's body when it came be taken home. Achilles ordered his servants to wash and anoint the body, but he first took it to a place where Priam should not see it [in its mangled and disfigured state]… Afterwards Achilles himself placed the body on its bier, and he and his servants carried it to the wagon. Achilles sobbed as he did so, invoking his dead comrade, 'Do not be angry with me, Patroclus, if even in the house of Hades you hear that I have allowed his father to ransom Hector's body. The ransom was a worthy one, and you shall receive your due share.'

The Fall of Troy

Even with both Achilles and Hector now dead, the war raged on unabated, until Odysseus came up with his cunning plan. The Trojan horse has so embedded itself in the popular consciousness that today a 'Trojan' refers to a computer virus that, like the wooden horse at Troy, gets within the protected area and opens it up to all sorts of nastiness from the outside.

And in Troy, when the Greeks did finally get within the walls, the extent of that nastiness was profound. Profound enough for Schliemann in the modern era to claim he had found evidence of the violence of the Greek sack of the city. There was a general massacre of the male population, which was almost to be expected. However, many women were killed as well, and not simply in the passion of the moment.

Greek Outrages to the Laws of Gods and Men Included:

Polyxena, human sacrifice The youngest daughter of Priam was cold-bloodedly sacrificed by Neoptolemus who cut her throat at the grave of Achilles, for the Greeks believed it was she who revealed the secret of Achilles' vulnerability to Paris. For this Neoptolemus was doomed in turn to die. (At the hands of Orestes, the son of Agamemnon, as it happened.)

Infanticide The infant son of Hector was thrown from the walls of Troy so as to extinguish the hero's family line.

Desecration In their fury the Greeks did not even spare the temples of the gods from the general destruction.

Cassandra raped One of the most shocking events – from a Greek perspective – was the sacrilegious rape of Cassandra by an Ajax (not the hero mentioned above but another of the same name sometimes called 'the lesser Ajax'). Cassandra had fled to the sanctuary of Athena and clung to Athena's statue so hard that it toppled when Ajax minor pulled her off it and proceeded to do the deed then and there.

Given that the Maiden Goddess had strong views about people having sex in her temple (see Medusa), the rape on the premises of a supplicant under her protection was hardly going to pass without comment. The horrified Greeks wanted to distance themselves from the event by killing Ajax minor on the spot, but he saved himself by clinging to the very statue he had defiled.

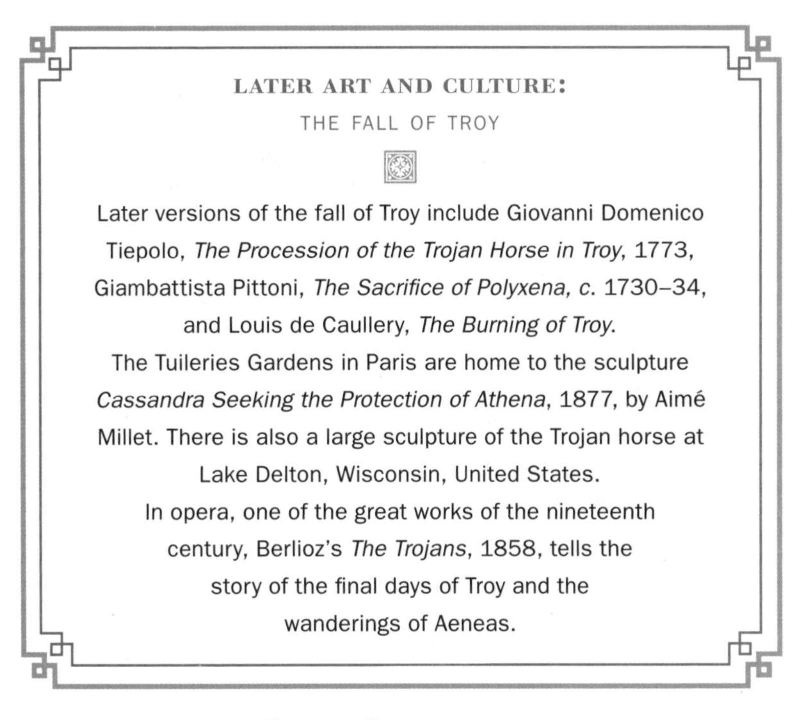

LATER ART AND CULTURE:

THE FALL OF TROY

Later versions of the fall of Troy include Giovanni Domenico Tiepolo, *The Procession of the Trojan Horse in Troy*, 1773, Giambattista Pittoni, *The Sacrifice of Polyxena, c.* 1730–34, and Louis de Caullery, *The Burning of Troy.*

The Tuileries Gardens in Paris are home to the sculpture *Cassandra Seeking the Protection of Athena*, 1877, by Aimé Millet. There is also a large sculpture of the Trojan horse at Lake Delton, Wisconsin, United States.

In opera, one of the great works of the nineteenth century, Berlioz's *The Trojans*, 1858, tells the story of the final days of Troy and the wanderings of Aeneas.

Divine Retribution

'A return fraught with grief, that shall I give the Achaeans.'

ATHENA TO POSEIDON, EURIPIDES

TROJAN WOMEN 65

The conduct of the Greeks at the fall of Troy so outraged Athena and Poseidon that they actively turned against all but the best-behaved of their former protégés. The withdrawal of their protection left Apollo and Aphrodite a free hand with the rest. Apollo was known for flamboyantly unrestrained vengeance, while Aphrodite was no less nasty for being subtle. Few Greeks made it home alive. Some sample cases include:

Ajax minor

The ship carrying the disgraced rapist predictably came to grief on the return voyage, but the 'hero' struggled to safety on one of the same rocks that had wrecked his ship. He was loudly praising his ability to save himself despite the gods when Poseidon split the rock with his trident, and Athena finished him off with a lightning strike.

Agamemnon

Aphrodite took a special interest in his case. Under her influence, the wife of Agamemnon had taken a lover, Aegisthus, in her husband's absence. Clytemnestra also carried a grudge for the fate of her daughter Iphigenia. Agamemnon was relaxing in a bath when his wife dropped a net over him to prevent his struggles and dispatched him. By some reports she killed Cassandra at the same time. The long tradition of murder, rape and incest in the family was continued by Agamemnon's

Orestes murders his mother's lover, Aegisthus.

children, Orestes and Electra, who ganged up on Clytemnestra and Aegisthus in revenge. Orestes was pursued by the Furies until Athena, in a monumental triumph for civilization, persuaded the Furies to defer to the judgment of a human court (which acquitted him).

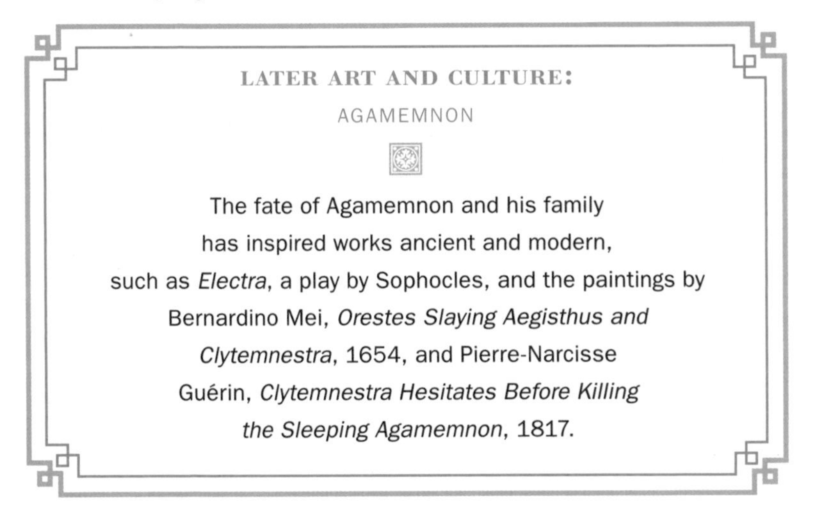

LATER ART AND CULTURE:

AGAMEMNON

The fate of Agamemnon and his family has inspired works ancient and modern, such as *Electra*, a play by Sophocles, and the paintings by Bernardino Mei, *Orestes Slaying Aegisthus and Clytemnestra*, 1654, and Pierre-Narcisse Guérin, *Clytemnestra Hesitates Before Killing the Sleeping Agamemnon*, 1817.

Diomedes

Diomedes had various adventures on his way home, but still enjoyed the protection of Athena, and so (for example) escaped by the skin of his teeth from being sacrificed to Ares when wrecked on an unfriendly shore. He finally got home to discover that Aphrodite had arranged for his wife to become unfaithful. In disgust the hero left once more, eventually ending up in Italy. Aphrodite continued to protect Helen, whom Menelaus found himself unable to kill, and indeed Helen long outlived her vengeful husband.

The epic voyagers

Odysseus the Greek and Aeneas the Trojan both struggled to find home. Odysseus sought his ancestral kingdom and his beloved Penelope, while Aeneas searched for a new home for his surviving Trojans. Almost the last tales of the Heroic Age are stories of the long homeward voyages of these two men, to which we now turn.

Going Home

The *Odyssey*, by the Greek poet Homer, and the *Aeneid*, by the Roman poet Virgil, come chronologically at the end of the Heroic Age, and focus on one hero apiece. Each of these sagas is a *tour de force* of the world of myth as well as a travelogue of the magical Mediterranean world, featuring bizarre creatures, exotic peoples and a landscape packed with wonder and hazard. What Homer and Virgil have done superbly, this chapter will not attempt to imitate. Its purpose instead is to give an overall framework to these epic journeys, so that readers who are vaguely familiar with incidents such as the Land of the Lotus Eaters, or Aeneas and Dido, can see these episodes in their overall context.

The Odyssey

Tell me, O Muse, of that ingenious hero who travelled far and wide after he had sacked the famous town of Troy. Many cities did he visit, and many were the nations with whose manners and customs he was acquainted; moreover he suffered much by sea while trying to save his own life and bring his men safely home; but do what he might, he could not save his men.

HOMER *ODYSSEY* INTRODUCTION (TRANS. SAMUEL BUTLER)

Since no one had done more to bring about the fall of Troy than Odysseus, the wily hero should have known better than to expect an easy ride home. Hera and Apollo were thirsting for vengeance, and even Zeus was annoyed by what the Greeks had done to Troy. All of which meant that Athena was hard-pressed to keep her protégé in one piece. Under these circumstances, crewing Odysseus' ships was essentially a suicide mission, but at least the crewmen could expect luridly colourful, extremely varied and highly unusual deaths. The story as told by Homer is convoluted, with multiple flashbacks and digressions. Straightened out into chronological order, here is what befell Odysseus on his way home.

1 *The Cicones*

Hard-pressed were we by their attack, for they
were as thick as leaves, or summer flowers.
HOMER *ODYSSEY* 9.48

The first stop on the way home was at Ismaros. As was perfectly standard for Mycenaean Greeks, Odysseus' men attacked the nearest town – that of the Cicones. They slaughtered the men and cattle, and divided the women and treasure among themselves. Odysseus was unable to get his men to cease enjoying the spoils before the rest of the countryside was roused to arms and fell upon the marauding Greeks. The battle-hardened veterans of Troy gave a good account of themselves, but were forced to flee.

2 *Lotus Eaters*

Whoever ate of the honey-sweet lotus …
wished only to remain among the lotus eaters,
feeding on the flower, and forgetful of his homeward path.
HOMER *ODYSSEY* 9.95

Zeus for the first time showed his disapproval of the loutish conduct of the Greeks, and hit Odysseus' little fleet with a powerful storm that sent the ships far off course. With the sails torn to shreds and fresh water expended, the sailors put ashore in North Africa. There, they met the lotus eaters, the people (as the poet Tennyson memorably puts it) of 'a land in which it seemed always afternoon'. All who ate of the lotus became promptly demotivated, languid and uncaring of friends or home. Odysseus eventually managed to get his crew back on board by providing external motivation through physical pain. Weeping bitterly and tied to their oars, the crewmen set sail again.

3 *Polyphemus*

A monstrous being who shepherded his flocks,
but lived apart and alone, never socializing,
and with his heart set on lawlessness.
HOMER *ODYSSEY* 9.189

Odysseus and crew blind the Cyclops Polyphemus.

This monstrous Cyclops was a child of Poseidon, and had a violent nature, having already murdered a son of Pan who was his rival for the love of the nymph Galatea. He was warned to beware of Odysseus, but when the hero blundered into his cave, the quick-witted adventurer gave his name as 'Nobody'. When Polyphemus added murdering and eating Odysseus' crewmen to his faults, the hero got the monster drunk, and stabbed him in his one eye with a stake. Polyphemus cried out to his fellow Cyclopes that 'nobody' was hurting him. Thus reassured, the other Cyclopes went back to sleep. The next day, the surviving crewmen escaped by clinging to the undersides of Polyphemus' sheep as they left his cave to pasture. This injury to his son added Poseidon to Odysseus' ever-growing roster of divine foes.

4 *Aeolus, the lord of the winds*

So we came to where dwelt Aeolus, son of Hippotas,
dear to the immortal gods, on a floating island,
with walls of bronze and sheer cliffs.

HOMER *ODYSSEY* 10.1

There are several characters called Aeolus in myth, but Homer describes the lord of the winds whose home Odysseus and his (by now somewhat depleted) fleet happened upon. Odysseus was his normal charming self, and enjoyed the hospitality of Aeolus for a month. Aeolus then speeded his departure with a west wind that wafted Odysseus and his men almost back to Ithaca. Odysseus had also been given a large bag, tightly sealed. Thinking the bag contained gold, the sailors opened it while Odysseus slept. In fact it contained the east, north and south winds, and with the west wind almost expended, the other winds blew the ships right back to where they had started on the isle of Aeolus. Aeolus refused to help a second time, and Odysseus' feelings about his crew at that moment may have eased his pain at their later deaths.

Aeolus has given his name to various products pneumatic in the modern era, but is more famous for his 'windbag', which has become personified and gone into politics.

5 *The Laestrygones*

In the water they speared the men like fishes
and took them home to be a loathsome meal.

HOMER *ODYSSEY* 10.125

After a weary time rowing, the fleet found a secluded harbour. This turned out to be a trap where man-eating giants threw boulders to smash the ships below, then harpooning and eating the men. Only his own ship, which the cautious Odysseus had moored outside the harbour, escaped the carnage.

6 *Circe*

She smote them with her wand, and they had the heads,
and voices and shapes of bristling swine, but their minds
remained unchanged even as they had been before.

HOMER *ODYSSEY* 10.240

Circe was a daughter of Helios, the Sun, and the sister of Pasiphae, the mother of the Minotaur. She was also a powerful enchantress. She drugged the hero's men and turned them into pigs. (Or, in the opinion of the Victorian poet Augusta Davies Webster, Circe removed the disguise that makes men seem otherwise.) Odysseus himself escaped transformation because Hermes, one of the few gods still on Odysseus' side, gave him a sacred root that countered Circe's potions. The sacred root was called 'moly' and is probably the origin of the modern exclamation 'holy moly!'. Thereafter Circe was putty in Odysseus' hands, and he and his re-humanized crew enjoyed a year of feasting and frolics before they put to sea again.

7 *The Underworld*

How did you, still alive, come to be below in
the murky darkness? Hard is it for those
that live to behold these realms.

HOMER *ODYSSEY* 11.155

Instructed by Circe, the involuntary adventurers went north to 'the city of the Cimmerians, fog-bound in perpetual mist'. There, by one of the entrances to the underworld, Odysseus performed arcane rites that allowed him to speak to the prophet Tiresias. Tiresias pointed out that the enmity of Poseidon was a powerful challenge to anyone planning on sailing home, yet sail Odysseus must, or suitors would arrive to court his 'widow' Penelope, and eat her out of house and home.

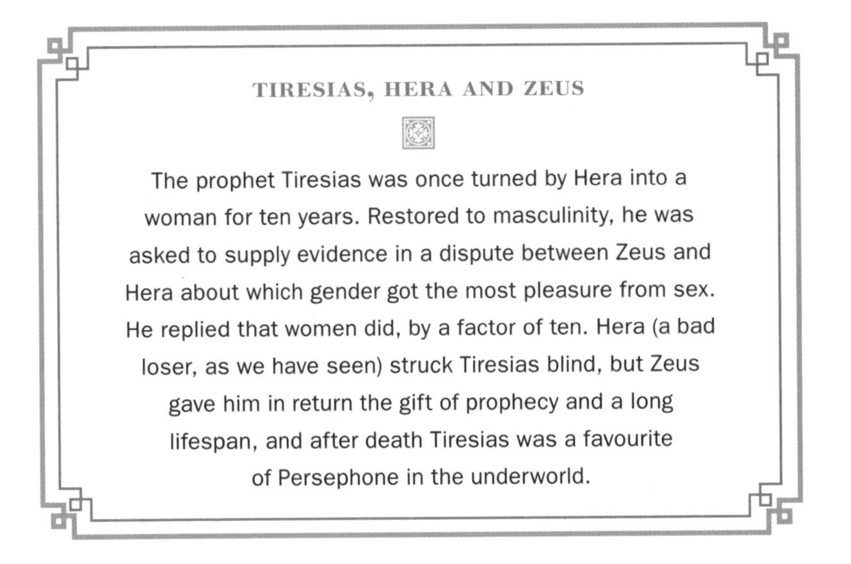

TIRESIAS, HERA AND ZEUS

The prophet Tiresias was once turned by Hera into a woman for ten years. Restored to masculinity, he was asked to supply evidence in a dispute between Zeus and Hera about which gender got the most pleasure from sex. He replied that women did, by a factor of ten. Hera (a bad loser, as we have seen) struck Tiresias blind, but Zeus gave him in return the gift of prophecy and a long lifespan, and after death Tiresias was a favourite of Persephone in the underworld.

8 *The Sirens*

The Sirens beguile with their clear-toned song,
but about them is a great heap of bones from rotting corpses,
and round the bones the skin is shrivelling.

HOMER *ODYSSEY* 12.45

A doomed siren falls as her song fails to lure Odysseus.

Warned of these creatures (p. 138) by Circe, Odysseus blocked his men's ears with wax, and ordered himself tied to the mast to hear their song.

9 *Scylla and Charybdis*

She has twelve feet, all deformed, and six very
long necks, with an awful head on each one,
and in each head three rows of teeth,
thick and close, and full of black death.

HOMER *ODYSSEY* 12.45 ON SCYLLA,
THE MORE ATTRACTIVE CHOICE TO CHARYBDIS

Here Odysseus faced the unenviable choice of sailing past a whirlpool that might destroy his ship or a monster with multiple man-eating heads that would certainly kill six of his crew. Odysseus opted to lose six more men from his rapidly dwindling band. (Though Circe warned about Scylla, she forgot to mention she had created the monster herself from a fair maid whose lover she once fancied.)

10 *The Cattle of the Sun*

Friends, in our swift ship is meat and drink;
let us therefore keep our hands from those beasts
lest we come to harm.
These are the herds of the dread god, Helios.

ODYSSEUS TO HIS CREW, HOMER *ODYSSEY* 12.320

Next the ship beached on an island with fat, juicy cattle. In vain Odysseus warned his men that these should not be touched. But Zeus kept the ship trapped on the isle by an unfavourable wind, and eventually the crew gave in to temptation and ate beef suppers for the rest of their stay. Helios the sun god was outraged, and threatened to shine no more on the earth unless his dead cattle were avenged. Zeus promptly mustered a cloud over the ship, and blew it and the crew to smithereens.

11 *Calypso*

Odysseus, hapless man, is far from his friends
on a wooded, sea-girt isle, the navel of the sea.
There dwells a goddess … and ever with soft and wheedling
words she beguiles him to forget Ithaca.

HOMER *ODYSSEY* 1.44

The only survivor of the catastrophe was Odysseus. Clinging to the splintered mast of his ship, he eventually finished up on the isle where the nymph Calypso was imprisoned for helping her father Atlas in the war of the gods and Titans. Calypso and Odysseus hit it off, and the pair had a son together. However, Odysseus never ceased pining for Penelope and Ithaca, and after he had spent seven long years on the island Athena petitioned Zeus to order Calypso to allow Odysseus to leave. Calypso was devastated, but in later ages recovered enough to give her name to a catchy genre of Caribbean folk music and one of the moons of Saturn.

12 *Nausicaa*

Odysseus was about to enter the company of the fair-tressed
maidens, naked though he was and all befouled with brine.
Terrible he seemed to them and they fled …
but the daughter of Alcinous stood and faced him.

HOMER *ODYSSEY* 6.127

Nausicaa encounters a naked Odysseus.

The sight of Odysseus on the water gave grim satisfaction to Poseidon, who immediately set about changing 'on the water' to 'under it'. The boat was smashed by storm and wave, and even the best efforts of Athena were barely enough to allow a naked and battered Odysseus to crawl ashore on an unknown beach. Here in the morning he was wakened by the sound of the princess Nausicaa and her maids playing. Though the maids fled at the sight of Odysseus, young Nausicaa stood her ground, and as she had accompanied her staff to the beach to do the laundry, fresh clothing was immediately available for the hero. Odysseus was wined and dined at the court of Nausicaa's father, and the traveller regaled them with an account of his adventures (which account takes up a significant portion of the *Odyssey* of Homer). Then the king gave Odysseus a boat that rowed him safely home.

Ithaca

There I found Odysseus standing among the corpses.
Those he had slain stretched all around him on the
hard floor heaped one upon the other; a cheering
sight which would have warmed your heart.

NURSE TO PENELOPE, HOMER *ODYSSEY* 23.45

Meanwhile, Penelope, wife of the absent Odysseus, had problems of her own. Odysseus was missing, presumed god-smitten, which meant that the palace was overrun with suitors for the hand of Penelope – and more importantly, the kingdom of Ithaca that went with it.

Despite the bitter protests of Odysseus' son Telemachus, the suitors abused the rules of Greek hospitality by overstaying their welcome and feasting and hunting daily. Penelope stayed in seclusion weaving a tapestry, and said she would choose a spouse when the tapestry was done. To delay the evil moment, she unpicked every day's work the following night.

Odysseus had learned caution after his decade-long, high-risk adventure cruise, and had no intention of boldly announcing his return before he had spied out the land. It helped that his experiences both in the Trojan War and its long aftermath had left him so weathered and worn that none but his faithful hound recognized him. Athena helpfully amplified these effects to make Odysseus look even more decrepit.

Penelope at her loom.

Telemachus had gone to Sparta to seek word of his father, and was a guest of the reunited Helen and Menelaus, who were apparently living in domestic harmony. Told by Athena to return (and to avoid an incidental ambush by the suitors en route), Telemachus met and joined forces with his father. Odysseus came to his own home disguised as a beggar, and there was mocked by the suitors. Together with Telemachus and Penelope, Odysseus arranged for a contest of archery, in the course of which Telemachus spirited away the suitors' weapons. The contest was something of a farce, as the chosen bow was the mighty bow of Odysseus, which none of the contestants could even string.

Odysseus took his turn to general amusement. This stopped when he strung the bow and shot an arrow through the target. He then shot arrows through suitors until he ran out of ammunition. Telemachus and some farmhands now joined in the general slaughter, which took some time as there were over a hundred suitors to get through.

Aftermath Odysseus and Athena had to use a mixture of threats and diplomacy to subdue the outraged families of those they had killed. Penelope recognized her husband when he described for her the bed he had made, and the pair settled down to domestic bliss. In a later legend, Odysseus is said to have gone voyaging again, and he may have been killed by the son he had had with Circe, who came looking for him.

LATER ART AND CULTURE:
ODYSSEUS (ULYSSES)

The *Odyssey* has been illustrated many times. Here, in narrative order, are some key examples: Jacob Jordaens, *Ulysses in the Cave of Polyphemus*, c. 1660; J. W. Waterhouse, *Circe Offering the Cup to Ulysses,* 1891;

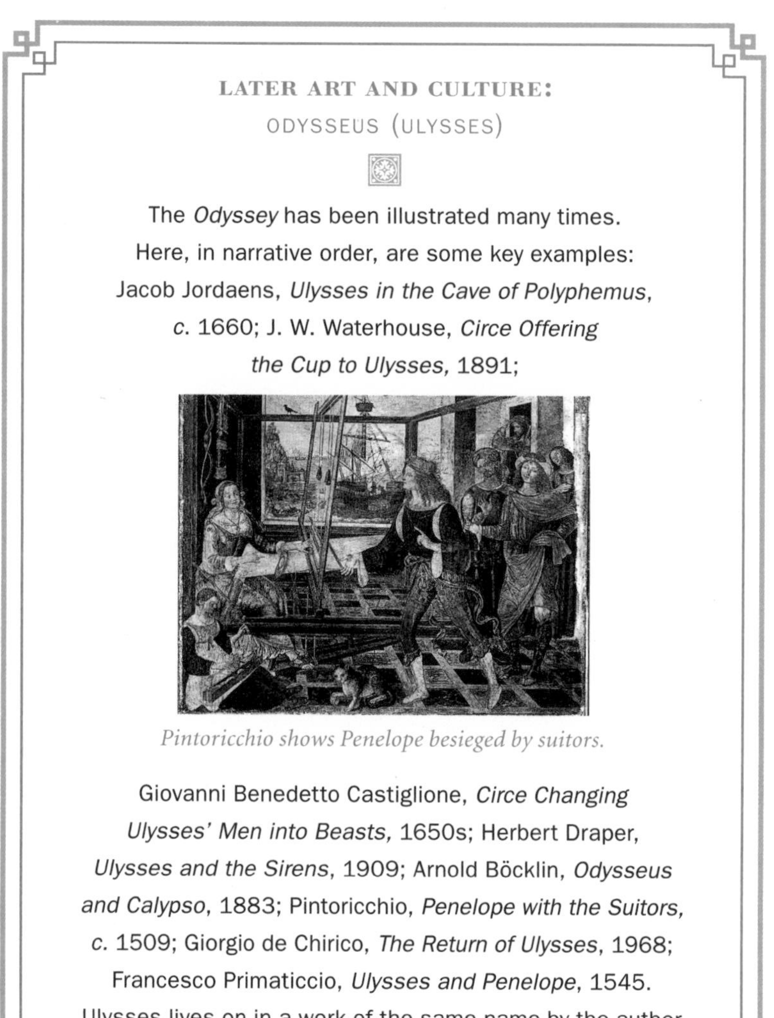

Pintoricchio shows Penelope besieged by suitors.

Giovanni Benedetto Castiglione, *Circe Changing Ulysses' Men into Beasts,* 1650s; Herbert Draper, *Ulysses and the Sirens*, 1909; Arnold Böcklin, *Odysseus and Calypso*, 1883; Pintoricchio, *Penelope with the Suitors,* c. 1509; Giorgio de Chirico, *The Return of Ulysses*, 1968; Francesco Primaticcio, *Ulysses and Penelope*, 1545. Ulysses lives on in a work of the same name by the author James Joyce written between 1914 and 1921 and published in episodes. (The section on Nausicaa led to a prosecution for pornography.) Those who do not know the legend of Odysseus find this epic work of Western culture even more incomprehensible than those who do.

The Aeneid

This man on land and at sea was helpless against
the battering of the gods, and the enduring,
savage wrath of Juno. He suffered much also in war,
until he could establish a city and bring
his gods home to Latium.

VIRGIL *AENEID* 3–7

Though written about a thousand years apart, the *Odyssey* and the *Aeneid* deal with contemporary subjects, so that Odysseus and Aeneas were both wandering the Mediterranean at the same time – and indeed nearly bumped into each other in Sicily. Both books cover roughly a dozen episodes. In the *Aeneid*, the first six parts describe the wanderings of Aeneas and the second six the bloody business of establishing a new homeland in a faraway country. As with the *Odyssey*, the *Aeneid* starts midway and uses narrative flashbacks, so the following chronological sequence has been brutally beaten out of Virgil's elegant verses.

1 *The Flight from Troy*

No tongue can describe the carnage of that night and the orgy of death. No tears could match the agony as the ancient city fell.

VIRGIL *AENEID* 2.360

When the Greeks penetrated the city walls with the wooden horse, Aeneas fought gallantly until Aphrodite (who from now on, following Virgil, will be referred to as Venus) informed the hero that he should concentrate on saving his family. With his aged father Anchises on his back, and his son Ascanius clinging to his leg, Aeneas escaped the burning city. He went back for his wife Creusa, but she had already been slain. Gathering a band of his fellow exiles, he built a small fleet and fled the Trojan shore.

Aeneas leaves Troy with father and son.

2 *The Mediterranean Tour*

As soon as we could trust the ocean we crowded
to the beach and launched our ships into the smiling
seas and the whisper of the breeze.
VIRGIL *AENEID* 3.69

First the Trojans planned on building their new city in Thrace. After unwelcoming omens, they moved on to Crete. Next they considered settling in the region where Pergamum was later founded, but (after a clash with the Harpies) Aeneas had a revelation that he should go west to Italy. Sneaking around the Greek peninsula, they made landfall on the west side of Greece at the city of Buthrotum, which was currently ruled by another Trojan refugee, Helenus, who had wed Andromache after the death of Hector. Helenus warned the Trojans to detour around Scylla and Charybdis, and in so doing took them to the island of the Cyclopes. Here the Trojans picked up a member of Odysseus' crew abandoned during the escape from Polyphemus, and made their way to Sicily, where Anchises died. Before his funeral games could be celebrated, a storm blew the ships to Africa.

3 *Dido*

Dido is queen of the realm; she abandoned her city of Tyre,
fleeing her brother; her woes are too long for recital.

VENUS TO AENEAS, VIRGIL *AENEID* 1.33

Dido, a refugee queen from Phoenicia, was busy building the city that would become Carthage (though some spoilsport modern archaeologists have pointed out that the earliest settlement of Carthage seems to be several centuries later). The queen received the refugees hospitably, but became collateral damage in the ongoing feud between Venus and Juno (Hera). Juno, a supporter of Dido and Carthage, proposed to Venus that Aeneas and his Trojans should settle in that city. This, Juno well knew, would forestall the destined foundation of Rome and the eventual fall of Carthage. A love-struck Dido consummated her passion for Aeneas in a cave outside the city. But Mercury (Hermes) came to remind Aeneas sternly that his destiny lay in Italy, and Aeneas was ever obedient to his destiny. Dido was devastated by the news of her lover's impending departure, and the episode culminated with the abandoned queen lighting her own funeral pyre and immolating herself on it, all the while eloquently and imaginatively cursing Aeneas and his posterity.

4 *Sicily*

Thrice hail, O sacred father … It was not given to you
that you should be at my side as I quested for the
boundaries of Italy and the lands allotted us by fate.

FUNERAL ORATION OF AENEAS FOR ANCHISES, VIRGIL *AENEID* 5.80

The Trojans returned to Sicily to celebrate the funeral games of Anchises. Juno made another attempt to sabotage the founding of Rome by persuading the Trojan women that they should make their home in Sicily and literally burn their boats to stop their menfolk wandering off. Though the attempt was averted, some Trojans opted to stay in Sicily and Aeneas bade them farewell before sailing out – straight into the teeth of a storm that Juno had prepared for him. But however much Neptune (Poseidon) disliked Trojans, he disliked interference by others in his domain even more, and to spite Juno he guided the little fleet to safety.

5 *Landfall*

Hiding in the tree's dense shade is a bough, and it is golden,
and all the leaves are golden, and golden is the stem.
VIRGIL *AENEID* 6.146

Aeneas landed at the point where Daedalus had constructed a memorial to his son Icarus after his (literal) flight from King Minos (p. 153). Aeneas consulted a Sibyl – a prophetess – who told him 'I see wars, horrid wars, and the Tiber frothing with much blood'. Aeneas was told he must travel to the underworld (which is easy – in fact inevitable) and return (which is a lot harder). To make his escape he must bribe Proserpina (Persephone) with a golden bough from the forest.

The Golden Bough in this myth is the eponymous title of the epochal study of myth, magic and religion written by Sir James George Frazer in the late nineteenth and early twentieth centuries, and of an evocative painting by J. M. W. Turner (1834).

6 *The Underworld*

Oh Dido, I swear I was forced to leave …
how could I have known that my departure
would have caused you such terrible grief?
AENEAS ON MEETING DIDO IN THE UNDERWORLD,
VIRGIL *AENEID* 6.460

After some difficulty with Charon, Aeneas entered the world of the dead. Like Odysseus, who was also visiting the underworld at roughly this time, Aeneas saw old friends from Troy. He also met his father, and had an embarrassing encounter with his former lover Dido. Anchises introduced Aeneas to his Roman posterity, including the future Romulus and Julius Caesar, who were currently in the queue of those awaiting rebirth (see p. 48).

7 Latium

We ask only a modest home for our gods,
a strip of shore, where we will harm no one.

THE FOREFATHERS OF THE ROMAN EMPIRE
SUPPLICATE KING LATINUS, VIRGIL *AENEID* 7.227

Sailing on past the isle of Circe, the Trojans reached the mouth of the Tiber and a land ruled over by King Latinus. Latinus had a daughter called Lavinia, whom prophecy had declared would be the source of major strife. Latinus was keen that Lavinia should be someone else's problem, and was trying to marry her to someone as unrelated to his own people as he could find. So far Turnus, a Latin styled as 'the Italian Achilles', was the only candidate for the hand of this stormy petrel, but Latinus was wily enough to see the problems inherent in giving his daughter and a legitimate claim to the throne to a potential rival. When he heard that the Trojans were looking for a wife for their leader, Latinus leapt at the chance to offload his troublesome offspring.

8 *War (Part I)*

Behold, you now have your quarrel, securely
entrenched by the horrors of war.

ALLECTO TO JUNO, VIRGIL *AENEID* 7.549

Juno could see the fated birth of Rome becoming ever more imminent, and redoubled her opposition. She encouraged Turnus and Amata, the wife of Latinus, to oppose the marriage of Lavinia and Aeneas, and further stirred the pot by getting Allecto, one of the Furies, to cause trouble between the Latin countryfolk and the Trojans. Finally, over the bitter protests of Latinus, his people declared war on the Trojan band. Diomedes, the Greek hero of the Trojan War, had also settled in Italy. Turnus sent a message inviting the hero to join in a return match with his old foes, pointing out that with Lavinia, the Trojans were back at their old game of stealing other people's wives.

9 *Evander*

Evander took him to the Capitol, wild and ragged with woodland undergrowth, where now all is golden.

EVANDER SHOWS AENEAS AROUND THE FUTURE SITE OF ROME, VIRGIL *AENEID* 8.350

Aeneas turned to Evander, king of the Arcadians. Evander was a son of Mercury (Hermes), one of the main patrons of the founders of Rome. Furthermore, both Aeneas and Evander could trace their descent to Atlas, making them distant relatives. On the other hand, half the heroes of the age could also claim Atlas as an ancestor, so Aeneas was mainly banking on the fact that Evander and Latinus were traditional enemies. Evander urged Aeneas to bring the Etruscans into their coalition, and Venus intervened to give Aeneas a set of armour forged for him by her husband Vulcan (Hephaestus).

While Venus was equipping Aeneas, Juno sent Iris (a more anti-Trojan envoy than the solidly pro-Rome Mercury) to Turnus. She urged him to attack the Trojan camp while Aeneas was away. The anti-Trojan coalition was also joined by the warlike, Amazon-style Queen Camilla.

10 *War (Part II)*

Trojans, are you not ashamed to be once again under siege, cowering from death behind walls?

VIRGIL *AENEID* 9.598

When the attack on the Trojan camp was beaten back (ten years of practice had made the Trojans very good at defending fortifications), Turnus tried to burn the Trojan fleet, and so incurred the wrath of Rhea, for the fleet had been built with timber from her sacred grove. The attack on the camp met with a spirited Trojan foray, and though Turnus fought like a demon, he was unable to break the defences. Ascanius fought well, but Apollo, worried about the future Roman race, advised the son of Aeneas to step back from the fighting. Back on Olympus, Jupiter had to cope with impassioned petitions from both Venus and Juno. He opted to stay out of the struggle completely and let events take their course.

The character of the siege was changed when Aeneas arrived with Etruscan reinforcements, and became a true Homeric battle with heroic encounters and mass casualties on each side. In a repeat of Hector's killing of Patroclus, the friend of Achilles, Turnus slew Pallas, the friend of Aeneas and son of Evander. To defend Turnus from Aeneas' inevitable wrath, Juno lured him from the battlefield, but the disappearance of their champion threw the Latins into disarray.

11 *Negotiations*

You will never get me into such a battle …
Join your arms in a treaty,
and take whatever terms you can get,
but at all costs avoid an armed clash.

ADVICE OF DIOMEDES TO THE LATINS,
VIRGIL *AENEID* 11.260ff

Aeneas cremated Pallas with honours, and offered terms to the Latins. Diomedes meanwhile had sent messengers saying he had not enjoyed his last war with the Trojans, and certainly did not want another. Turnus returned and rallied the war party, and hostilities resumed.

12 *War (Part III)*

This is my fate – you have conquered.
Enjoy what fortune has given you.
TURNUS TO AENEAS, VIRGIL *AENEID* 12.930

Queen Camilla now went on a rampage through the Trojan forces, supported by Diana (Artemis) who was her patron. On Camilla's death, however, the Latins fell back, and fighting continued until, as a last throw of the dice, Turnus issued a challenge to Aeneas that they settle the issue man-to-man. Sadly for Turnus, by this point Juno and Jupiter had done a deal. The Roman project would go ahead, and Juno would cease harassing the Trojans. But she demanded that Aeneas' people must befriend the Latins and take their name. The agreement was sealed, and so was the fate of Turnus. With his death, the epic ends.

The End

The Heraclides

Sons of Heracles (Hercules), these were a brood so numerous that they constituted a separate race. Driven from their homeland, they were told by the oracle at Delphi that they must wait 'until the third crop' before they returned. This 'third crop' was the third generation of the clan, who swept into Hellas with fire and sword and divided the kingdoms of Greece among themselves.

The mythological episode of the return of the children of Heracles has sometimes been associated with the so-called 'Dorian invasion', the historicity of which is much disputed. On one view it was the arrival of Dorian invaders from the north that put paid to Mycenaean civilization. Greece was plunged into a dark age, and the civilization which emerged centuries later had only confused memories of the preceding era. It was these memories which they collected into myth.

LATER ART AND CULTURE:

AENEAS

Dido and Aeneas by Purcell, first performed in 1689, is one of the greatest British operas. And as can be seen from the following list, the Age of Exploration evoked memories of the earlier voyages of Aeneas: Andrea Sacchi, *The Death of Dido*, 1600s; Mattia Preti, *Aeneas, Anchises and Ascanius Fleeing Troy,* 1630s; Claude Lorrain, *The Landing of Aeneas at Pallanteum*, 1675; and *Aeneas and Dido in Carthage,* 1676; François Perrier, *Aeneas and his Companions Fighting the Harpies*, 1646–47; Luca Giordano, *Aeneas and Turnus*, 1600s; Giovanni Battista Tiepolo, *Aeneas Introducing Cupid Dressed as Ascanius to Dido*, 1757; J. M. W. Turner, *Dido Building Carthage*, 1815.

Claude Lorrain shows Aeneas landing in Italy.

The foundation of Rome by Romulus and Remus

In Italy, the children of Aeneas and Lavinia settled into a town called Alba Longa. However, many historians consider the town to be a place marker where ex-Trojans could remain until the foundation of Rome – which the Romans were very clear happened on an exact date three centuries after the fall of Troy. There is a huge debate amongst historians as to the reality of the Roman foundation myth.

In its most mythical form, Rome's foundation legend claims that a deposed king's daughter, a Vestal Virgin, was violently seduced by Mars and later gave birth to the twins Romulus and Remus. The infants were thrown in a basket into the Tiber, and were found washed up on the banks of the future site of Rome by a she-wolf. The wolf suckled the twins until they were rescued and raised by the shepherd Faustulus.

The hard-headed Romans had some trouble with this, and there is a parallel legend which claimed that 'Mars' was in fact the king of the time, raping his rival's daughter in an anonymizing helmet. When popular opinion prevented the despoiled Vestal or her children from being executed, the pair were handed to a shepherd and raised by his prostitute wife (*lupa* meant both 'she-wolf' and 'prostitute' in Latin).

In both versions of the tale, Romulus and Remus realized their true origins when they grew up, and gathered the local youths into a small army which overthrew the false king and restored their grandfather to the throne of Alba Longa. They then gathered the youths together and set out to found Rome.

Most historians dismiss even the more sordidly realistic version of the legend as complete fabrication, but some others point to the mounting archaeological evidence that supports the essential elements of the tale. If true it is, there is certainly no clear-cut division, but it may well be that the founding of Rome on the morning of 21 April 753 BC marks the exact point when mythology ends and history begins.

Further Reading

It's easy to find copies of the great epics of myth. Homer's *Iliad* and *Odyssey* can be found both in paperback form – for example *The Iliad* (Penguin, 2003) translated by E. V. Rieu and revised by Peter Jones, and *The Odyssey* (Penguin, 2006) translated by Robert Fagles and revised by Bernard Knox.

Those who want to read these in a form close to the original (and with the Greek version on the facing page) should look at the Loeb versions *The Odyssey*, Loeb Classical Library 104 and 105 (Harvard University Press, 1919) translated by A. T. Murray and revised by George E. Dimcock, and *The Iliad*, Loeb Classical Library 170 and 171 (Harvard University Press, 1924) translated by A. T. Murray and revised by William Wyatt.

It's also possible to find out-of-copyright books by searching the internet. Other books deal with rarer parts of the great story of mythology, such as Hesiod's *Theogony and Works and Days* (Oxford University Press, 1999), translated by M. L. West. (This contains useful annotations and explanations for the non-classicist.)

It says something about modern misunderstanding of mythology that most retellings of the ancient myths are written as children's stories, but adults who want an accessible version of the stories might like *Myths of the Ancient Greeks* edited by Richard P. Martin (New American Library, 2003), or Robert Graves *The Greek Myths* (Penguin, 1990).

Other more general discussions can be found in:

Lucilla Burns, *Greek Myths* (British Museum Press, 1990)
Richard Buxton, *The Complete World of Greek Mythology* (Thames & Hudson, 2004)
Paul Cartledge (ed.), *The Cambridge Illustrated History of Ancient Greece* (Cambridge University Press, 2002)
Malcolm Day, *100 Characters from Classical Mythology* (Barrons & A. & C. Black, 2007)
Jane F. Gardner, *The Roman Myths* (British Museum Press, 1993)
Bettany Hughes, *Helen of Troy* (Cape & Knopf, 2005)
Mark P. O. Morford & Robert J. Lenardon, *Classical Mythology* (8th ed., Oxford University Press, 2007)
and the indispensable William Smith, *Dictionary of Greek and Roman Biography and Mythology* (London, 1894)

Sources of Illustrations

All line drawings are from 19th-century sources.

Alinari Archives 11, 43; D.A.I., Athens 181; Antikensammlungen, Basel 149; Staatliche Museen Preussischer Kulturbesitz, Berlin 138; Museum of Fine Arts, Boston 104, 109, 121, 122; National Gallery of Scotland, Edinburgh 91; Galeria degli Uffizi, Florence 15; Kestner Museum, Hanover 1; Landesmuseum, Kassel 103; Archiepiscopal Castle, Kremsier 86; British Museum, London 153, 159, 167, 176, 205; National Gallery, London 108, 166, 210; Royal Academy of Arts, London 219; Tate, London 76, 132; Museo del Prado, Madrid 19, 102; Staatliche Antikensammlungen, Munich 22, 35, 178, 207; Gallerie Nazionale di Capodimonte, Naples 147; Museo Archeologico Nazionale, Naples 2, 38, 52, 93; Metropolitan Museum of Art, New York 16, 131; Ashmolean Museum, Oxford 29; Cabinet des Médailles, Bibliothèque Nationale de France, Paris 163; Musée du Louvre, Paris 3, 28, 47, 55, 61, 79, 81, 88, 124; Musée d'Orsay, Paris 141; D.A.I., Rome 128; Scala, Florence 21; Musei Vaticani, Vatican City 27, 118, 139, 164, 186; Earl of Pembroke's Collection, Wilton House, Salisbury 114; Martin von Wagner Museum, Würzburg 192, 212

Index

Page numbers in *italics* indicate illustrations